AIMED SOLAR AND LUNAR RETURNS

*To André Barbault,
my great master*

Ciro Discepolo

AIMED SOLAR AND LUNAR RETURNS
What you can do when you cannot leave

Ricerca '90 Publisher

Translation and editing: Luciano Drusetta and Ram Ramakrishnan
Graphic design: Pino Valente
Cover picture: Courtesy NASA/JPL-Caltech.

Copyright © 2009 Edizioni Ricerca '90
Viale Gramsci, 16
80122 Napoli - ITALY
info@cirodiscepolo.it
www.solarreturns.com
www.cirodiscepolo.it

In the very moment of our birth our entire destiny is written in our birth chart down to the smallest detail – but we can change the screenplay.
Ciro Discepolo

Gli astri non sparano mai a salve.
Ciro Discepolo

The birth data of the people mentioned in this book proceed mainly from Lois M. Rodden's database and from Ciro Discepolo's archives. Other birth data are taken from web-based databases.

Astral maps and calculations are produced by the exceptionally precise astrological software **Astral** and **Aladino** (also referred to as *Module for the Automatized Research of the Aimed Solar Returns 'RSMA'*).

Preface to the English edition

Active Astrology is well know all over the world, thanks mainly to my previous books in English (http://www.cirodiscepolo.it/english_corner/English_corner.htm), together with several other works published in Italian, English, French, German, Spanish, Hungarian, Slovenian, and Russian.

Many of my readers have urged me to have this volume published in English. Unlike other works of mine, this volume does not explain how to 'aim' the relocation of a map of Solar Return: it rather tells you what to do if you can not leave for an aimed birthday and you wish to make use of the technique that I called 'exorcism of the symbol' – or more properly said: 'exorcization of the symbol'.

I trust that you can find good, practical, and useful pieces of advice in these pages.

This volume contains also certain chapters similar to (but not the same as) a previous book of mine titled *Astrologia Attiva*. Here I've added several chapters and I've revised and expanded other sections.

As a support to the explained theory, I have also added some astrological portraits of universally known historical personalities such as Giacomo Casanova, Luigi Pirandello, and Ernest Hemingway.

Before you start browsing this volume, I would like to remind you that you can always join my blog (http://cirodiscepolo.blogspot.com/) with queries or comments in English or in the Italian language. There you'll actually find a sort of an 'extended family' made up of my passionate followers, colleagues, pupils or people who simply are fond of Active Astrology – they will be able to help you go on and deepen your studies of Active Astrology.

Yet another thing though. This is probably my very last book in English, as a publisher. In future, if my readers from the States, the United Kingdom, Canada, Australia (and so on) wish to read my works on the rectification of the time of birth or on the dating of events within the frame of the twelve month of a given Solar Return, they should mention these works of mine to publishers urging their translation into the English language. This is the only way in which they will be able to go on reading my works in their own language.

I wish you all a fruitful pursuit in the deepening your understanding of this wonderful topic called Active Astrology, which is not *The* Truth, but it is surely Truth.

Ciro Discepolo

Naples, the 6th of February 2009

Preface

This book is addressed mainly to those who can not leave for a relocation of their birthday, or who believe they cannot. For I believe that it's somewhat of a prejudice. The reason for the prejudice that leads people not to leave is mainly due to the fear of flying on an airplane, or the conviction that it's too expensive. Talking about Aimed Solar Returns, many people attack me fiercely with a wide range of reasons; while they are only unable to admit to themselves that they simply fear from flying. I would recommend to them to make an effort to overcome such a taboo: considering that we are at the dawn of the third millennium, it appears to be something absolutely anachronistic.

During my twenty-eight years of deploying approximately eleven thousands of ASR's I have helped even aged mountain people from Aosta Valley fly for the first time, and without any companion, on the route Rome-New York! Sometimes a few drops of Valium, or a double whisky before departure are enough to overcome any fear... So why should we renounce the possibility of living ten times better because of a simple, little, insignificant taboo? I dare say that every day I do my utmost to convince new reluctant people to relocate their SR.

Some of my opponents used to speak ill of me, claiming that travel agencies pay me royalties... And since this year my daughter Luna started working at a travel agent, this gossip has become a certainty in their minds... Beyond the wit, the reality is that being perfectly convinced of the validity of my method, day by day I do my utmost to offer an extra source of light to those who want to see. To those who claim that they cannot afford a travel abroad, I stress that nowadays you can go from Europe to America with one million Italian Liras *[TN: corresponding to more or less 516 Euros]*. After all, how many pizzas should you give up in two months, in order to make your year change radically?

Nonetheless I'm not wishing to discuss this notion further. I repeat that this short volume is mainly addressed to those who – for one reason or another – can not or do not want to leave to relocate their birthday. Let me underline another couple of things for the sake of clearness. As I have already explained on other occasions, my school, called *Active Astrology*, consists of that particular way of using astrology in the exactly opposite way to those who drop into an armchair throwing up their hands and exclaiming to the stars: "I submit to fate!" *Active Astrology*, on the contrary, spurs people to show their fist to the sky, saying: "I'll die hard!" In order to carry out such a purpose, in my opinion you have only two choices: changing your place on the day of your astrological birthday, or adhering to the notion of the *exorcism of symbols*. In my previous works *Trattato pratico di Rivoluzioni solari, Esercizi sulle Rivoluzioni solari mirate, Transiti e Rivoluzioni solari, Nuovo Trattato di Astrologia*, and *Rivoluzioni Lunari e Rivoluzioni Terrestri* (these are only the main ones, two of them are also available in the English language: *Transits and Solar Returns* and *Lunar Returns and Earth Returns*) I have developed to its highest point the implications of only the first of those two choices. In this volume I have broadly explained how to exorcize the symbols in Astrology, while continuing to stress the fact that this practice can not guarantee the same results as an aimed birthday. What I mean is that if you are willing to leave and relocate your SR, you can achieve satisfactory results; while if you don't leave and you rather try to relieve the negative effects of a bad Solar Return by means of the exorcism of symbols, you will only attain partial results, and you might not be fully satisfied with them.

Let me add that reading the following pages should be done only after having read the above listed works, because together they jointly represent the real essence of *Active Astrology*. Above all, in connection with *Transiti e Rivoluzioni Solari* (*Transits and Solar Returns* in its English version) I find it crucial to make a further clarification with reference to the notion of pessimism and optimism. After reading it, most people have accused me to be a prophet of doom, an incorrigible pessimist dominated by bleak visions of Apocalypse.

Well, if that was a book of alarm and admonitions, this is the book of hope. After all, in order to propose a remedy I *had* to depict the dangerous abysms that people can meet in their life. Now, I don't really think I'm a pessimist. At least, I don't think I am more pessimistic than one should be. On the contrary: I find I am a pragmatist – which is something quite different. And leaving aside such philosophical considerations: do you *really* think that a pessimist might be able to 'send' hundreds of people around the world every year, aiming for a better year? Well I wouldn't say so! *Au contraire!*

Furthermore, I would like to point out the fact that I have never claimed that you should expect tremendous tragedies *every time* that the 12th, the 1st, and the 6th House play a role in the chart of Solar Return! For if it were so, it would be the same as pretending that every second or third year you are run over by the tramway and lose your arm! In fact what I really intended is a quite different notion. I claim *that every time* you suffer from disgrace – lesser or major ones – you find the 12th, the 1st, and/or the 6th House involved in the Solar Return of that year. Please do not tell me that there isn't a huge difference between the two claims. Now, somebody could object as follows: If a disgrace is not absolutely certain, then why should we change our place of SR? This is my answer: Since we cannot reckon in advance the real extent of the devastation implied in a bad Solar Return, why shouldn't we relocate it anyway in order to avoid any possible trouble? Often people don't relocate and they believe that things have turned up gorgeously for them, while they have suffered serious damages without even realizing.

In this preface I would like to focus on another question: the language I use. Even through the English translation, you may have noticed that my way of speaking is direct, open; let me say: frank. A famous Italian poet, perhaps Giuseppe Ungaretti or Salvatore Quasimodo, once declared: "I started writing out of hatred for Gabriele d'Annunzio!" Well I might say the same for my last works, in connection with certain astrologers following a 'psychological school'.

Approximately two or three years ago I happened to deliver a speech on Astrology in an astrological club, where I had been invited by two of my former students. There I chanced to glance at a bulletin board containing a list of recommended books for the members of that club. I saw a lot of books of a theoretical-philosophical kind, and no title from my works. "Is it possible – I wondered – that among over fifty books I have published so far (well, actually there were a little less at the time) I haven't written anything worth for these people?". This is why I inquired of my former students as follows: "Isn't it true that when you read a book on transits written by some famous 'philosophical' author you can read a good piece of literature; you can enjoy a high-sounding lofty language; and most importantly you can learn – verbiage? For the standard interpretation given to any transit, be it Mercury conjunct with the Sun or Neptune opposite to the Moon, is always the same and it looks like this: *You are in a very unique moment of your life in which you need to present the budget of your existence in order to understand that blah blah blah...* I don't know if those people consulting such books or their authors are human beings of the same genre as those who consult me; but unless one is making horoscopes of Martians, normal ordinary folk do not want to hear such nonsensical readings! They rather want to know if their shop would be successful; whether they would be able to pay the rates of their loan or their son would stop taking drugs; and so on. And if people consulting you are similar to those consulting me, what would you tell them if you studied about transits in books like these?" This is the reason why I have written plenty of pages using a style that is exactly opposite to the one used by those sorts of astrological bibles: I mean to make practical observations, aimed on facts. This is what I have tried to do with this volume as well, the one that you are about to browse, or read, or study.

This volume also tries to give other good bits of advice that are not strictly connected with the notion of the exorcism of symbols: about certain technical problems that everybody encounters when they deal with *Active Astrology* (for example, the problem of the 'gap').

Let me add yet another point before closing this preface. Those who wish to deal with *Active Astrology* should not search for the evidence of its validity in the events of my private life. In fact, my birth chart is extremely tough as far as my health is concerned, and I believe that if I am still alive, it's thanks to the constant application of my own rules upon myself. I won't probably live a long life, but this should not mislead you as far as the validity of *Active Astrology* is concerned: simply try it on yourselves and on your dear ones, and you'll become convinced that it really works.

This volume is partially inspired by an ancient work of mine titled *Il sale dell'astrologia [TN: The Salt of Astrology, not available in English]*. Yet, only one of the chapters contained in that book has been included in this volume.

In the section on transits you won't find those of Jupiter. For the transits of this planet, just remember that they imply a dramatic fall of the native's critical sense and in order to avoid their worse effects, you should simply recommend to those consulting you (or induce in yourselves) an increased level of diffidence.

Let me dedicate these final lines to express my gratitude to my friend Lorenzo Vancheri: he proofread this volume with the precision of Virgo also offering precious pieces of advice on its contents.

Ciro Discepolo
www.solarreturns.com
www.cirodiscepolo.it

Naples, the 4th of February 2009

1.
Praise of escape

From time to time, I hear somebody object to the notion of Aimed Solar Returns, saying that he/she prefers not to turn his/her back on the problem, because he/she rather wants to face it instead. This is actually a pseudo-heroic attitude. I believe that it is inspired by certain drawing-room psychoanalysis that certain beginners have re-interpreted in their own way. According to them, man should always show an ever active, responsible, watchful, assertive and fighting attitude against the thousands of troubles in his daily life. Still according to this Freudian-like way of reasoning, man's problems are virtually always of an endogenous kind: that is to say, they are self-born, i.e. produced only by the distorting visions of one's own mind. This corresponds to claiming that tumours, partings from our beloved ones, losses of personal freedom or even mournings can not simply exist unless we necessarily consider them to be compulsory materializations of our own inner phantoms.

This reminds me of the 1995 science fiction film *Twelve Monkeys* starring Bruce Willis. The heroine is a psychiatrist who quarrels with her professor and master, objecting to his aprioristic scepticism, and denying that psychoanalysis can play the rule of the Gospel, i.e. that it cannot be able to establish what is real and what is a product of the imagination in any single human event. If we wished to find the traces of an historical inspiration of heroic orientation, we should get to the very root of the myth and go alongside it again step by step until our days, mentioning classical heroes such as Lancelot and Ivanhoe, or icons which are closer to our days such as Superman or Mickey Mouse.

In the entire – laic or religious – history of the world it is possible to keep trace of this sort of basic teaching towards a daring behaviour against bad luck: man must fight against his own fears, as well as against the products of his fears. Of course, considering the very title of this volume,

I basically agree on this approach; nonetheless I keep a distance from it as far as the operational methods are concerned. In fact it is not granted that the best way, the most efficient way of being active is holding a rifle or drawing your sword: for often escape is really the best weapon! French physician, writer and philosopher Henri Laborit exposes this point of view in his essay *L'Éloge de la fuite*, which I've read in his Italian edition *Elogio della fuga* by Oscar Mondadori. This is what Laborit writes. "When she cannot struggle against the wind and the sea any longer to keep her route, the sailing ship has only two choices: she can go storm sailing (i.e. the jib aback and the bar to leeward) which eventually causes her to go adrift; or escape from the storm sailing before the sea and with a minimum of cloth. Often, escape is the only way of saving the ship and the crew when you are far from the coast. Moreover, it allows you to discover unknown shores peeping out from the horizon when the waters get calm again."

So, escape. Yes, escape – because despite the celebrated heroes of hundreds of Western or action films, against the stars, man can do much more by escaping than by waving a hatchet. Then his salvific power consists in avoiding the *radiation wind* literally *falling* against him. Before a cloud of radioactive particles, it should be always wiser running away than showing your breast and muscles. I have been claiming this for years. A female friend once asked me, "So we have to escape always?" and I replied, "Well, if by *escaping* your life gets better – then why not *escape?*"

Let us consider Mr. Laborit once again, and let us try to understand his thought better. Even if in its practical implication his point of view is far from ours, still we share the same basic notion – escape. As a scientist, he considers man's life mainly as the product of the processes of his nervous system. He explains human behaviour mainly in relationship with what he calls *the search for dominance* or the so-called *instinct of property*. In his modern, laic and scientific version of the ancient motto *homo homini lupus* (man is a wolf to man), he believes that the origin of the mechanisms on which our diseases and our self-destruction are based, stands in the human being's instinct for dominating other beings, and he proposes his own direction of escape. Let's see them in details. "... Now, the space in which this action takes place is occupied also by the others. So it becomes necessary to avoid confrontation, because from confrontation it necessarily originates a hierarchical order of domination that stand very little chances of being fulfilled, for it alienates his own desire from the others' desire. On the other hand, subduing means accepting, with submission, the psychosomatic pathology that is necessarily originated by the impossibility of acting according to one's pulses. Rebelling means being the cause of one's own ruin, because rebellion – when carried out as a group – immediately reconstitutes a hierarchical order of submission within the group. And the rebellion of the individual leads rapidly to the abnormal generality – which considers itself to be the holder of normality – to the suppression of the rebellious one. So there's no other way than escape.

One can escape in different ways though. Some people make use of the so-called 'psychogenic' drugs; some others use psychosis; others suicide; others, single-handed navigation. Perhaps there's one way more: escaping into a world which does not belong to this world - the world of imagination. The risk of being pursued there is the least. There you can own a vast land of gratification, some would call it: narcissistic. It never minds, because if you escape into the world of imagination, submission and rebellion, dominance and conservatism lose their anxiety-inducing character for you as a fugitive, and you would consider them as a play in which you may take part without fear, in order to have the others accept you as 'normal'. In this world of reality it is possible to play up to the limit of breaking off with the dominant group, escaping and establishing relationship with other groups if necessary, and maintaining untouched your own imaginary gratification: the only essential one, safe from the social groups.

Only the fugitive behaviour would let you remain normal with yourself, until the majority of men who consider themselves as normal would unsuccessfully try to become normal by trying to establish a dominance – the dominance of an individual, a group, a class, a nation, a block of nations and so on. In fact, experimentation proves that the state of alert of the pituitary gland and of the adrenal cortex (which – if it persists – is the cause of the visceral pathology of the so-called 'psychosomatic' illness) is typical of the dominated ones, or of ones who try unsuccessfully to assert their own dominance; also, of the dominating ones who try to maintain an objected dominance. All of them should be considered abnormal ones then. In fact it does not appear to be very normal to be suffering from stomach ulcer, sexual impotence, hypertension, or any other of the hundreds of depressive syndromes that are so frequent today.

And since a stable and unquestioned dominance is rare – thank God! – you can clearly see that if you wish to go on being normal, you cannot but escape far away from the hierarchical competitions. So wait for me: I'm coming too!"

According to Mr. Laborit then, man must defend mainly against other men, and he must escape confining himself in an imaginary world. While it is my opinion that man must mainly defend himself from the stars; and he can do it in a very productive way, by means of the aimed birthday. Also the technique that we have called 'exorcism of the symbol' may serve this purpose, but it has to be used mainly when you aren't able to relocate your Solar Return.

I guess that the Reader would react in the most obvious way, that is, claiming: "But this means having a paranoiac vision of life!" I realize that things appear to be exactly so, and I wonder whether it is worth at all to object to such a claim. So I better counter-question as follows: "Could you support a different, yet equally credible, vision of life?" In other words, do you really believe that our worldly path in this universe resembles or vaguely recalls the story of a life as depicted in a film of Frank Capra? I mean, life as a dispenser of joy? Life as the carrier of pleasure and delight? Or life rather as a neutral entity, witness of a mainly flat existence, without any trauma? What model do you believe sticks more to reality? Personally speaking, before my eyes I see that when you wake up every morning, not only do you have to defend yourself from your siblings, but you must also erect shields against pollutions, natural catastrophes, the attacks of microbes, germs, illness and diseases of all kinds, and …… the list is endless.

Am I paranoiac for thinking so? If those who think so are paranoiac, so am I. But if looking at things this way means simply facing reality without demagogy and without the false positivism of certain political – both leftist or rightist – currents, then let us prepare for survival and let us look for methods for our everyday life; let us delete from within us the hypocrisy that makes us think that a malignant tumour may be a rare event in the life of a human being. For the truth is that tumours as well as judicial errors or losing one's job are not rare events in the life of men and women. In fact they are simply the 'playfield' within which we move along that handful of seconds that we are allowed to live during our worldly path. By relying on the exorcism of symbols or the aimed birthday does not mean to aspire to become immortal! It simply means to defend better, exactly what we do when we wear a scarf in winter. Nothing more, nothing less.

You may know that I am fond of cinema. One movie film in particular may well represent what I am writing: *Mediterraneo*, Gabriele Salvatores' film that won the Academy Award for Best Foreign Language Film in 1991. The film begins with a quote from Henri Laborit's book, dedicated to "All those who escape."

The metaphor deployed in the film is that of a small group of Italian sailors. During WWII, they are ordered to occupy a small, remote island of Greece. The military 'occupation' would soon become a wonderful oblivion in which the heroes forget everybody and everything, feeling the pleasure of abandoning themselves to a reality made of dreams, fantasy, football matches, sky and uncontaminated sea.

The 'escape' that I am proposing in these pages is much less poetic and inventive, still I believe that is may be extremely useful for your destiny.

2.
The reasons for a vocation

I discovered astrology at the age of 22, during my military service at the airport of Latina in 1970. I dipped into it immediately and with a great passion. I understood that the only way to learn astrology is not by studying dozens of books (which I actually did for many hours a day, yet).

On the contrary, you have to practise it on the field; you have to meet hundreds of people and cast their natal charts; thus making mistakes and learning by mistakes. I don't think that there is any better way to learn astrology. Before meeting somebody I studied his/her chart for hours, dropping notes and wondering how he/she would look like; what would his/her character and cultural interests be, and so on. I eventually met the consulting person, whom in the great majority of cases I didn't know before, and my real study began after he/she had gone away. Then I reconsidered the whole trying to understand what I had mistaken, and why. Such training course was giving me good results and I noticed that, even if the path I was stepping into was boundless, every day I was advancing a little further.

Astrology had become my great passion; it had an even stronger charm on me than informatics – the other nourishment of my soul. But there was one thing that I wasn't able to accept and I couldn't stand at all: often I met people who were to face very hard transits and evidently dramatic situations – and I could do nothing for them! To hide them the truth? This was against my principles: I didn't want to deceive them. To tell them the truth – well I had to, but how? How could I face then their disappointment, their fears? That was the most impelling knotty problem I had to solve if I wanted to keep being an astrologer. During those years I also undertook my first Jungian psychoanalysis and I used to read loads of books on psychology. Very soon I got fascinated by the concept of «constellating a symbol» or, as I named it later on: «exorcization of a symbol».

In psychology to constellate means to activate, i.e. to bring something to life. Once I happened to read with an extraordinary interest the preface that Gianfranco Tedeschi, a Jungian psychoanalyst and a school founder in Italy, wrote to the Italian paperback edition of Jung's study on schizophrenia (Psicologia della schizofrenia, Newton Compton Italiana).

You'll read more about it a little further in this book; then you'll understand how this example can be considered the origin of a good portion of my practice of astrology, which consequently goes under the name of «exorcization of the symbol».

While I was greedily absorbing those readings I also studied the Solar Returns. From the very beginning I discovered that it was possible to change them, even in full, by simply being somewhere else on the day of your birthday. These two coincident discoveries lit a sparkle in me – the desire to follow a way, to try to make light, to check up on some possibilities. I had found a semi-hidden path and I was trying to light it up with a weak torch. That would be my future way. I would never leave it. I'm still trying to improve it every single day since then.

The exorcization of symbols and the Aimed solar returns are the foundation of my Active Astrology.

As my last lines for this chapter, I would like to emphasize that the techniques that I have explained are for controlling a circumstance, not for solving possible basic problems. The latter must have their solution in a different environment: for example, in psychoanalysis.

3.
To antagonize and to potentiate

I'm sure that the more watchful readers and followers of astrology cannot ignore this current situation. We, the authors, are aligned essentially on three almost incompatible positions that eventually determine one's personal way of understanding and pursuing astrology. The first, yet not the most important school claims that astrology is an instrument of knowledge of the human psyche and it doesn't allow the least possibility of prediction. Those who think so argue that Saturn and Uranus have nothing to do with John Smith even if John Smith is being robbed of all his goods the very same moment when these two planets cross the threshold of his natal 2nd House. It's the same as implying that transits, Solar Returns and primary directions are good for nothing.

The second sort or 'school' of astrology fully admits the power of transits, to such an extent that it is considered useless to 'apply yourself' because everything is already written in your natal chart; and no one can do anything against fate. Finally, here comes the third school: those who think like me: namely, that transits, Solar and Lunar Returns, and primary directions work faultlessly, but you have got the chance to antagonize these forces: i.e. to fight against them. Of course, everything that I have written in my previous books – and above all in this one – has been borrowed partly from Tradition, partly from my master André Barbault's teachings. It also derives partly from the results of astrological research, partly from my personal experience of almost thirty years of activity; and partly from the personal way I have arranged those pieces of information together, amalgamating them with some aspects of Jungian knowledge, which has been guiding me since the beginning of my studies. I am sure that we can and we must try to weaken the negative transits and to strengthen the positive ones with all the means at our disposal. We can do it mainly with our own knowledge; with the enlightenment, which is the highest form of emancipation at our disposal. Secondarily, we can use the techniques that I have already described elsewhere and that I am about to complete here, in this synthetic work.

The main operation that I am going to describe is what I call the *exorcism of the symbol*, or if you prefer, the *ritualization of the symbol*.

"A miracle," was the cry of a great part of my students after reading the Italian translation of *Schicksal als chance* [Destiny as Choice] by Thorwald Dethlefsen, published in Italy by Ed. Mediterranee. Still, much of what my German colleague wrote had been published previously in my books over the last two decades, with the exception of the part about reincarnation - something I don't believe in at all.

Let's start from the beginning, by recalling the example that I have already reported in one of my writings, first described by the analytical psychologist Gianfranco Tedeschi in his preface to the Italian edition of Jung's study on schizophrenia (*Psicologia della schizofrenia*, Ed. Newton Compton Italiana). In his preface, Dr. Tedeschi talks about a Jewish student of medicine in Rome, who had started to manifest symptoms of mental dissociation years before: he had begun to behave like a priest of ancient Jerusalem.

Dr. Tedeschi told him that he himself was a Jew too, thus they could celebrate the holy rites together on condition that they strictly followed the rules: fasting first of all; purifying themselves; wearing the right dresses; spreading incense; reading the original scriptures, etc. They did so for many months until the young man abruptly asked: "All this is interesting, but - what do the Jews do today?" From then on, having regained interest for actuality, the young man was dismissed from hospital to begin his psychoanalysis with Dr. Tedeschi - who tells the reader that the young man recovered completely and eventually graduated in medicine. The doctor had constellated the symbolism that was pressing from inside the patient: this way the problem had been 'exorcized'. Let us consider two further examples whose central characters are two female clients and good friends of mine. The first one is a university professor with a vast general culture and a good knowledge of psycho astrology.

During a transit of Saturn over her natal Venus she was left by the man she loved. She felt such a devastating pain that in order to cope with it, in order to detain it somehow, she went into mourning and dressed in black for one whole year. To those who asked her the reason of such a choice she used to answer: "I've lost my love." She went on for one year, exactly the same time required for Saturn to pass beyond her natal Venus; then she went out of mourning - back to normal life. The second case is another lady professor, as cultured and intelligent as the former. As the transit of Saturn on her natal Venus approached, she asked me what she could do to avoid losing her love. Her partner lived in a distant town; they met on a regular basis, say once every fortnight. I advised her to meet as rarely as possible, even further: not to meet at all during the entire coming year. They did so. Thus Saturn *'was given'* what it required: sentimental mortification, subtraction of loving enthusiasm, temporary dearth of sentiment and sex. Then Saturn passed over and everything turned back the way it used to be.

In both cases we can say that the given procedure was to make the 'ghost' act; which in psychoanalysis is defined as the 'technique of restraining the field'. In the case described by Dr. Tedeschi the principle of identification was employed too - a Jew was the student, and a Jew was the doctor. This procedure has been invented neither by me nor by Dr. Tedeschi or by Jung: it belongs to the rites of any religion; it can be applied very often with excellent results; and it can be compared to the principle of homeopathic medicine *similia similibus curantur* (the similar cures the similar).

Can we state that all the cases must be treated the same way? "No." The above mentioned Thorwald Dethlefsen suggests to wear black, to visit cemeteries, to meet grave people and so on, in order to cope with a transit of Saturn, say, on your natal Sun. But my personal experience and even the teachings of psychoanalysis don't agree with it. In fact, in many cases one must employ a prosthetic technique: i.e. a technique of compensation. Let me explain. Let's say that the one who copes with the mentioned transit of Saturn is a native Pisces whose Sun or Moon is afflicted by an aspect of Neptune. In this case we are before a psycho labile individual; an extremely fragile person; an emotional sponge who fully absorbs the atmosphere around him/her. It is not wise to advise such a person to read *Les Misérables* by Victor Hugo and/or to associate with sad people. On the contrary: we'll ask him/her to meet healthy happy people and very equilibrated persons; to watch amusing films such as the American comedies; to read Wodehouse's works all the time.

For we must never think that everything has to be read, interpreted and developed in one direction only. Some people react better to allopathic medicine than to homeopathic; similarly we should use the exorcism of the symbol with the strongest individuals and the compensatory technique with the weakest ones. Sometimes the two principles can be combined. In the case of the fragile and vulnerable lady born under the Sign of Pisces, we'd advise her to find help in certain medicines used in psychiatry while spending a few months in deep solitude. The basic principle of the *exorcism of the symbol* is the notion of sacrifice: exactly the same concept that thousands of years ago, made the Greek pastors select and sacrifice the best lamb of their herd in order to contain Zeus' wrath. The bottom line is that you have to pay your due in the same analogical direction of the symbol and in an expectedly adequate extent in order to discharge the transit. So if you are a female and Uranus transits on your natal Mars in the 5th House, it wouldn't be sufficient to have a dentist fill your cavity - but it would be expectedly enough to undertake an operation and have your some-year-old uterine fibroma removed. The primary advice that I prefer giving is to 'anticipate' the transits; to 'offer the sacrifice' when the transit is about to arrive.

Another extraordinary instrument of self-defence in the critical periods – or at least a good way to strengthen the highly promising periods – is to use the Solar Returns in an 'aimed' way, or one could also say, in a 'targeted' way. That is, to choose the most suitable astral situation to spend your birthday with: i.e. the best annual sky which the horoscope of your following year derives from. For many years I have been advising my clients to use this technique and I have tried it out myself several times – always obtaining excellent results.

I suggest considering the consulting client's general situation about one month before his/her birthday, i.e. when the previous year is coming to an end and the astrologer is adequately updated about the facts that characterized the astral map of his/her prior *return*. On the other hand, one month before the birthday one has got time enough to organize even a very exotic travel. My personal technique is to cast a dozen of Solar Returns maps ranging from Los Angeles to Tokyo scanning all over Europe. If none of them is suitable I explore some 'extreme' territories such as Siberia, New Guinea or Easter Island. Further, in this book, you'll find suggestions on the right way to proceed, based upon practical cases.

As my last lines for this chapter, I would like to underline that the techniques that I have depicted are for controlling a circumstance, not for solving possible basic problems. The latter must have their solution in a different environment: for example, in psychoanalysis.

Remark:
Let me express my gratitude to Dr. Antonio Speranza, of the Jungian school, for discussing with me the events described in this chapter, and for giving me very useful advice.

4.
The problem of expectations

If you decide to put in practice *Active Astrology*, the problem of expectations is surely the most important problem that you will face. It is a matter of fact that when you try to convince anybody to relocate his/her Solar Return, you will be forced to describe a little bit about the possible results that can be achieved with an Aimed Solar Return. And what you say will surely be translated by the listener with precise scenarios: some people would see a lot of banknotes; others would fancy sexy lovers; still others would see their enemy die, and so on. One year later it would be impossible not to face the effects of your listeners' unaccomplished expectations. And whatever you may say, your client would be always reluctant to accept your explanations, while he/she would more easily accept you reading of the achieved results. As an example of this, I quote an exchange of letters between myself and a deceived client, as published in the issue # 28 (October 1996) of my quarterly bulletin of astrology *Ricerca '90*. The readers, being acute and cultured people, made their reflections on it.

Dear Mister Discepolo,
As you know, I've been following your studies on Aimed Solar Returns for some years. I've always appreciated your spirit of being a attentive and conscientious researcher, aiming to undertake your own theories to an experimental verification.

Therefore if I write to you, simply as a reader of your works, it is with the spirit of collaboration and it is not my intention of being argumentative. Keep my words as a criticism 'from inside', with the following preliminary remarks:

1) I do not set myself up as an 'astrologer', not even a beginner. So please excuse the modest technical contents of my remarks.

2) the year of the last SR has arrived, yes it has. But as Spurinna the haruspex would say: it isn't over yet (although it will be over soon, namely on the 5th of August).

Perhaps you have already guessed the reason why I am writing to you. My 'aimed' Solar Return, which I relocated last year in London in order to place my Ascendant of SR in my 5th House radix thus avoiding its being in the 6th House (as it would have been if I had remained in XY), has not worked at all.

I know that you trust 'in stars more than in human beings' and I don't feel like objecting. I only hope you trust me when I say that during this last year no 'determinantal' episode has happened – your famous 'headlines on the newspaper', neither in my sentimental life nor in the field of diversion and play. The only exception may be a short episode – lasting one week only from New Year's Eve to Epiphany – consisting in a fleeting, furtive *rendez-vous* with my former girlfriend. And anyway, this episode had been precisely announced by the transits of the faster planets over my 5th House radix.
But almost the same had already happened – with the same girl and anyway, for a longer span of time – also last year by midmonth of June, and also in that occasion it had all finished without consequences. This authorizes me to reach the conclusion that nothing relevant has actually happened to me along this year!

It is extremely hard for me to find out any other event related with the symbology of the House, even more: of the whole Aimed SR! Perhaps the only exception – but it's an episode that I mention for the sake of meticulousness – it that at the beginning of December I bought a Personal Computer and a software package of professional astrology. This is the most typical diversion for a Uranian individual, and it may be probably linked to the fact that my 5th natal house lies almost entirely in the sign of Aquarius. In fact, exactly during those days Uranus was significantly entering that House!

Although this event may have implications in a more or less remote future – obviously in connection with the transit of Uranus and its duration – it is a matter of fact that this episode hasn't really meant for my eyes, in the scale of the events of the whole year (which is the most important scale of evaluation, since we are tracing the balance of a SR), the least importance. In fact I had already written down my doctoral dissertation with the computer in 1989, and I had bought and used other computers in the past.

The stellium in the 7th House of SR, on the contrary, has expressed itself in a rather consistent way in the direction of an increased pugnacity in my field of profession. On the other side, at least so far, it hasn't fulfilled the promise of the trine with the conjunction of Jupiter and Moon in Sagittarius in the 10th House. So everything confined to a slight up-tuning of the usual permanent conflict that I always find in my professional activity. But this could be reasonably due to the arrival of Saturn in my 7th House radix. Moreover, for some time this planet has also been creating a wide trine with my very feeble natal Sun in the 11th House – and it could also be due to the contemporary transit of the faster celestials in my 6th and 7th House somewhere during February and March.

I wouldn't really be able to find out anything else of relevance, corresponding to the 'tune' of the year; except a sequel of micro-episodes that have nothing to do with the Asc. in the 5th House radix or the stellium in the 7th House, for they can be rather – and promptly – explained in terms of the transit of faster celestials in the Houses of my birth chart.

At a certain point I have even considered the hypothesis that, by mistake, the Asc. of SR might have fallen in the 4th House rather than in the 5th House. On this assumption I was able to recall several episodes that pointed to the possibility of it being true: for instance, a sequel of small enhancements in my domestic habitat. Still, it was much more reasonable to explain them with the contemporary transit of Jupiter in my 4th House radix.

Yet I thought to myself, I once aimed a SR in Bangkok in 1991, and it turned out to be a full success. So how can it be that a theory supported by evident theoretical and – I can testify it myself – practical pieces of evidence, could work sometimes and fail at other times?

That year (1991) was really important for me. It started around mid-September with an episode of crucial conflict in my job, which led me to the end of that same year of SR to open the doors to a change of job which I really would appreciate. And around mid-December, it went on with me buying a small flat; and a few days later I engaged in a 'prestigious' betrothal – obviously promised by my natal Venus in the 10th House, in a wide conjunction to the MC. Then, around mid-January, I was presented with a shift to the new flat: a really decisive emancipation! Eventually, that year closed brilliantly with me winning a competition for a teaching chair – with my registration in the roll.

If you look at it again, perhaps it is not impossible to read those events 'against the light' – or at least some of those events – as mere expression of the transits:

1) My winning the competition for a chair: Jupiter on the Asc. exactly during the days of my effective registration in the roll (around mid-October 1992). Please note that Jupiter in my birth chart is in the 9th House and trine to the Asc. – and as everybody knows, the 9th House is connected to the teaching at a University. And during the days of the exams, Jupiter had been conjunct with the triple conjunction of Uranus-Mercury-Pluto in the 12th House, thus heralding – obviously – a hard commitment to studying.

2) My estate acquisition and the contemporary sentimental episode (respectively on the 20th of December and on the 13th of December of 1991): Uranus Neptune in the 4th House in wide opposition to the Moon Cancer in the 10th House (please note that the Moon is in wide conjunction with Venus Gemini in my birth chart).

3) On the day (the 17th of September 1991) of my decisive quarrel with my boss (a quite well-known, powerful and aggressive woman, as confirmed by my natal Moon-Cancer in conjunction with Mars, in the field of profession):

the Sun was over the Asc.
the Moon, in conjunction with Uranus in the 4th House during those

hours, was also opposite to itself

Mercury was conjunct with its radix position, with Uranus, and with Pluto in the 12th House

Jupiter had just entered the 12th House (a 'lucky' misadventure).

The next birthday announces an important year, since the Asc. of SR will lie in the 10th House radix. Even so, the SR only seems to be emphasizing events that other astrological events may well underline! In fact let us focus on what will happen after March, when

1) The conjunction of Uranus-Jupiter in my 5th House radix opposes my natal Sun in the 11th House and create a sextile with Saturn in the 7th House (exactly on those days Saturn is also precisely trine to my Sun), as well as another sextile with Pluto in Sagittarius, which by then might also be able to create another trine with my natal Sun: for the first time in my life, and for a very few days.

2) Neptune enters definitely into the 5th House creating a wide supporting conjunction with – just in case there were any need of supporting – the conjunction of Jupiter-Uranus.

As you can see, the 5th and the 7th House are heavily involved, which have been kept 'silent' during this SR. Also the 11th House is involved, the House in which my House lies. As I've already underlined, I'm not an astrologer. Nonetheless I think I can forecast that something important is to happen in my sentimental life or in the field of diversion and play. If it doesn't, I am afraid that I'll start doubting the validity not only of the aimed SR's, but of astrology itself as a tool of forecasting.

And if it weren't so – i.e. if what I take as hypothesis really happened – could we claim (and this is the conclusion of my question to you) that if – say – we placed the Asc. of SR into the 9th House rather than the 10th one, in the importance of the events of the year the symbolic value of the latter would overcome what the slower and more relentless pawns are already developing in the silent celestial chessboard?

Your sincerely,
signature

Dear Doctor ...

I'll try to reply to your letter in full, and I hope that my reasons will satisfy you, although I am afraid that it won't be easy. It won't be easy, because first of all I don't understand whether your 'constructive criticism' refers to the Aimed Solar Returns or to Solar Returns in general. For at the beginning of your letter you make a reference specifically to the former, while as you go on you seem to object to all the Solar Returns: even those that certain – a little bit bemused – colleagues of mine cast for the native's place of birth, rather than for the place where the native is actually at the moment of the astrological birthday.

So let us proceed and make certain points clear. I realize that the first problem, I mean the most important one that an astrologer of my school must face daily, is the problem of *expectations*.

Perhaps the entire degree of satisfaction or dissatisfaction of the client, one year after the previous consultation with the astrologer, depends on this point. In the past years it has happened to me several times – I have also written about it – that I have 'promised' important years to people who later on complained because they had seen *no money* during those twelve months. But – who had ever mentioned money to them? When I described to them the potentialities of an important and constructive year, I am sure that I haven't, for I intended much different things. Sometimes it's the opposite that happens to me: I announce a black year and the client, one year later, merrily claims that it hadn't been so. I remember that once I forecast a bad year to a young homosexual who used to have several occasional intercourses during the year. I warned him yet, but maybe he thought about AIDS.

Perhaps this is the reason why he actually had a very detrimental year with several troubles; nonetheless his eyes were sparkling with joy as he claimed that it has not been a bad year - for he hadn't taken the terrible virus. So you can understand that beyond any objective fact, if you want to establish whether a SR had worked or not, it is important to understand what one really expects. I also would like to make it clear what I mean by 'the headlines on the cover page'.

When I explain to a client the effects of leaving or placing the Ascendant of SR in a certain House, I make use of this type of language because I hope that he/she understands me better: "By placing the Asc. of SR into your natal 4th House, what we do is that the headlines of your 'captain's log', the one describing the events of the twelve months from one birthday to the following birthday, will be: 'Habitat'." Now, what happens quite often is that my listener misunderstands, and in his mind his own personal 'captain's log' becomes as important as a national daily paper.

I will try to explain this another way. If I forecast 'officially stamped paper, troubles with bureaucracy, with the law' he links this to the cover page of a daily paper and he eventually thinks that he will be mentioned by the TV news because, say, the Prime Minister had accused him of something. In reality, what happens is that he quarrels badly with his brother-in-law. A simple, banal, bad quarrel with his brother-in-law. He would then object, "This is what you call a 'cover page'?" Yes, of course this is what I call the cover page, if that has been the most important event in the year of the native.

Who ever told that every year you suffer from mourns or you upgrade to new jobs or new love affairs? There may be very flat years in which the most important event for each of us may be taken as 'absolutely trivial' by the less smart journalist writing in the paper of your neighbourhood. What I mean is that the SR does not tell lies.

When it heralds the prevailing subject of the year, the most significant one, it does so without considering that this subject may or may not be well accepted by the addressee. Now let us consider your specific case. What I notice is that when we were discussing it - you and me together, we gave a very different reading of your next SR. My goal was to avoid you a 6th House of SR, while you probably – perhaps rightfully – were dreaming of very satisfactory events connected with the notion of love in the 5th House. Now, after everything has taken place, could we really claim that the SR has told lies? It is my opinion that it hasn't. In your letter (as well as in the card annexed to the letter) you claimed that this year you devoted yourself to the computer more than in the previous times, thanks to an astrological software; you also devoted yourself to the study of law – as a hobby. Now, any activity carried out as a hobby, for fun, is it not something specific of the 5th House? You say that in past times you had already used the computer to write your doctorate.

Well, but it was not the same thing: then it was an assignment, now you used it for pleasure. It is not the fault of the SR if you fancied that the 5th House would materialize, say, through a very graceful female colleague for whom you particularly care. There has been no graceful girl, but there has been a practice of hobbies during the year. You might say, 'Nothing worth the headlines!' Who says so? Can you mention other important events that marked the twelve months we are talking about? It is you who write, in your letter, 'Nothing else to notify'. So, if you *have nothing else to notify*, why don't you want to admit that these have been the prevailing events of your SR? Nonetheless there is another point that you have forgotten to notice, while it has a great importance. You live in Bari, so haven't you noticed that the 6th House would have played an important role in your SR of Bari, implying a sequel of different troubles, while having relocated it to London you had suffered from none of those troubles? So you can see, it's what I said: as I projected this ASR my goal was to avoid all the troubles that you had faced if you had spent the SR at home in Bari; while you probably were fancying of one year of voluptuous sentimental affairs. You also claim that the extremely pleasant events that happened to you during the SR of Bangkok would have taken place anyway, even if you had stayed home, for they had been provoked by the transits.

Well, I invite you to make a very simple test. Stay home, I mean in your town, when you'll have your next positive transits together with an Asc. of SR falling in the 12th or 1st House of your birth chart, and let me know. Please believe me, if I say so it is not my intention of being argumentative either.

If I feel 'flamed' on certain questions it is only because I believe that thousands and thousands of positive feedbacks cannot be deleted by the pessimistic declaration of one person – although a very trustful person as you are – who feels deceived because his own expectations did not come true. Lastly, if you allow me, I would respectfully like to make an ironic remark on your last sentence: "... I think I can forecast that something important is to happen in my sentimental life or in the field of diversion and play. If it doesn't, I am afraid that I'll start doubting not only the aimed SR's, but astrology itself as a tool of forecasting." Maybe a psychoanalyst would invite you to ask yourself what uncertainties may hide behind this menace of yours. I often receive this menace from people who consulted with me.

To them and to you, dear Dr. ..., I would like to answer as follows: "Whom do you think you are hurting? Do you want to keep without light? Keep going like that!" But I don't say so, for I know that you are a serious man, and above all you are a man of studies. So I am sure that you will reconsider the things under the point of view that I have proposed to you. Perhaps you'll find that the SR has not failed in doing its job.

Nevertheless, by writing so I don't mean that this system is a perfect one and that it doesn't need any adjustment! As Terzio would say in Federico Fellini's wonderful film *The Voice of the Moon*: a slight amendment should be done to our satellite, after all.

Your sincerely,
Ciro Discepolo

5.
Jeoffrey's theorem

What has Jeoffrey to do with our subject? You'll see it soon. Active Astrology is not only a matter of choosing places and moments at the right time: it is a matter of synergies – in the widest meaning of this term. You've got to choose if you wish to grasp chances – this could be the motto of Active Astrology. In other terms, it may be a matter of not trying to tilt windmills, but taking decisions instead – in order to achieve good results always, and to go with the stream.

So let us consider an exemplary case. She is a young woman with a quite detrimental stellium of celestials including Venus in the 12th House: her life is a sequel of sentimental fiascos. She shows the tendency of establishing liaisons with mentally or physically ill men. I remember a particular event also. Two parents consulted me with despair because their only daughter, a nurse in a hospital, had an affair with a disabled. After years of this liaison, she left that young man, but to her parents' discomfort, she started a new relationship with another disabled man a few months later. Many women with similar astrological values as the lady mentioned before tend to choose as their partners weak, suffering, usually ill and sometimes even strongly neurotic men. They usually do so almost unwillingly.

They aren't usually satisfied with that, and in fact their relationships usually break in short time. And this is what Jeoffrey has to do with this story. Do you remember *Angelique*? It's a series of French historical adventure books. The protagonist is a beautiful young lady who has got to marry a lame with a wooden leg and huge scars disfiguring his face. Now, you may remember that the gorgeous lady, after overcoming the first visual trauma, got to know this man's tenderness, passion and virility, so she ended up with falling in love with him for the rest of their life. What I mean is that Active Astrology should teach girls having a strong stellium in the 12th House to select their own Jeoffrey as a mate. For if they aimed for the classical Prince Charming, looking like Leonardo DiCaprio or Brad Pitt, they would surely doom themselves to a misery of suffering and humiliation. While if they looked for a 'Jeoffrey' – i.e. a semi-disabled one, a man with a little mental or physical handicap – they would even reach a happy life, at least from the point of view of love. After all, is it so bad to live with a lame partner, or someone blind in one eye, or a diabetic to whom you should give three injections a day? Is it so significant a hindrance if all the rest is fine and you really love each other? For one must live in practice his/her astrological elements concerning the 12th House – and as I said before, one cannot tilt windmills.

Now let me show how this rule can be applied to another case. One day a woman comes to consult me whose birth chart shows a very bad conjunction (exact to the degree) of Saturn and Mars in Cancer, in her 4th House. I asked what were the terrible things that had happened to her in connection with her parents and her home. She answered that she had lost both parents in the first five years of her life. She had also moved more than twenty times in her life, taking in account the children's homes from which the law had forced her to leave. "But, she told me, now I've solved my problem. They won't me able to give me notice to quit any longer – I am about to buy a house and this will solve my problem." I strongly advised her against that.

I explained to her that her terrible birth conjunction could have expressed itself even worse if she had bought a house. Perhaps she might buy the house and find out that there's asbestos in the walls; she might lose hundreds of millions in the purchase; she might even run the risk of losing her house for a procedural vice. "So, asked the woman in despair, what should I do?" "You should, said I, pay a rent in a house or a flat with a known basic problem: a hindrance that lets you discharge your conjunction Mars-Saturn day by day, every day. For example, you could live in a flat of the sixth floor of an old building without lift. This way you would suffer day by day, but nobody would kick you out of that house, and you wouldn't run the risk of throwing hundreds of millions out of the window." I gave the same piece of advice to a famous Italian dancer who used to live in Paris.

His natal Saturn is in the 9th House of his birth chart: stars would have suggested him not to leave his birth place ever. He lived in Paris, but in an old building, in a mansard on the very last floor of an aged building – without lift. "I must absolutely find a place on the first floor", he said, and I replied, "No you should not. If you really want to stay in Paris, remain where you are– do not tease the devil: he's constantly waiting in ambush."

6.
The added value

As far as Active Astrology is concerned, I cannot keep silent about an important (or at least, it's important in my opinion) reality that I've never mentioned so far. It's the notion of 'added value' – that is to say, something to which we give an additional meaning beyond its specific, basic value. Carl Gustav Jung used to say that the subjective reality is equivalent to the objective reality. Therefore, if you are an optimist you stand better chances of finding a wallet on the street; while if you are a pessimist you run a higher risk of falling down the stairs. I am convinced that each man has got his own rhythms in his life: you must make your utmost to find out what are your own rhythms.

For example: after several years of observations, I have personally become convinced that Tuesday is a very tough day for me; while on the contrary, Thursday corresponds to a day in which things go better for me. You may argue that these are only fantasies and imaginaries from my side, but I can assure that I have collected several pieces of evidence. For example, when I was a soldier I was punished three times: it was Tuesday on every occasion. On Tuesdays I had certain serious accidents by car. My first daughter also had an accident on Tuesday, and my wife once delivered by Caesarean also on a Tuesday. Beyond those 'objective' meanings I have probably added also meaning of an 'added value' to the specific reality of my life. In other words, I admit that I may have 'charged' the Tuesdays of meaning, so now Tuesday perfectly matches this pattern. At this point it doesn't really matter whether Tuesday is really a detrimental day for me, or it merely matches my own inner projection.

The result is the same and I know that my weeks are kind of split in two halves. For they usually seem to follow a sort of diabolic pattern: matters start entangling on Monday evening, they literally flop on Tuesdays, and they leave a sequel of little disasters on Wednesdays. Then my silver lining usually arrives on Thursdays and my week shows a neutral trend for the following days. Each individual should find out his/her own rhythm, which is not necessarily based on the days of the week. I often happen to meet people who swear that to them everything turns into a fiasco, say, every year in April or in December; while others claim that their life becomes worse every third year; others say they have problems every leap year. Each of them proves to me the validity of his/her point of view based on the precise dates of dramatic events of their life: and I believe them, for the reasons that I have just explained.

I have never been able to throw light on the astrological implication of those rhythms. But I believe that this is not really important, because it's life itself which teaches you to beware of a certain day, or a certain month, or a certain year. It is surely not due to the simple equation Sunday-Sun, Monday-Moon and so on: for I know many people for whom Tuesday is a wonderful day, while Thursday is a harmful day. When we get to find out the reason of such spans of time, we should follow the logic of Active Astrology and behave accordingly. For example during your 'bad days' you should never undergo an important medical examination, or go to a job interview that could influence our future occupational life, or attempt a reconciliation with your beloved one.

Of course I don't wish to make up the theory that such a conviction should block you to paralysis on a regular basis, preventing you from doing anything at all! I simply find it reasonable not to ignore this alternation of 'good' and 'bad' times, and behave more prudently in the 'bad' ones. If you learn to understand the intrinsic value of the days, you'll surely live better.

7.
A complete failure

If you apply it well, Active Astrology is certainly able to improve the quality of your life. Obviously, within the frame of precise limits. What I am about to tell you may prove that on certain occasions, not even a miracle can really save you. This is the case of Sandro, a young man from Veneto. He comes from a very good family and he graduated brilliantly. Fig. 1 shows you his birth chart. The first time we meet he assured me that he was born exactly at 11:05 pm.

He is definitely confident about it, and – he said – he is particularly sure of those 'five minutes'. Since then I met him several times. He used to ring me almost daily, and sometimes he called me at different times on the same day. He used to tell me how his life develops despite the hindrances – he says – caused by a brother with whom Sandro has a very bad rapport. Sandro's ugly conjunction of Mars and Saturn (one of the most detrimental aspects in a birth chart, I dare say) seemed to support his given time of birth during all those years. He also had a very bad relationship with his sister-in-law. Every year, Sandro relocated his Solar Return always aiming at the place that I suggested to him.

Things seemed to develop quite well, although he usually claimed his dissatisfaction, until something terrible happened during the years in which Pluto was transiting over his aforementioned bad natal conjunction, while at the same time Neptune was passing over his natal Mercury. A very strong heap of celestials on the very day of his birthday prevented me from being able to determine a suitable place for his Aimed SR and to save him from the huge risks that I foresaw for his health, from my astrological observation post. So I resolved to place that ugly stellium in the 2nd House of the SR.

Of course I warned Sandro that during the following twelve months he should drastically 'turn off the taps' of his outgoing money, not to transfer any money for whatsoever reason. As I told you before, also during that year Sandro used to phone me almost daily. I used to answer as a friend, for if I summed up all the minutes that I devoted to him on the phone, I might rightfully say that I gave him as a present a good portion of my job. During those conversations, Sandro never mentioned to me anything special happening to him.

Unluckily, he eventually talked about it only years after the disgrace had happened. More or less, based on his late report, things turned out like this. His father had a huge amount of money (billions of Italian Liras) and gave 50% of it to Sandro and 50% to his brother. This is when a 'friend' of Sandro got to know it and suggested, more or less as follows: "What are you going to do with all that money? Don't be silly! If you leave them in a bank they'll yield only a pittance! Give them to me, I will fetch you a tidy sum!" Sandro did not tell a word to anybody: not a single word to his parents, not a word to me and not a word even to his confessor, I suppose. He simply wrote a cheque and left all his capital in the hands of that scoundrel. You can imagine what happened afterwards. A few years later Sandro accosted the vulture, who claimed to have lost everything in wrong speculations.

Sandro realized that he was totally ruined and that he cannot take any legal action against his 'friend' because his signing the cheque hadn't been extorted in any way. Later on, when Sandro told me the terrible thing which had happened to him, I tried to fix it up with a sequel of good Aimed Solar Returns one after another; but the damage was so huge that I did not achieve any positive result. I don't know anything else. At the end of 1997 Sandro expressed to me, in an ungenerous telephone call, as much ingratitude as a human being can feel for those who have only tried to do good. In other worlds, he insulted me violently, thus ending our relationships.

As a conclusion of this dramatic story, I have tried to read the events with detachment. After all, I said to myself, my duty was above all to save Sandro from the huge risks for his health. By placing that terrible stellium in the 2nd House of SR I knew of course that he would run serious financial risks, but I could not guess that

- he would not follow my advice not to relocate money, especially not to make any expense;
- he would embark on a crazy enterprise without saying a word to his father or to me;

- he would draw a cheque of an incredible amount without asking himself what he was doing;

- that his time of birth was wrong. In fact, after the tragedy had already happened, he asked for his officially registered papers of birth, and after recalculating his birth chart on the registered time of birth, we realized that his detrimental conjunction of Mars and Saturn was not in his natal 3rd House, but in his 2nd House.

This sad story should teach something to all of us. It should teach that before any other consideration, in dealing with Aimed Solar Returns the astrologer becomes responsible for extremely important events: therefore we cannot 'let the children play with the rifle'. Secondly, it should teach that no Aimed Solar Return can save us from certain disasters. No matter how experienced the astrologer is: facing certain events, neither a pilgrimage to Lourdes nor the intervention of Padre Pio could help. Sandro's story is a very bitter one. I sincerely believe that even more than the obnubilating Neptune, it was the devil himself who suggested him to sign that cheque. I cannot say anything else, because it would be out of the scope of this volume. Also because I am not really prepared in this field: but I do firmly believe that Evil exists and that he's constantly setting traps for us. Otherwise how could we explain such a case like Sandro's? Please take into consideration that he graduated with a first class in economics!

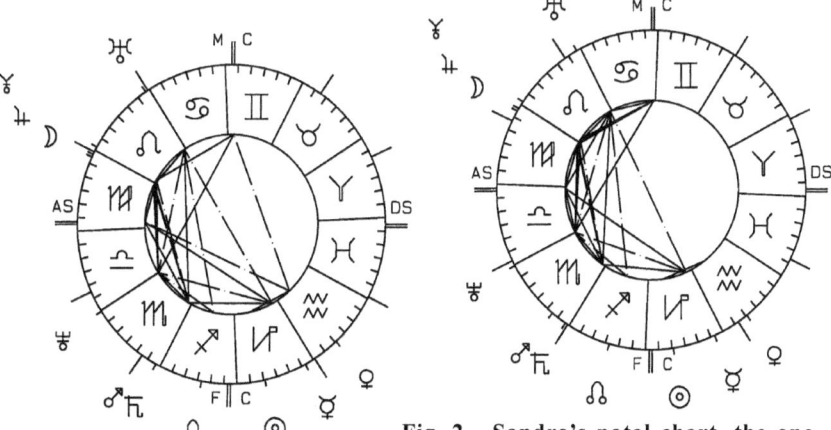

Fig. 1 - Sandro's natal chart, the one I've worked on for years

Fig. 2 - Sandro's natal chart, the one corrected with the registered hour of birth

8.
On the precision of the time of birth

Not always is it clear for the Reader which is the range of precision within whose limits one should operate when studying an Aimed Solar Return. Of course I refer to the precision of the time of birth. We must then make a distinction between, say, the Sun or Mars of SR risking of lying in the 12th House of SR, or the Ascendant of SR risking of lying in the 12th House of the natal chart. Perhaps a practical example will help me explain it better. Consider the subject whose natal chart you can see in fig. A1. Fig. A2 shows the same natal chart of the same individual, but considering an anticipation of half an hour in his time of birth. Now let us consider two different Solar Returns. The native spends his 1978 SR in Savona, Italy; and his 1979 SR in Athens, Greece. The table shows all the longitudes required for the examination of this case. Let's start from his aimed birthday in Athens. Fig. A3 shows the chart of SR, while fig. A4 shows the same chart based on the anticipated time of birth. As you can see, it is legitimate to doubt about a possible presence of the Sun in the 12th House of the SR relocated in Athens. In fact if the native were born half an hour earlier than his declared time of birth, in Athens the Sun would precisely be in the 12th House of the SR. In fact the Sun is 19° Scorpio, while the cusp we are considering, in Athens, is 17° Scorpio – that is to say, the Sun is two degrees 'below' the cusp. Now let us consider his SR in Savona, in 1978. Fig. A5 shows that the Ascendant is 19° Virgo while his natal cusp of the 12th House is 24° Virgo. Now what the astrologer asks to himself is, what if the native's time of birth is wrong? What if, say, he was born before? What would happen then? Could the Ascendant of the SR be in his natal 12th House? As you can see in fig. A6 this could not happen. In fact by recasting his SR for an earlier time of birth, the newly drawn Ascendant is 14° Virgo and the cusp of the 12th House is 17° Virgo: three wide degrees of safety. In fact in my practice I have always noticed that the relationship Ascendant/cusp of even one degree may be safe, while in the relationship Sun/cusp or Mars/cusp it is much safer to consider a margin of three or four degrees. The absolute values would change if we considered an Ascendant falling in a sign of slow ascension, but the logic would remain the same. So remember that the extremely dangerous degrees in which the Sun or Mars of SR should never be, are the last degrees of the 12th House, the first degrees of the 2nd House, and the last degrees of the 5th House.

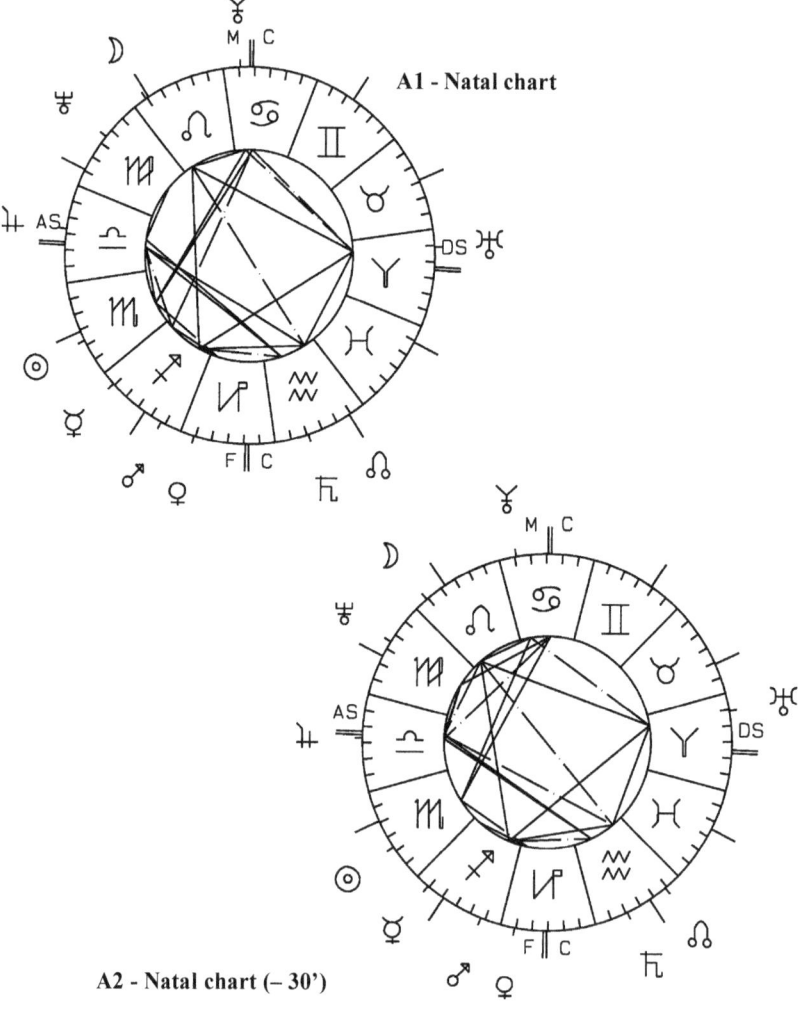

A1 - Natal chart

A2 - Natal chart (– 30')

ON THE PRECISION OF THE TIME OF BIRTH

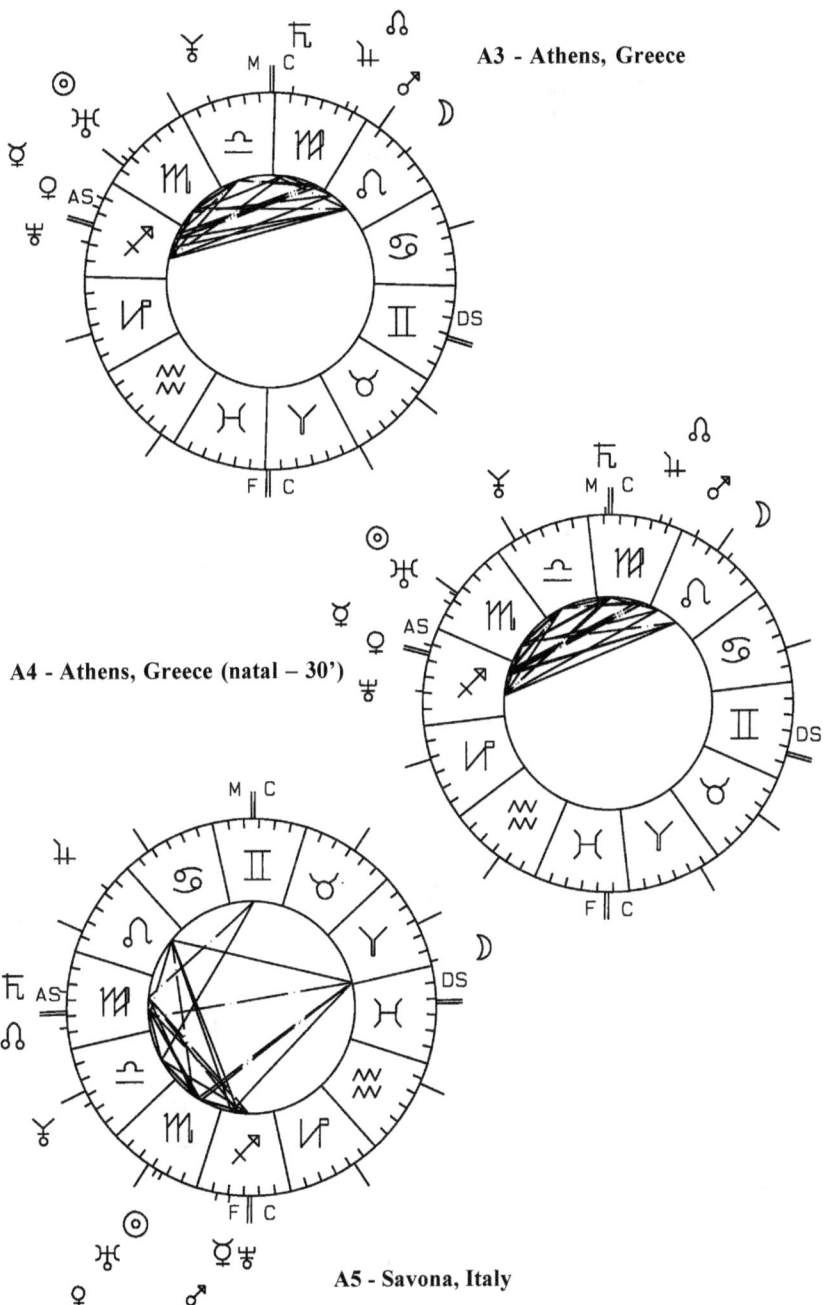

A3 - Athens, Greece

A4 - Athens, Greece (natal – 30')

A5 - Savona, Italy

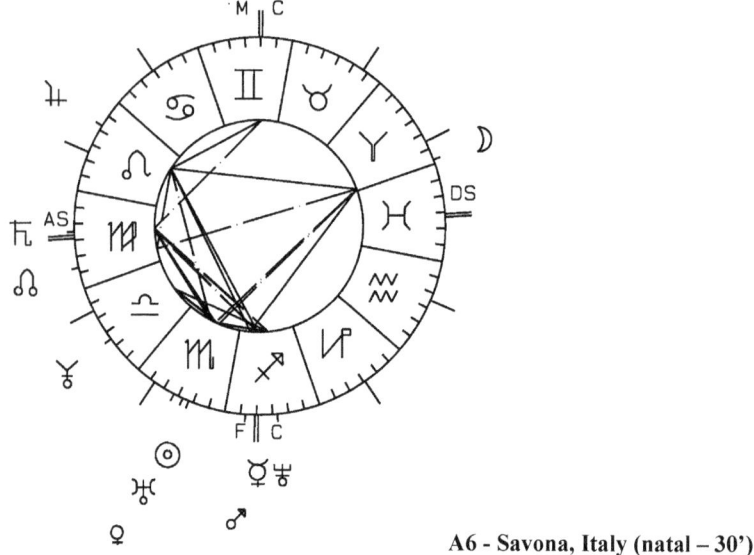

A6 - Savona, Italy (natal – 30')

Fig. A1	Natal Sun	19° Scorpio
Fig. A1	Cusp of the 12th House, natal	24° Virgo
Fig. A2	Cusp of the natal 12th House, 30 minutes earlier	17° Virgo
Fig. A3	Cusp of the 12th House in Athens (1979)	23° Scorpio
Fig. A4	Cusp of the 12th House in Athens, 30 minutes earlier	17° Scorpio
Fig. A5	Ascendant in Savona (1978)	19° Virgo
Fig. A6	Ascendant in Savona, 30 minutes earlier	14° Virgo

9.
The 'gap'

In a map of Solar Return you have what I call 'the gap' when, for example, the Sun is almost on the cusp between the 5th and the 6th House, and Mars is almost positioned on the Descendent, or vice-versa. Please consider the chart in the following page. When the subject happens to have a Base Solar Return like this, (I mean, the SR cast for the place where he, or she lives normally), there is no use in wasting time trying to correct it with a slight relocation, because the only chance is to change completely to another part of the world; another time zone.

For if you relocate slightly eastward you end up putting Mars deep into the 6th House, while if you move slightly westward it's the Sun that you place deep into the 6th House. Both positions are quite dangerous. As you can see from the following example, the native has a similar situation if he spends his SR in Salerno, where he has settled down; but things are even worse if he relocates in Otranto (eastward) or Genoa (westward). An astrologer who suggested him not to move at all would make a serious mistake: in fact even a difference of 10 minutes in the time of birth could be enough to have that Sun or that Mars placed in the 6th House of the BSR.

Let us consider another subject. The charts in the page following the next one belong to subject #2, whose SR of Naples shows the Sun very close to the cusp of the 6th House, and Mars quite close to the 1st House. As you can see, it is not sufficient to relocate in Jerusalem, where Mars would be clearly in the 1st house. And neither Madrid is a suitable place for relocation, because there the Sun would be placed in the central area of the 6th House. A solution consists in changing the ASR of many time zones: in Flores in the Azores the Sun of the subject's SR would be safely in the 7th House, while Mars would be safely far from the 1st House.

AIMED SOLAR AND LUNAR RETURNS

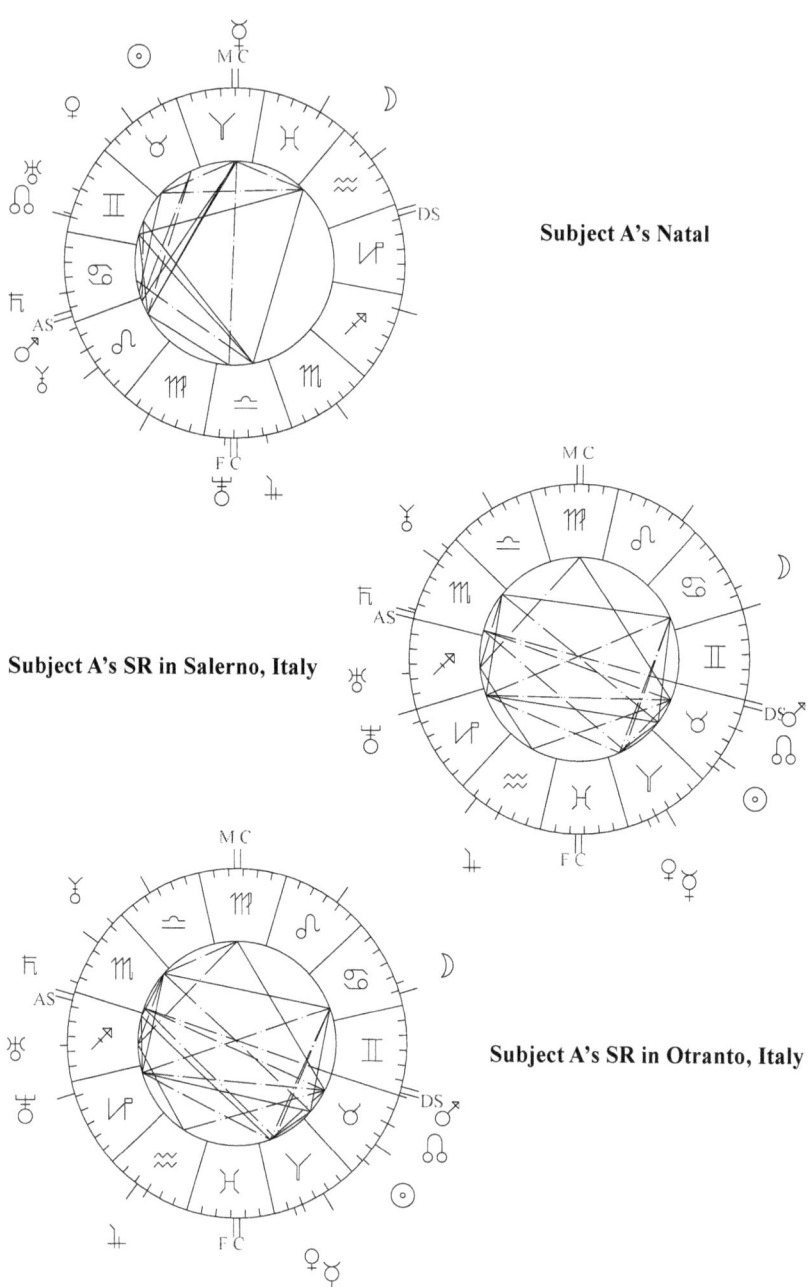

Subject A's Natal

Subject A's SR in Salerno, Italy

Subject A's SR in Otranto, Italy

THE 'GAP' 53

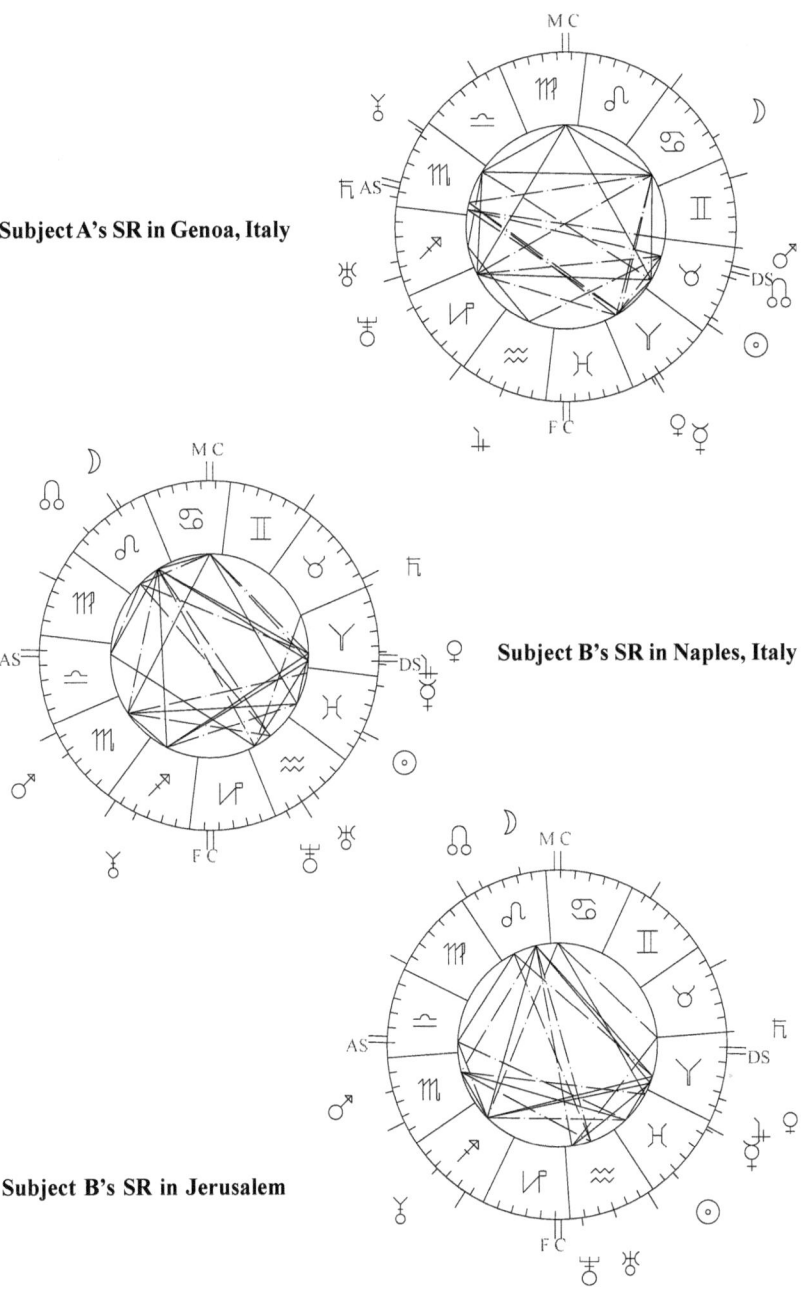

Subject A's SR in Genoa, Italy

Subject B's SR in Naples, Italy

Subject B's SR in Jerusalem

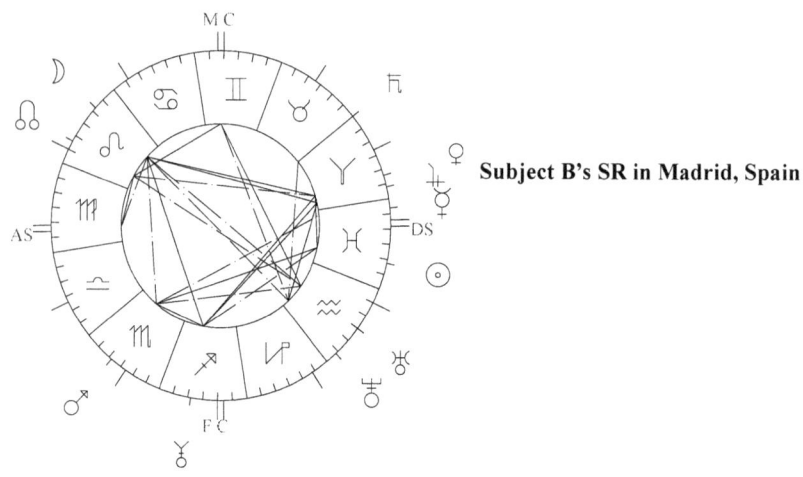

Subject B's SR in Madrid, Spain

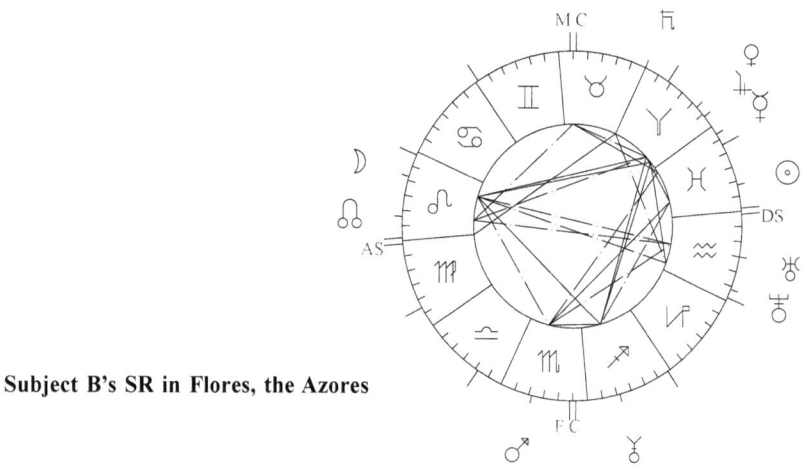

Subject B's SR in Flores, the Azores

10.
When the natal Sun is in the 10th or in the 9th House

Those whose natal Sun is in the 10th or in the 9th House live with the frustration of being unable to place their Ascendant of Solar Return in their natal 10th House, for if they do so their Sun of SR lies in the 12th or the 1st House of SR. This may be explained by the fact that those people are somewhat 'kissed by good luck' from their very birth, thanks to the fairly good position of their radix Sun.

Therefore they should not expect further help from life. But of course, this way of reasoning is merely academic: it does not want to face such implications as karma or similar. So in these cases you can still relocate by aiming a slightly less powerful combination as the Ascendant of SR in the 10th natal house: for example, by placing the Sun or Jupiter or Venus in the 10th House of SR. It is not the same, but it helps. If you place the Sun into the 10th House of SR though, be careful not to leave the Ascendant of SR in the 12th or 1st House of the native's birth chart.

But if the subject was born with the Sun in the 9th House, not far from the MC, not always it is possible to place the Ascendant of his/her SR in the natal 10th House. It is the case of the young man from Emilia-Romagna whose charts you can see in the following page. In 1996 he would have had a very bad Solar Return if he had remained in his place of residence: he would have had the Sun, Mars, and Saturn in the 12th House of the SR.

Apparently it was impossible to avoid those positions and place his Ascendant of SR into his 10th natal House. For example, by relocating in Athens, Greece, he would have had the Ascendant in the 10th House, but he would have had also the conjunction Sun-Mars over the cusp of the 12th House: a very dangerous thing! In fact, a difference of 10 minutes in his time of birth would have been enough and he would have had this conjunction deep in the 12th House. What could we do then? A huge displacement of latitude was required. And so we did. By relocating his SR of 1996 in Johannesburg, South Africa, we achieved an Ascendant perfectly in the 10th House and the conjunction Mars-Sun very safely indeed far from the 12th House. Saturn all alone in the 12th House is not particularly alarming.

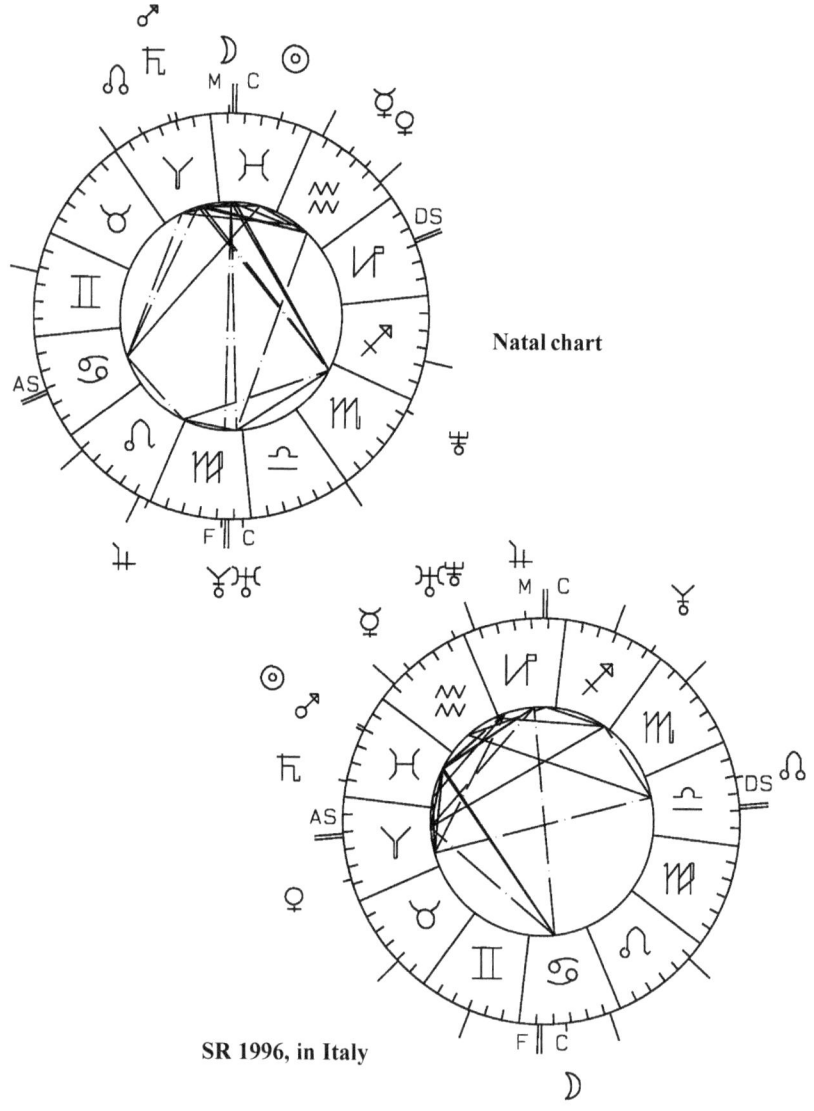

Natal chart

SR 1996, in Italy

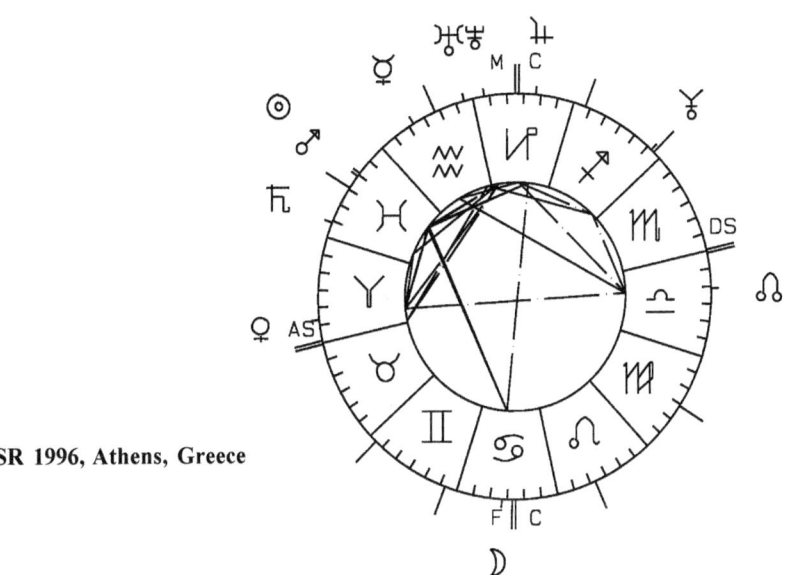

SR 1996, Athens, Greece

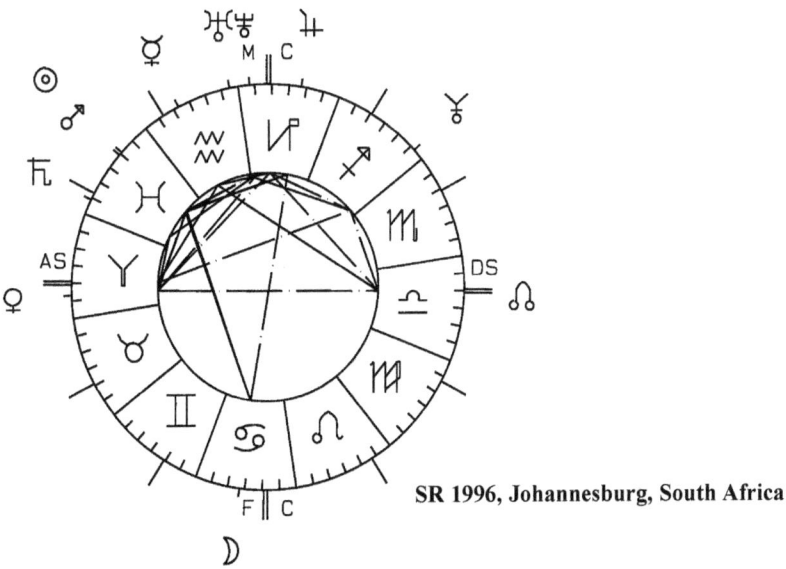

SR 1996, Johannesburg, South Africa

11.
The case of Mrs Smith

What could you do when your interlocutor is absolutely deaf to all of your suggestions? Probably nothing. Some people born with their Sun in Taurus are so resistant to any external influence that one would wonder why they consult astrologers anyway. So let us call this subject Mary Smith.

Mary is a hairdresser and she's been trying to survive among a sequel of troubles: she's in deep crisis with her husband; she's full of debts because of a shop she perhaps opened too early in consideration of her real possibilities; and she suffers from depression as a consequence of all this. Earlier I had already tried to convince her to relocate and have a good ASR, but in vain: she always opposed and had a total, fierce, and unreasonable reluctance to aiming her birthdays. She simply didn't want to hear about relocation. Fig. 1 shows her natal chart.

Among other details, you can notice that when she consulted me once again in spring 1998, Saturn was entering her 8th House – a quite certain herald of recrudescence of her financial troubles. Fig. 2 shows her terrible Solar Return of 1997-1998, with Mars conjunct with the Ascendant of SR, and the Ascendant of SR lying in her natal 12th House. The result was a really hellish year. She understands astrology a little bit, nonetheless she insists: I'll never relocate a birthday! Her following SR is shown in Fig. 3. You can see that detrimental conjunction Sun-Mars in the 6th House, announcing yet another bad year in all sectors of her life – job, money, health, and so on.

Despite it all, Mary is inflexible. She refuses even to displace the conjunction Sun-Mars out from the 6th house by travelling, say, to Lisbon. In a case like this, any astrologer practising Active Astrology would desist and see her to the door. Nevertheless I don't forget that under certain aspects, the astrologer develops a mission similar to the one of a medical doctor. So I gather all my energy and make a last effort to help her anyway. Thus I suggest her to concentrate, to focus, to 'aim' at the only positive area announced by her following SR: namely, the 4th House with Venus and Jupiter in it. My suggestion to Mary is to try and sell her current shop because it is in a charming but isolated area of the town.

I suggest her to open another shop in a perhaps poorer, but surely more populated urban area. For I see that in the following year (i.e. the twelve month from her next birthday to the following one) she would have good luck in real estate, and since I adhere to the principle that it is always necessary to 'aim' at something, I point to a transaction in the field of real estate that be successful for her.

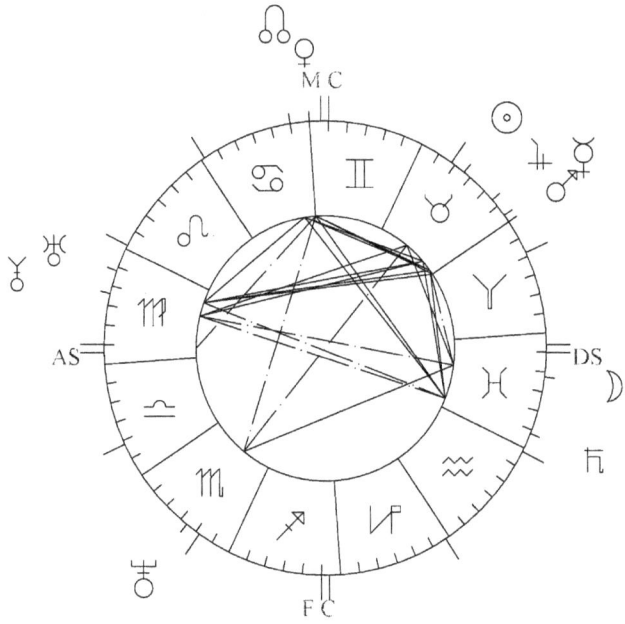

Fig. 1 - Natal chart

THE CASE OF MRS SMITH

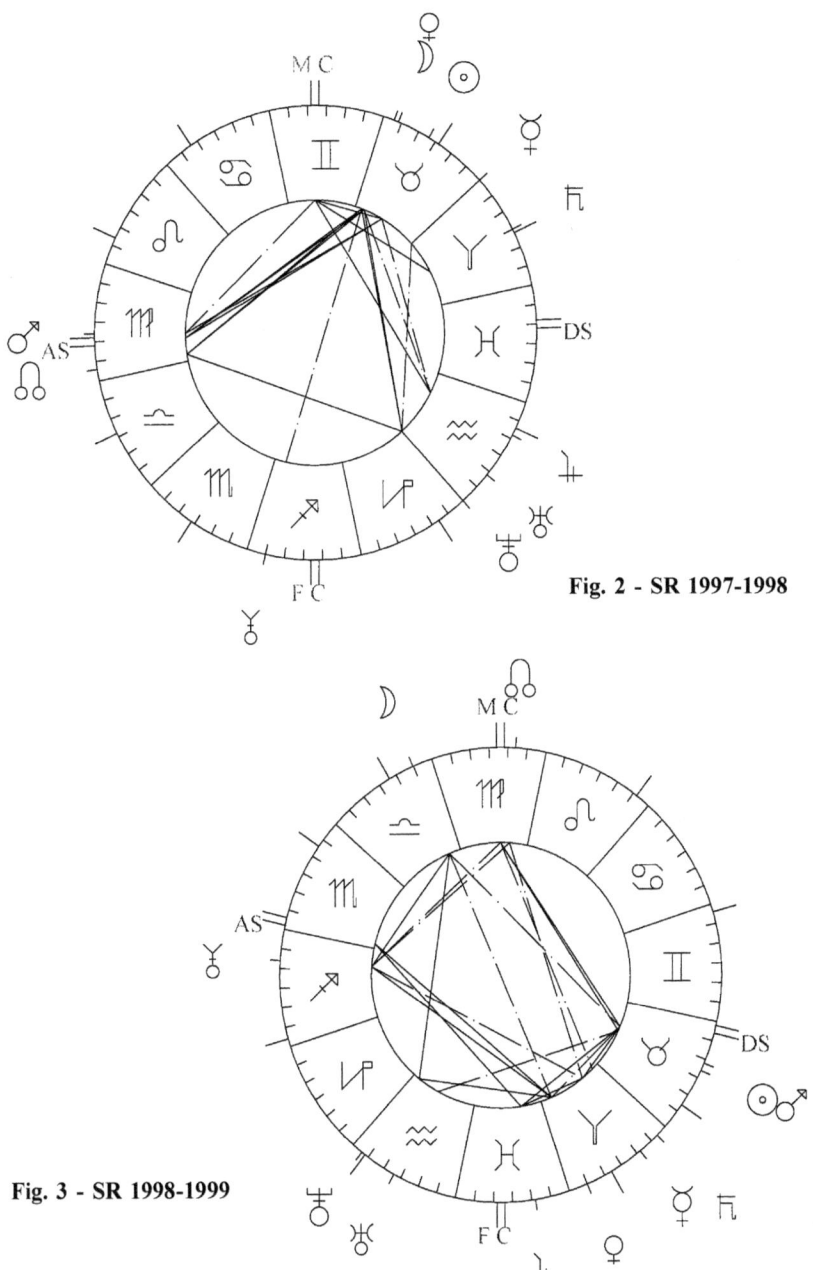

Fig. 2 - SR 1997-1998

Fig. 3 - SR 1998-1999

12.
An easy case and a hard case

What I like to introduce now are two cases: the first one, a quite easy case to be solved; the second one, a really hard one. By following the description of the solutions proposed in each case you can have an idea of how you should reason while searching for a suitable place where to relocate a Solar Return.

Subject A is a twenty-eight-year-old man who owns a hotel. He is preparing to perform important financial transactions. I examine his case at the end of March 1998, with the aim of suggesting to him an aimed birthday for summer 1998. Before anything else, I notice that Saturn is entering his 8th House, which could correspond to an important financial expense from his side. Moreover, I also see that in his Solar Return of 1998-1999 he would have Jupiter in the 7th House, trine to the Sun: this could help him very much in making good commercial transactions.

His Base Solar Return – the one he would have if he remained in Italy in the place where he usually lives – is a really bad one, due to Mars in the 1st House, conjunct with the Ascendant. It is a shame though, because the Ascendant itself lies in his 10th natal House, which would favour the trine Jupiter-Sun very much, by means of a powerful synergy with it. The solution to this case is easy: Lisbon. There we leave the Ascendant in the 10th House and moreover, we place Jupiter in the 10th House of SR, trine to Venus and Mars; the latter planets leave the extremely dangerous 1st House and occupy the 2nd one.

To all this you can add what I wrote about the 'added value' and about the 'magical' relationship that I have with Lisbon, whenever I suggest that place to somebody for relocation. The whole picture is definitely very good. The only doubt that I have is about Mars: it might fall in the 1st House if the native would have been born a little later than the time of birth that his mother gave to me. But it is a risk that we must run: for a young person it may be important to correct his/her own time of birth, even if is at the cost of some trouble.

The second case is the case of Subject B. He is a well-known professional man from Emilia-Romagna dealing with quite wide financial operations. His natal chart shows evidently that (at the end of March 1998) Saturn is about to transit over his MC radix: it is a quite tough transit for a man so exposed professionally and financially as he is. His Base Solar Return in Emilia-Romagna has a stellium with the Sun and Mars in the 8th House of SR: it surely has to be changed if you want to avoid the subject's financial fiasco. If you have read my volume *Transits and Solar Returns* you know that in this case I will never even try to place the Ascendant of a Solar Return in the 10th House radix; so I try to place Jupiter in the 10th House of SR instead. I achieve this result by relocating in Honolulu, but I realize that that place is not suitable because Mars would occupy the 12th House, and the Sun would be in the 1st house of SR.

Then I try to find out a suitable place a little more eastward and westward from there: say the Marquesas Islands and the Fiji Islands. Unluckily the former aren't suitable because there would be a stellium in the 12th House there; while in the latter Mars would be too close to the 1st House; furthermore, Jupiter would go out from the 10th House there. So I try to place Venus in the 10th House of SR. I try Los Angeles, California; but I renounce it because I would have a very bad Saturn conjunct with the MC there.

So I try a little bit eastward, say El Paso: Venus would remain alone in the 10th House, but I would also have the Ascendant of SR falling in the 1st natal house there. At this point, there's no use in trying further with enhancing the 10th House of the SR. Therefore I proceed by searching a neutral Solar Return, or a SR as neutral as possible. So I try and relocate it in Flores, the most western island of the Azores. To be sincere, here I achieve more than a merely neutral ASR: Venus in the 8th House protects money, and Jupiter in the 6th House protects job.

I could end my quest here. But this is exactly where I have to make further considerations. In fact there are astrologers, who suggest people to perform strange and painful treks in the middle of nowhere, say 500 miles in a Jeep in the jungle, with the only aim of achieving a perfect trine or sextile. Of course they do wrong, in my opinion. This way of acting is wrong, for different reasons. First of all, because the time of birth of the subject is never known with great precision: therefore those additional forty days of forced march might prove to be absolutely useless. Also, because perhaps those astrologers look after the decimal digits but they overlook the whole numbers: so they achieve a perfect trine between celestial and leave the Ascendant of SR lying in the 1st house of the subject's natal chart.

And last, because in a SR it's much more important in which House the celestials are than the angular aspects among them. If you wish to have evidence of this, consider a gorgeous Mars in the 6th House of SR and then you tell me whether the subject with such a SR has or hasn't terrible troubles. Back to our example, it should be mentioned that Flores is a quite difficult island to reach: the only way to reach there is flying in a small, always full, ten-passenger-airplane that often doesn't even take off on windy days.

So I'll eventually suggest him to spend his SR in the island of Horta, where Mars is closer to the 8th House but where it is possible to land in any weather condition with a comfortable DC Super 80.

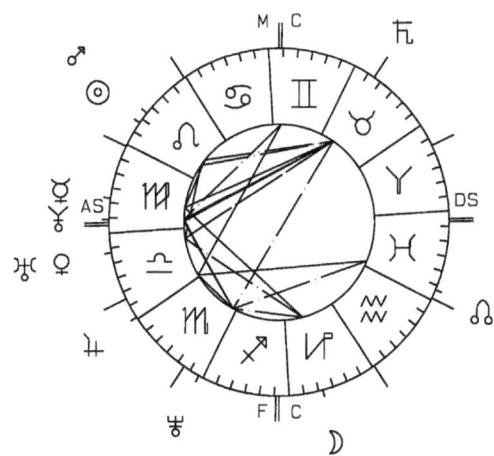

Subject A

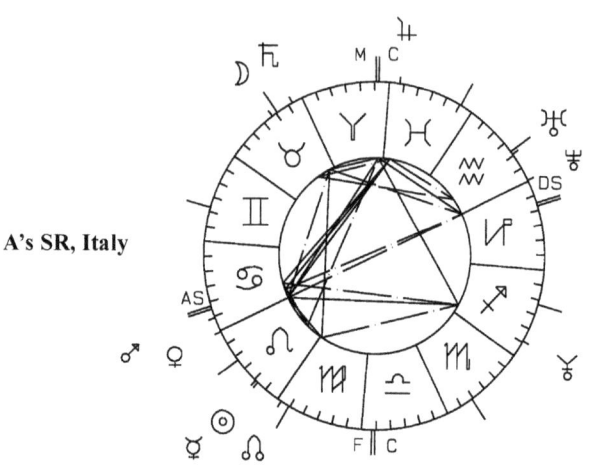

A's SR, Italy

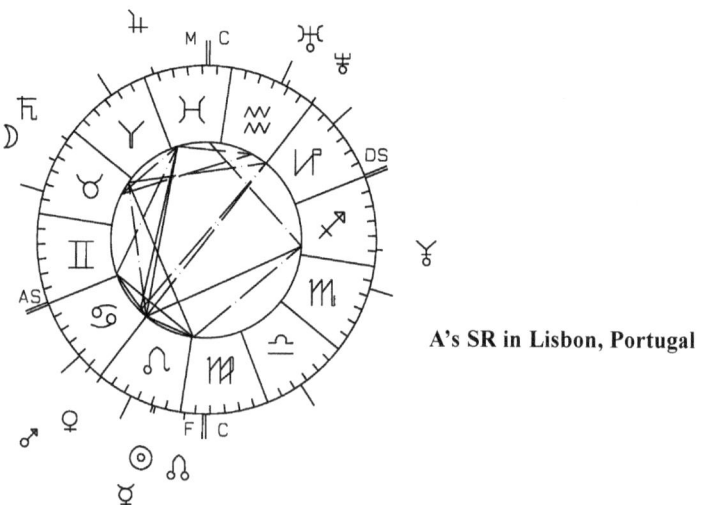

A's SR in Lisbon, Portugal

AN EASY CASE AND A HARD CASE

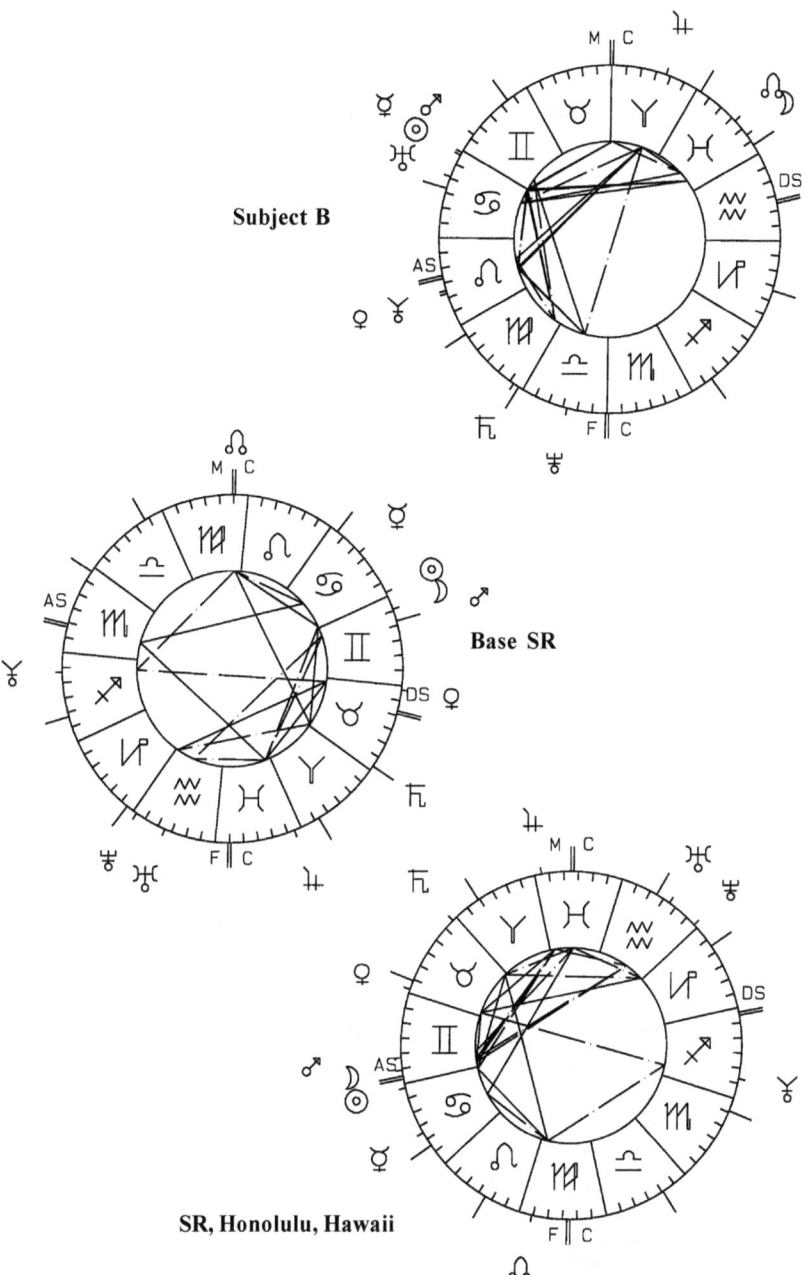

68 AIMED SOLAR AND LUNAR RETURNS

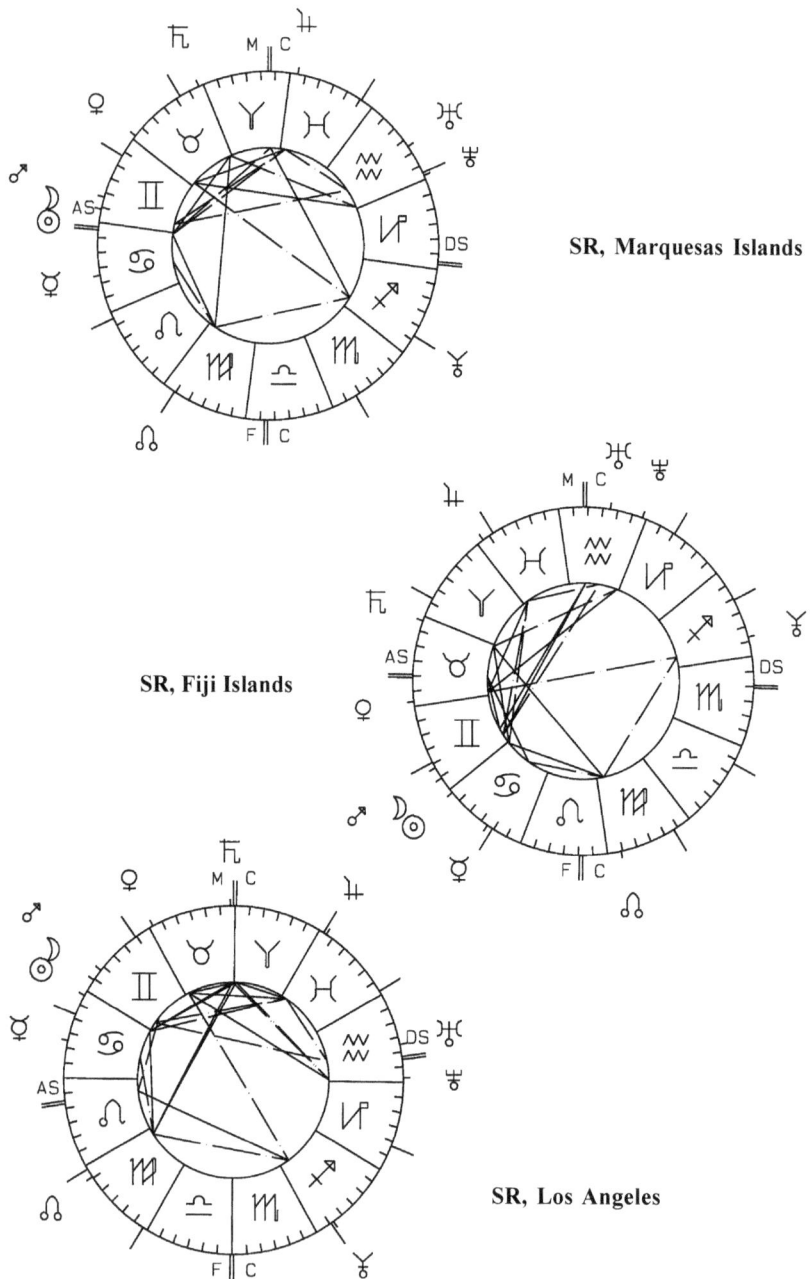

SR, Marquesas Islands

SR, Fiji Islands

SR, Los Angeles

AN EASY CASE AND A HARD CASE

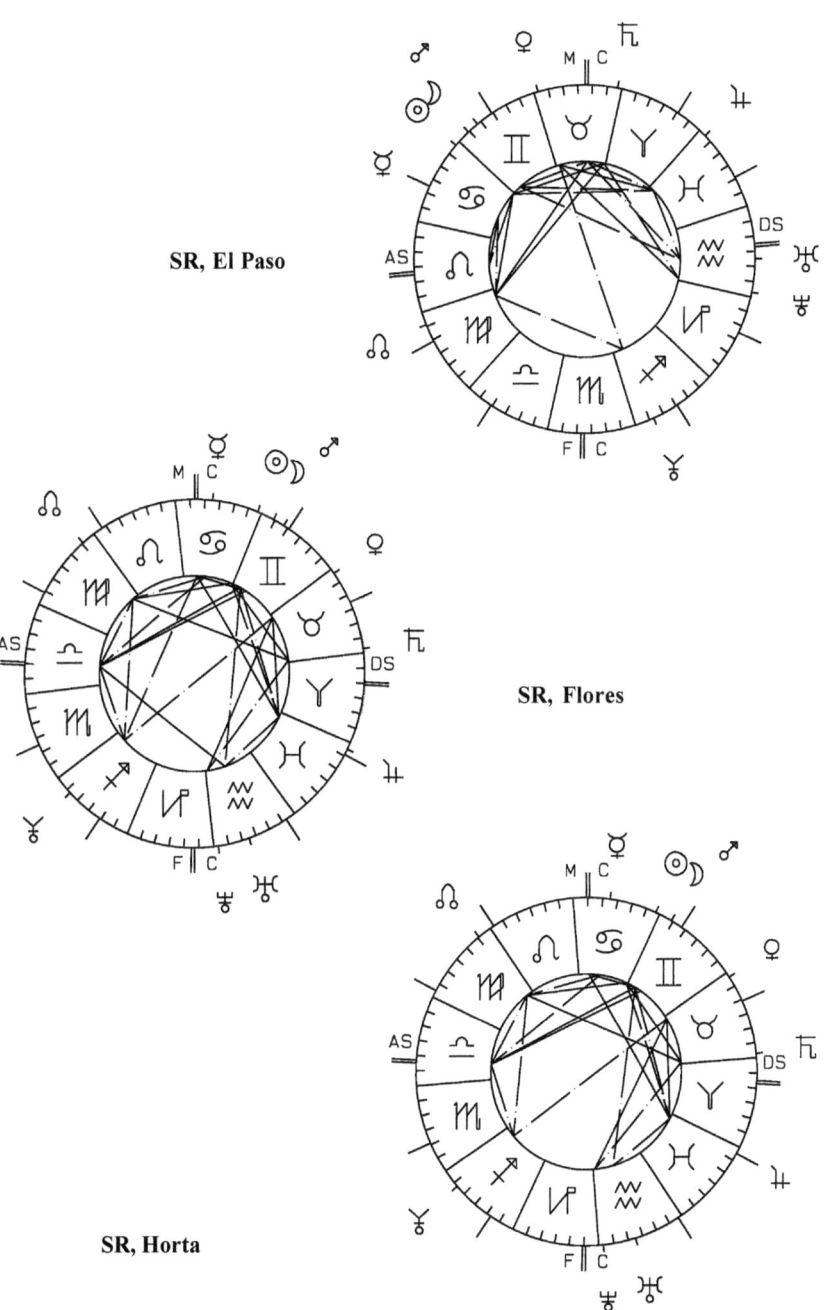

SR, El Paso

SR, Flores

SR, Horta

13.
Stardust

How you can use the principle of Synchronicity at its best

In his studies, Carl Gustav Jung theorized the existence of the so-called principle of synchronicity, which should explain the reality of the world besides – not against, or instead of – the principle of cause and effect. I give a few examples. Say that I hit a bottle with a stone. The bottle breaks up in pieces and this is a typical case of cause (me throwing the stone) and effect (the bottle breaking up in pieces). Now let us consider an example of synchronicity as exposed by Jung himself.

A man goes and buys a blue dress. The shop owner makes a mistake and sends to the buyer a black dress – exactly the same day when the buyer's brother dies. This is how Jung explains the principle of synchronicity: *when two or more events take place almost simultaneously, and they are mutually connected by the same preceding analogical meaning, yet they are independent from the respective causes that have produced each of them.*

Death and the colour black have a common analogical stock preceding each of them. The fact that the shop owner sends the black dress to the buyer exactly on the very same day when the latter suffers from serious mourn, of course, is a circumstance which is independent from the causes that have produced the two events: the shop owner's mistake, and the buyer's mourn.

In our daily life we had better take in good consideration this huge piece of truth discovered by Carl Gustav Jung. Its most banal application consists in directing your antennas if you wake up and find out that everything turns out badly in the morning: you may be constelling a bad moment, so the best that you can do is to stay home and read a book.

A more aimed application of this principle can be found in the chronicles of the media. For example you may remember that in summer 1997, within the span of few weeks, dozens of passionate climbers had died on the Italian Alps – both professional and non-professional ones. Under those circumstances, if you had wished to go and perform climbing on those days, you should have remembered the principle of synchronicity and you should have absolutely avoided that – thus you would have saved your own life.

By reasoning this way, we must still not forget numbers and proportions. So if during the same week three different aircrafts fall down or crash in three different areas of the globe, it is absolutely illogical to avoid flying: in fact there are thousands of daily flights all over the world, and the probability theory is on our side – it has been proven that it's easier to die in your own bathtub rather than in an air crash.

Little Chinese acupuncture

Many years ago I happened to read a quite interesting volume, written by Pietro Orlandini and published in Italy by Rizzoli: *Cutaneous acupuncture*. The author, a medical captain during the WWII, took part in many campaigns and battles, also in Ethiopia. There he recollected – under a special perspective – the point of view of the medicine of many shamans and of ancient native tribes.

He mainly focused on a notion which is quite similar to those exposed in this volume. He practices skin acupuncture, i.e. the 'little Chinese acupuncture'. That's to say, he pierced a series of needles (about twenty) in the cork of a bottle. Then, say that a patient suffered from molar tooth pain: he tapped the needled cork on the jaw above the aching tooth. As he explains in his book, by doing this Mr. Orlandini sent a series of signals of little pain (caused by the needles on the cork) to the patient's brain.

This 'saturated' somehow the 'pain channel' and prevented the main pain from reaching the 'central unit' of the patient's suffering. This is what he had seen many native do, in their villages where they didn't have painkilling pills: they assured him that this method really works.

So he resolved to study those applications for years, and he got convinced that they do work, according to the Latin motto *dolor dolorem trahit*, which may be translated as 'one worry drives out another'. I'm confident that the notion is clear and I see no reason for spending further lines on this subject.

The four variables involved

While evaluating the events in connection with your 'aimed' steps, do not forget to consider the variables involved. Our historical, visceral opponents haven't the slightest intention to include the influence of celestials among the variables involved.

On the contrary, our most fanatical and blind supporters forget that there are several variables involved, besides the influence of those pebbles spinning over our heads. In 1997 the Italian TV broadcasted a show where this subject was partially discussed. On March 30 (Easter) at 23:45 the channel Canale 5 broadcasted the show called *Corto circuito*, conducted by Daria Bignardi and Gian Arturo Ferrari. The theme of the discussion was 'bioethic'.

Philosopher Giacomo Marramao, Catholic priest Roberto Colombo, Muslim Gabriele Mandel, and biologist Mr. Boncinelli – with whom I used to work together at the CNR (National Research Council) in Naples in 1967 – and a writer whose name I don't remember were talking about this intriguing subject. They also discussed of cloning or 'clonage', as the biologist preferred to say. It was an interesting debate, under different points of view. It turned out that there's a fear (but who fears? Man? The Church?) about creating 'doubles' of human beings, although – luckily – everybody agreed that this is nonsense.

Nevertheless, the extremely educated guests of the TV show forgot to underline an important detail: the relationship between man and the stars. Let us forget about the issue of soul: I don't mean that this is not a problem. I simply mean that it would lead us to sterile discussions, absolutely useless at a practical level.

So let us consider other issues. All the guests seemed to be more or less convinced that there are two variables preventing, at a practical level, the chance of two individuals being absolutely identical. In fact, they claimed, two human beings can only be apparently similar: like the monozygotic twins.

The two fundamental variables they talked about are: 1) the genetic background, i.e. the information contained in the deoxyribonucleic acid, and 2) the historical background, the latter teaching us that a human being is influenced by the geographical, economical, political, social, and cultural conditions of the time and the place in which he/she was born and in which he/she grows. At this point a little *coup de théâtre* took place. The biologist doctor Boncinelli brought into play a new variable, which to my best knowledge had never been mentioned in previous debates on this subject: the connection among the neurons at an intrauterine level would take place in an absolutely random way. This way it would determine in itself that absolute uniqueness which characterizes any individual human being.

He wasn't granted enough time to explain his notion in depth; but it seems to me that what he meant to say, from his absolutely and rightfully lay point of view, was that the third variable is nothing else than the soul. We may call it soul or we may try to define it in a more specifically biological way; but the bottom line is that it is a third variable involved. And what about stars? Have we forgotten that the astrological one is the fourth variable, and perhaps not the least one?

Dice are not loaded

One of the most frequent criticisms against my practicing the Aimed Solar Returns during the course of the years is the following: "How can you know whether an ASR has really worked or not, since one can not know how things would have turned out if the native wouldn't have relocated the SR?" This seems to be an unassailable argument, but in fact it is totally feeble.

After anything else, you should realize that in this 'game' the dice aren't loaded, because all the rules are written down in advance. In my volumes, which everybody can read since decades, you'll find all the rules that I propose for a correct reading of the Solar Returns.

Very often those rules fight against the rules of the astrological tradition: for example, when I say that the Ascendant of SR lying in the 1st House of one's natal chart is one of the worst tragedies that may happen to a human being.

Now, when someone comes and consults me and I explain to him/her what will happen if he/she doesn't relocate the SR, I make reference to written rules: being written down, such rules cannot be changed depending on the astrologer's needs. I make an example. Say that John Smith is having Mars in the 6th House of his next SR. I say to him that he should expect a very hard year, a hellish one, with troubles in every field of his life. But I also add that if he relocates and places that Mars in the 5th House of SR, he'll have troubles only in the field of love or in relationship with his kids. So say that John Smith leaves to relocate. After twelve months from his 'aimed birthday', if John only complained about his son failing at school, do you think that there would be any doubt about how Mars had really worked? I don't think so! Of course, somebody (perhaps Werfel) claimed that there is no sufficient evidence for those who don't want to believe, and any piece of evidence is superfluous for those who wish to have confirmations at any cost.

Therefore, it may also be that some of my opponents might even get to swear that black is white, for the sake of opposing the fact that ASR's do work. But I don't really care. The most important thing is that some people are on the level: with *bona fide* they really want to see whether this wonderful tool of 'safety' works or not.

To them I say, make an objective examination of the year and you'll be able to see for yourselves whether it has worked in the right way. I am extremely confident that the results will prove me right.

The expired passports
Often our internal resistance to renewal is much stronger than the apparent will of sitting at the steering wheel of our own life in order to produce a decisive turn. So, often it happens that those who should leave for an Aimed Solar Return maintain a strong front of inner opposition within their own soul. Many of the most incredible things have happened to me in connection with the above mentioned manifestation. May times, people to whom I had suggested a relocation of their SR arrived late at the check-in, so they stayed at home instead.

Probably Sigmund Freud would be turning in his grave, if he only knew of how frequent and how crystal-clear are the cases of those who suffer from high fever at the last moment. Another trick for not leaving, played by our unconscious, is when at the last moment people realize that their passport has expired or that they are whishing to travel with their children, but they are legally separated and they 'forgot' to obtain the other parent's approval for their kids travelling abroad.

But when the 'devil' has decided that something 'must not' happen, he can use any means. The most recent, disconcerting case has happened to a female friend of mine. She is a rather unlucky woman, stricken by a clouded destiny that only in recent times has started to show her its silver lining. She had to leave for her first relocation or aimed birthday, but she was struggling against a great deal of anguish: I can't afford it, where would I get the money from? I'm frightened at the idea of flying, how could I take a plane? I've never been far from home, how will I overcome…? At the end all her problems got solved by her little baby: he was supposed to travel with his mother, but evidently he was receptive to his mother's anguish and at one o'clock of the night before the departure, he got a fever of 41°C – thus giving a turn to her standstill situation. This is one of the reasons why I suggest you to leave always five or six days before the day of your birthday, while you can travel back immediately after it (for 'after' has no importance at all).

The year before the 10th House

If you have a Solar return whose Ascendant lies in your natal 10th House, the following year is quite treacherous. First of all, it is a treacherous year because in the overwhelming majority of the cases, the Ascendant of the following SR usually falls in the 12th or in the 1st House of your natal chart – both combinations announcing a hard, troublesome, tough year in any sector of your life.

And if you have just had the experience of a SR with its Ascendant in your natal 10th House, the problem is even sharper because you usually feel so satisfied with a year of good events or – at least – of lack of problems, that in the majority of cases you don't even think of asking for the astrologer's advice any longer, and you may end up with spending your next, detrimental SR at home. Life is always an oscillation between *yin* and *yang*, darkness and light, negative and positive; so it is logical that one relaxes after a year of living positively. I had this unlucky experience myself, years ago. I had had a birthday with the Ascendant of my ASR in my natal 10th House, in Lisbon, and I was studying my next Solar Return: the Sun would be in the 11th House, approximately 4-5 degrees above the cusp of the 12th House.

My registered time of birth is 6 o'clock a.m. – I thought, if I was born twenty minutes earlier I'll have the Sun in the 12th House. On the other side, I reflected with exaggerated optimism, why should my time of birth be twenty or more minutes before 6 o'clock? So, also in consideration of the fact that things were going wonderfully for me, especially my health which is the thing I care the most, I pampered myself with a brand new watch and I renounced to relocate my SR. Unluckily, only few months later, finding out that I was having a really horrible year, I realized that I had good reasons to doubt on my real time of birth.

Also many other people have lived such a situation: for all of them the fact of having had a terrible year was due – almost exclusively – to their feeling of wellness caused by their previous, gorgeous ASR.

So the Ascendant in the 10th House works similarly to Jupiter lavishing presents but at the same time lowering dramatically your critical sense: it makes you behave without diffidence in any circumstance, even where diffidence would be required.

Beware!

When I was a boy, a virologist once observed my upper lip covered by an ugly herpes and said, "Beware…" I was so young that his comment got me unprepared. Had it happened now I would have said, "Beware of what? And how?" How many times have you heard people warning you this way, with this generic and at the same time terrorizing 'beware'? 'Beware of smoking', 'Take care of your liver', 'Take care of your heart'… Beware, take care – but how? Unluckily, in my life I've dealt with the troubles of friends whom I lost early; friends with a bad heart who followed a series of medical prescriptions spanning from a strict diet to a precise pharmacological prophylaxis, up to a severe and detailed behavioural protocol in which all of their physical activities got monitored and disciplined: from sex to work.

All in vain. Some people are convinced that you can avoid all the troubles of this Earth by means of a correct alimentation… while I happened to meet with followers of macrobiotics who generated a baby with Down syndrome.

Of course nobody can claim to be a master in this ranking; I mean nobody can claim to possess the truth, the key to immortality and to inerrability. Yet, a scale of values can be established in this field. Within the means of prevention, I believe that the Aimed Solar Returns are on the top of the ranking. I am confident – I am *convinced* in fact – that in a scale of values 1 to 100, the ASR's score 100 points against the 10 points that can be reached by being wary of food; by driving your car or riding your mobike carefully; by respecting the Law; by avoiding egoism in order to avoid losing your beloved ones; and so on. I believe that nothing can be compared – not even remotely – to the salvation power of an ASR. In the stricter meaning of the term, an ASR is not a miracle. It simply scores much more than any other form of insurance.

For example, it is much safer than a double-layer condom in a risky sexual intercourse. The terrorizing, vague and useless 'Be careful…' of medical doctors is worth nothing if compared to the magnificent results that can be achieved by relocating the map of your Solar Return. Taking Mars away from the 12th House of a SR and displacing it in the 11th House of the SR is one thousand times worthier than taking a pill of *digitalis* every day of your life. Relying on ASR's implies also having a quite wide breadth of mind.

If you suffer from cirrhosis, a glass of whisky kills one hundred times more than fish-fry. Similarly, an ASR is worthier than one hundred pilgrimages to Lourdes or ten heart surgeries in Houston. So "Beware…" yes: beware of where you are spending your birthday!

A question from the Italian newsgroup of Astrology

The reason of this study comes out from the fact of having found, in the subjects that I have examined, awful Solar Returns (that's to say, SR's whose Ascendant, Sun, Mars, or a stellium, were occupying the 12th, 1st, or 6th House) without having had any *serious consequence* at the end of the twelve months. In the majority of the cases they simply had a fair-to-middling year, a tolerably good one.

Saying so I don't claim that Solar Returns don't work – on the contrary, I'm a supporter of this wonderful means of forecast. I want to say it quite clearly: especially in the cases of the 12th House playing a role in the SR, I have registered some health problem in the subject; or the subject dealt with volunteering during the year, or he/she had to visit his/her parents at hospital, or he/she had to undergo therapies.

As far as the 1st or the 6th House are concerned, some subjects showed concern for their own aspect: for instance they changed hair-dressing; they started wearing glasses or they bought new-styled glasses; some of them became fatter, some other became slimmer (1st House); some found a job, other changed their job; some joined a gym; some dealt with their pets etc. (6th House).

So how can it be that only to me have happened dozens of cases without any serious consequences? I myself have had years with Mars, the Sun, or the Ascendant of SR occupying the 1st House - without registering anything negative. And in his *Trattato pratico di Rivoluzioni solari* (ed. Ricerca '90), Ciro Discepolo himself talks 'almost well' of Mars in the 1st House of SR, claiming that it is 'like putting a tiger in the motor' although you can run the risk of getting hurt – while I didn't bang up anything, not even a toe! In this newsgroup I've read Carmen's experience on the dangerousness of the a.m. Houses. If it were possible,

I would like to get more testimonials on this (only from attentive students of the Solar Returns, please).

Those who would like to testify about particularly negative – or positive – years but they aren't able to cast their own S.R., if they wish they can send to me their birth data (they may remain anonymous if they wish so) and I'll cast their chart myself thanks to the wonderful software package called *ASTRAL* (let me say congratulation to Ciro Discepolo, Luigi Miele and the other developers for the newest 32-bit version for Windows 95) and study their case.

Remember though, give me your data only if you are sure about your exact time of birth, and of course tell me the year to be considered, and where you spent your birthday relevant to that year. Thanks to everybody for your precious collaboration.

Alfio Strano

Reply:

Dear Alfio

May I take the opportunity of your request of clarification and clarify something that evidently is not clear – maybe because I haven't explained it well in my volumes on Solar Returns. I have never claimed that EVERY TIME there are negative values of 1st, 6th, and/or 12th House you loose your arm or your leg in a collision with a tramway coach.

For if it were so, considering that the above mentioned combinations are quite frequent, we should all die before reaching the age of twenty. I meant it a bit differently, which is that ALL THE TIMES that you suffer from terrible disgraces, you see the occupation of the 1st, 6th, and/or 12th House in the relevant SR.

You should make the following test. Collect the data of your female and male friends who have suffered, in a given year, from detrimental mourn; clashes with the Law; financial upsets; who have lost their job; who have lost everything; and so on. Then you check out how many times, in those years, for them, the Sun or the Ascendant or a stellium or Mars of the SR occupied the 12th, the 1st, or the 6th House. Let me know then. At this point you may wonder, If those combinations are not always deadly, why should we be concerned? Well, I believe that since we cannot get to know how many bullets are there in the cylinder of a revolver gun, it is not convenient to play Russian roulette with our own temples.

Furthermore you should consider what follows. Many people tend to play down the damages they receive from life.

Do you know that here in Italy about one million people are afflicted with hepatitis C and among them, many don't even suspect they have got it? From time to time I happen to deal with the SR of a husband and a wife and, for example, I get to know that one betrays the other while the latter knows nothing about that.

And if you ask the latter, *What happened to you during the year*? He or she would answer, *Nothing, absolutely nothing*. And last but not least, I have explained several times that the serious troubles of health may be troubles of psychological health. If a boy fails at school and gets depressed, it is virtually certain that his SR has an occupation of the 1st, 6th, and/or 12th House. The same if a young man – with Mars in the 12th House of SR – spends two months of anguish fearing from having contracted AIDS in a risky intercourse. And maybe this is also Umberto Bossi's current situation: I don't think he has spent positive months knowing that he might be sentenced to life.

I hope I have been clear. Good-bye to everybody
Ciro Discepolo

A jigsaw puzzle

Making the best usage of Aimed Solar Returns and of the principle of exorcizing the symbols corresponds to a jigsaw puzzle on which your brain has to work hard. It is especially so in this context that we can talk of 'salt of Astrology' and that we can verify that our discipline is much closer to art than to exact science. I make an example. Say that you wish to relocate somebody's SR so that its Ascendant falls in his/her natal 10th House. But in order to do so, you realize that you have to leave Saturn in the 10th House of the subject's SR. So what you can do is suggesting to the subject to spend the year – starting from the very day of his/her birthday – making the utmost efforts, sweating, studying; joining stages or training courses to improve his/her professional level; suffering; bearing; in a word, activating as much as possible, i.e. *exorcizing* that position of Saturn in the 10th House.

The subject's personal record

One of the most difficult things to do within the frame of Active Astrology is deciding whether in a given year you can or you can not place the Ascendant of SR in the natal 10th House of a subject while, say, there's a transiting Saturn in opposition to his/her natal Sun. In other volumes of mine I have already explained that you have to be extremely careful in this event. In order to take a wide decision you must consider two fundamental factors, namely: what is the subject's profession or job; and two, are there also positive transits: say for example Jupiter conjunct with the MC.

If the subject is a state employee in a land registry office then he or she would run relatively little risk of losing his/her job. But if the subject is a politician, well then the risks are very high. There's yet another factor to be taken into consideration for this purpose: the personal record of the subject. Say that Mr. Smith with whose case we are dealing had already had a financial-economical collapse: without even interrogating the celestials, we would absolutely choose a safe Solar Return avoiding the Ascendant falling in the subject's natal 10th house.

We are going to pay for it in a future life

One of the most frequent objections that I have to face, especially during my lectures on Active Astrology, is the one related with *karma* and future lives. "If you prevent anybody from expiating his/her sins in this life – they object – in his/her next life you cause him/her to pay it double, and with interest." To be sincere, I find this way of reasoning absurd. As I have claimed several times, I don't believe in *karma*. Nevertheless let's argue, for a moment, that I do believe in *karma* and let us reason like those objecting people do.

My answer is a counter-question: You are walking on the street. You look up and you see a 100-kg vase falling down just over your own head. What do you do? Do you step aside and avoid it? Or do you think that you have to accept it, otherwise you'll pay it double and in your next life an even heavier vase would reach your head? I am confident that you move aside: and this is exactly what I do and what all the followers of Active Astrology do.

Resorting to an Aimed Solar Return is nothing more than moving aside in order not to accept the vase falling down from a balcony of the building.

Refrigerators in Alaska

Sometimes I happen to suggest the best moment for the opening of a commercial enterprise. This is not a frequent event, but it happens to me ten times every year. I have detailed the guiding criteria in my volume *Astrologia Applicata*; so I won't repeat them here.

I would like to underline the fact that from time to time, some of those commercial enterprises go wrong and those who consulted me complain. Of course they have all the rights to do so. On the other hand, I have all the rights to explain to them how things should be considered. The variables involved are not only of an astrological kind; there are many variable, including also factors of marketing. For example, say that John opens a delicatessen shop just besides other three shops of the same kind on that same street: it is extremely probable that his business won't develop at all due to the strong concurrency. Furthermore, if the opening of his shop took place in a period of economical recession like the one we had in 1993-1994, no elective or decisional horoscope would be able to save his business: it would be bound to disaster.

To exaggerate a little bit for the sake of clarity: regardless of the celestials, you should not sell refrigerators in Alaska. The following is the natal chart of a very unlucky man whose terrible conjunction Mars-Saturn in the 6th House has produced many a financial disaster in his life. He wanted to try once again, so on the date that I suggested to him, he opened a shop in a little place of Molise in which he produced and sold *croissants*. His produce was fine, people appreciated it very much. Alas, the inhabitants of that place are quite frugal people, so that this unlucky man faced his umpteenth fiasco caused by the absolute lack of clients. The moral of the tale: the best results can be achieved when you succeed in creating winning synergies. For example, during the transit of Jupiter over the natal Sun of a subject whose natal Jupiter is conjunct to his MC.

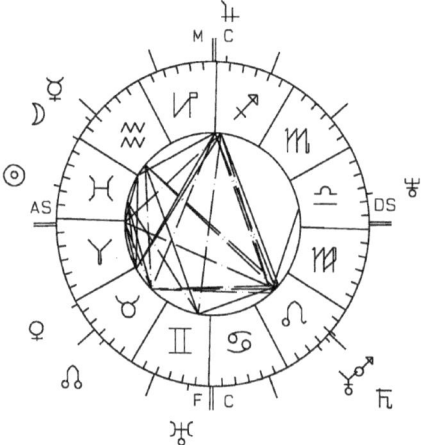

Natal chart of an unlucky man

14.
Transits of Mars

You should never underestimate them. One reason is that they can last for entire weeks or months. Another reason is that they can be responsible for real calamities, if they add to more intense transits. Their action is mostly maleficent.

In fact, Ancient – who didn't know the meaning of the world demagogy – called this planet *the little malefic*, in comparison with Saturn who was considered *the great malefic*. Similarly to the fever, which is always present in virtually all the diseases of the human being, Mars and Saturn stand out in virtually all the tragedies of the human being – in my opinion this says a lot about the maleficence of this planet. Therefore you had better have no illusions about it: when Mars passes over your head, at best you can exclaim, "Thanks God, I didn't hurt myself!" But it's a quite rare event.

Try and test it! For in the overwhelming majority of cases the rule is: you have *always* to give something to Mars, the ruler of Aries and Scorpio. Usually, it would be wounds, tears, rifts, lacerations, blood and so on. The nature of Mars is clearly of a destructive kind, and this is exactly how it behaves. Only in extremely rare cases it may play a constructive role. Usually this happens in those situations that require determined will, and with those natives who lack of willpower.

Only in these circumstances, when Mars transits over the native's Sun or Ascendant or Moon, it is possible – and only in few rare events – that the subject may become the protagonist of a leap in which he/she takes a brave decision and becomes able to get rid of years of stagnations and slothfulness.

Otherwise, Mars usually acts provoking tears, wreckage, destruction, wounds, and bleeding. There's nothing left other than testing what I've just written down.

Mars in a dissonant aspect with the Sun

When Mars creates a disharmonic angle with the Sun – including conjunction – at a theoretical level you should face a positive surplus of energy that you can spend just the way you prefer. Say that you can rely on a credit of energy and that you feel as strong as never before, whishing to employ this benefit somehow. So you leave home and you see a poor man lying on the street under his own motor bicycle.

He's unable to stand up, so you may help him. By doing so, not only you would do your daily good deed, as any member of the Junior Woodchucks should do – you would also make a good use of that bonus on which you can rely. With a less imaginative example, say that you can rely on it for bearing – better than usual – the whims of your chief clerk early in the morning.

You may even dare to give him/her a sharp answer, and then prepare for enjoying the usual calm for the rest of the day. On the other hand, if this transit of Mars adds to other dissonant positions in your natal chart and it also forms part of a bad Solar Return and Lunar Return, you run the risk of getting involved in an explosive situation with a final 'deflagration'. In the given example, the final explosion may be a very bad quarrel with your chief clerk, or with a colleague or with any other collaborator in your job; or perhaps with the policeman giving you a fine, and so on. In other words, on a day like today there's a special temperature in the air floating around you. You may get in serious troubles with the law, or with any other thing connected with what I call the 'officially stamped paper', including being in bad terms with your partner or with your mother-in-law.

Furthermore you may also hurt yourself. This can be in a real physical meaning of the term, i.e. you may cut while shaving; you may wound while dismounting a flat tyre; you may be run over on a pedestrian crossing; or when trying to open a carton box with inappropriate cutting tools. It is the least apt moment for urging a rise in salary. It is not the moment for trying to win over a superior, trying to behave friendly with him or her. On the contrary, you should try and exorcize this transit by performing hard but not dangerous tasks.

For example it may be a very good idea to chop wood; to move pieces of furniture from one floor to another; to empty shelves and arrange the books into carton boxes; to rearrange things in your attic or in your cupboard; to arrange the folders at office... It is also a very good day for making sports, provided that it is not something dangerous. For example jogging, trekking, marathons on the ground and on the water... Also going to the dentist would suit, as well as any other sort of operation such as incisions, removal of cysts, birthmarks, tonsils, etc. If you have to undergo a clinical examination under effort, such as certain heart exams, this is the best day to do so.

At most, I may say that any surgical operation is welcome during this transit, provided that you obey all the other rules given in my volume *Astrologia applicata* by ed. Armenia. The most important of those rules says that you should never undergo an intervention when the Moon is in the sign corresponding to the organ to be operated. For example, do not have your throat operated when the Moon is in Taurus.

This day – or these days – may also be apt for a good quarrel, provided that you cannot avoid it anyway. For example, it is very apt to give somebody a piece of your mind under the square Mars-Sun. If this Mars transiting in a bad aspect with the Sun also creates any angle with Saturn, it is also a good moment for making tattoos, piercing and so on, or for having them made on your skin.

Mars in a dissonant aspect with the Moon

In the previous section we faced an objective situation. I mean, the source of conflict given by Mars-Sun may or might produce a real laceration, such as for example the wreck of a car in a traffic accident; a bone fracture; a black eye caused by a punch; and so on.

While in the case of the transits Mars-Moon we are dealing, I may say, with a more ethereal dimension. It's still a form of 'belligerence', but such 'belligerence' may remain at a stage of temper: e.g. you may nurse a grudge against somebody or you may be in a bad mood, but you may not express it, or perhaps you would express it but in the least apt forms. Sometimes you feel your blood boiling, your heart quivering with indignation, fury, and anger. You would like to declare war to the entire world and you feel ready to burst out for nothing.

The great Swiss psychoanalyst Carl Gustav Young claimed that the subjective reality corresponds to the objective reality. This means that if you have war inside you, you meet war also outside you. Under this logic, at least it is convenient to invent real battles against anybody. If you wish to avoid war coming and visit you, you had better start war against somebody. It may be a neighbour, a colleague at work, a public organization, somebody who opposes our ideas, and so on. This simply means acting according to the Latin motto *similia similibus curantur*: like cures like, the fundamental healing principle of homeopathy. You'll surely feel like having more 'caffeine' and everybody around you feels that you are ready to jump for nothing.

Now, this is exactly the bottom line: do you wish to throw such an important energetic potential out of the window, or do you want to make good use of such energy by deploying it for anything that can be extremely productive for you? You cannot always rely on such an interesting determination. Therefore it is worth to try and look for the correct way to invest this stamina. Before anything else, you should direct your 'belligerence' against a female figure, or against any situation connected with the house (for example, quarrels with the neighbours). It is also a good period if you to get a load off your chest and preach your daughter, your sister, your mother... If you have to solve a situation by phone, you had better start your conversation like this: "I'm warning you, this is not a friendly call..." In other words, there's no use in wearing mantles of false pacifism if your blood is boiling with indignation.

So blow the trumpets and roll the drums. And if you have to shoot, shoot... There's moment for construction and a moment for destruction. Well, this is the moment for destruction, so behave consequently. If you can, you may also carry out heavy duties at home, such as chopping wood, moving pieces of furniture, fixing the roof and so on.

Mars in a dissonant aspect with Mercury

Here we deal with two different notions: on the one hand, the idea of effort (Mars) and on the other hand, the idea of communication (travel, telecommunication, etc.). It is possible that you should start for a journey against your own will, if you wish to exorcize this transit. You might cover a long-long distance while you really wished to stay at home. Sometimes travelling is a pleasure, with a brand new and comfortable car, and with a nice weather.

But if your car is old, if it doesn't work fine; or if the bad weather conditions (say, cold and lack of visibility) make the route uneven, then your journey may become rather uncomfortable and this may be the case when you make a sacrifice for the sake of the exorcization of this transit. So this is a good thing to do during this transit. Furthermore, according to the principles detailed in this volume the more you suffer in travelling, the more you 'discharge' this symbol. The negativity of the journey may also be connected with the reason of your moving around: for example, you may have to take a close relative to undergo a serious surgery; and in this case, in my opinion, no further explanation is needed. Often the objective aversion towards the journey may be caused by a specific reason which makes the travel harder or even unbearable: for example, you may have to travel together with your tiresome and haunting mother-in-law. In other cases this transit may imply the repair of your car or any other vehicle: this is another good way to exorcize this transit properly.

At another level, your journey may be only a virtual one. From this point of view, it may be connected with communication or telecommunication rather than a physical displacement of your body. For example, it is pleasant to browse the Internet searching for relaxing or – even better – for something to play with: but it may be less amusing to navigate on the WWW in order to carry out a precise assignment, perhaps something boring in which you can not use your creativeness, such as a repetitive job in which you may have – just to give an example – to delete a sequel of items from a list, one by one.

At a similar level you may try to exorcize this transit by making efforts of fixing up your printer, your mobile phone, or your satellite receiver by yourself, without even calling a technician. You may play the technician yourself by installing a satellite dish on the roof of your house. You can also invest your strength in compliance with the symbols Mars-Mercury by dealing with a brother, a sister, a cousin, a brother-in-law... You may have to take care of one of them, for example.

You'd attain the utmost from this transit if you took one of these relatives to run an errand a few hundred miles far from your own place. Last but not least, a clever trick to leave this transit may be to embark on a huge sacrifice and try to quit smoking; or withdrawing into a lonely room in order to write down a report, or to study for an important exam.

Mars in a dissonant aspect with Venus

The best way to exorcize a transit of Mars dissonant to Venus is to have se, much sex – you might 'gorge yourself' with sex. Mars is the synonym for strength and Venus stands for love. Hence the best way to constellate these symbols is to have much, healthy sex. This is valid regardless of the kind of transit, i.e. opposition or conjunction or square, it's the same. It is also important 'how' you make love. Each pair has his own fashion of making love, but he symbolism of Mars-Venus recalls a style of making love which may be considered a little bit 'violent' or 'virile'. According to this, during this transit it may a good thing to insert certain variation in your way of making love.

Also quantity is important – hence it would be a useful thing to have more frequent sexual intercourses until this transit lasts. Another way in which you can exorcize, or constellate, this transit is to manage – provided that you are able to do so – the creeping tension with your partner in love. This implies having a tense relationship, but not so tense as to provoke a real crisis.

When you act following the logic of exorcising transits, the most important thing is to keep always a good sense of humour, which above all allow you to consider thing 'from the outside', without feeling too much involved. If you follow this rule events would hardly overcome you; if you don't, you run the risk of becoming yourself a victim of your own ploys. If during these days you were able to handle a fairly argumentative relationship, this would not harm to your love affair – on the contrary, it would precisely benefit it.

Another way of constellating this transit may consist in helping your partner in carrying out heavy tasks. For example, say that your wife has to empty a whole case at office in order to allocate the files into another archive or in two-three cases. So you had better summon all your patience and go and help your wife even if this implies spending a couple of weekends for this purpose. Or vice-versa: if you have to arrange or rearrange your tools in the garage, she should help you to do so. In a similar attempt of keeping the situation (i.e. this transit) under control, you may exaggerate and indulge in some sort of pleasure.

For example you may have a special dinner with your friend, say for example a stag party, where you can indulge in intemperance and debauchery, overeating, and so on. This way you'd act perfectly according with the transit. Or, once in a lifetime, you may indulge in poker or any other gambling game – but remember to set a limit before, and then leave the game as soon as you reach the limit you had imposed to yourself. And now for something completely different: you may do your utmost for helping or giving assistance to a sister, a female cousin, or a young female friend of yours – and this has nothing to do with play and games, of course.

Mars in a dissonant aspect with Mars

You can only 'discharge' this transit making use of your own brute force. You can not mistake: you should chop wood, move pieces of furniture from one room to another, perform heavy physical tasks, sweating, sweating, and sweating over and over again. Any attempt of coming to terms with the symbology of this transit is doomed to failure. Under this transit you are bound to suffering at a physical level, so the more you suffer the better.

Let me be even more drastic and put it this way: if you don't sweat, you bleed. In fact, this transit may correspond to a period in which you find yourself laying on the dentist's armchair, who – with a drill in his hand – gives to the flaming ruler of Aries and Scorpio all that it wants. This is the aptest transit for being scalpelled, drilled, flayed, bled, and so on. You should have no doubt about it. The only thing that you should be concerned with is the ancient yet very good rule by Ptolemy: already in the second century before Christ, he suggested that you should never undergo any operation when the Moon is in the sign corresponding to the portion of body that you should heal – Taurus corresponding to the throat, Virgo the bowels, and so on.

If you find no heavy tasks to carry out and no lesser or major interventions to undergo (this would sound weird, after all), you may try to exaggerate a little bit and start quarrelling with your neighbour, with your fellow creatures, even if you don't know them personally. For example, with an ill-mannered deliveryman; an unpleasant telephone operator; the impolite assistant of a medical doctor, and so on. Instead of the heavy tasks, you may perform mechanical tasks or work with electricity, water tubes, motors, and so on. Another way of exorcising this transit is facing up situations: i.e. acting so that truth will out. Say that you feel a creeping friction in your relationship with somebody, but so far you haven't felt like facing up this unpleasant situation with him/her because if you did so, you would have an unfriendly and disagreeable confrontation, while your nature is of a pacifist kind. But you know: there's a time for peace and there's a time for war – and this transit marks undoubtedly a time for war.

Mars in a dissonant aspect with Jupiter

In this period you tend to hypertrophy and you suffer from a scarce critical sense. Your superficiality would grow consequently and you underestimate the difficulties that you have to face. Under these circumstances, prudent people would remain alone at home, doing their best to do... nothing at all. But if you did so, what would you give to Mars? Similarly to other cases, also in this case making sports may help. For example, archery would show you – and not only figuratively – how many times you can hit the bull's eye.

Under this transit something interesting happened to a friend of mine. It was during our mid-August holidays, and the event took place in one of those tourist villages in which they just organized a swimming competition. My friend took a deep breath, jumped into the water and started swimming. He was convinced to be the first but when he eventually emerged and opened his eyes, he sadly realized that everybody was before him, and that he was actually behind everybody else. This is exactly what may happen to everybody during this transit – and also losing your face in a sporting competition may help you exorcise the symbol of the transit.

Otherwise you can pamper yourself with a period of controlled intemperance, such as overeating with friends, yet without ever exceeding beyond the limits imposed by decency and by rational logic. You may also indulge in little crazy expenses; for example you may resolve to buy some new garment, and in this case you'd reduce the risk to the chance of paying 100 what really costs 70. In these days you may also donate your blood: it would be a wise and socially useful thing to do. And by doing so, you'd know if your blood is OK or perhaps something may be wrong in it, especially in connection with the liver, and do something to avoid further troubles. And last, you may renounce to a little but fix amount of your budget and devote it to losing it in gambling games.

Mars in a dissonant aspect with Saturn
During these days or months you feel nastier and perhaps you really are nastier, in so far that you natal chart allows you to be a bad boy or a bad girl. During this transit you should take those decisions that you normally are unable, or refuse to take. For example you may resolve to take your aged mother to a retirement home or to an old people's home, although this is something that anybody would hate. Yet it is something that you have to do under certain circumstances.

Nonetheless this is life: there are days for enjoying and there are days for suffering. And there are days of gathering consent and other days in which people consider you to be a fierce torturer. And this is exactly the case of this transit. So if there isn't any other possible solution, you should sacrifice this sort of lamb on the altar of Mars-Saturn: taking one of your dear old ones to the old people's home; parting from a dog cub or a pussy cat that you could not keep at home so that you have got to give it away; taking your dear suffering pet to the vet to have it suppressed – an act of mercy that, in my opinion, should also be allowed for those men and women who are suffering in the terminal stages of their illness. That cold SS torturer who sleeps within each individual – more or less depending on each natal chart – comes out during this transit and reclaims his right to existence. Hence, this period is apt for certain particularly delicate surgical operations, such as acting yourself as a doctor and give rescue to somebody who needs help because, say, his or her leg is broken, while you are waiting for a professional assistance to arrive.

On the altar of this transit you may also wish to offer a surgical intervention on your own body: it may be the meniscus, the knees in general, orthopaedic surgery, and above all – the dentist. Dentist-related suffering, their curing on the base of drilling, the laceration of the gums, their stitching up: all they are operations typically connected with the dissonance Mars-Saturn. The same can be told for demolitions. For example, if you have to demolish anything build without a planning permission, an unsteady external wall, or a former shelter for your dog and so on; but it also refers to the scrapping of cars and motor bicycles. And last if you have something unpleasant to tell to anybody, for example an unfriendly telephone call, declaring any sort of war etc. this is the right moment to do so.

Mars in a dissonant aspect with Uranus

This transit implies a sort of destructive or radically proactive energy tending to solve problems. Spurts of adrenaline seem to make all of your action 'sparkle'. You feel absolutely unsatisfied before anything that takes a longer time to evolve or develop. In fact during this transit you may become impatient, particularly with people who 'work' slower than you, or who don't understand what you say.

You tend to go straight to the core of any situation; during these days you are as loyal, sincere, and genuine as ever. You had better take advantage of this situation and bang the table with your fist: for if there are days for mediating, it is also true that there are other days for making war. Everybody has got situations that need to be removed radically, without any wavering, after sought, or weakness. This transit marks exactly this kind of 'bus stop' in your life. So you had better summon all your bravery and make a clean-up. So get rid of old and useless 'friends' and any sort of dead weight, including your own mental ballast. Hold your nose and wear brand new garments.

Get rid of your old taboos, obsessive manias, little fears of your being 'a very little man', and take a deep breath of fresh air even if this might cause you wounds. You'll have time to put in stitches to your lacerations later on. So the best way to discharge this sort of transit is to humour your nature of these days. And your nature of these days is, more or less, coherent with your basic nature. During these days or weeks you should make efforts to be as natural as possible, even in those occasions in which being natural means being brave. At any cost you should avoid any activity usually considered dangerous, such as riding bicycles and motor bicycles; skating; skiing; driving at high speed; climbing mountains; diving from high cliffs, and so on. Nonetheless, we have to give something to Mars and Uranus.

So you also had better try to go in for brave yet not really dangerous sport such as the kitesurfing. This is also a good moment if you have to undergo a little surgical operation with minimal sedation or anxiolysis. You will be also attracted by techniques and informatics; you may take advantage of this by opening the case of your desktop computer – although the successful result may not be guaranteed. This transit is also good if you have, for example, to support a relative of yours in a 'quarrel', for example against his/her neighbours.

Mars in a dissonant aspect with Neptune

During the transit of Mars on a dissonant angle with Neptune (including conjunction) you feel a sort of 'mental blindness'. This means that you tend to exaggerate a notion, an ideal, a point of view, a professional practice. The dangerousness of the transit we are talking about is totally inscribed in this sort of 'altered state of consciousness'. This leads you to behave in a way that you usually wouldn't do – unless you have already got this aspect in your very natal chart.

Those who are in a leading position of nations, countries, armies, mass movements and so on, they should be careful not to take any important decision during this transit, because otherwise their highly subjective decisions might provoke some sort of 'holy war', or 'one-way fanaticism'. So this transit is not something that can be solved with some Valium or *valeriana* or any other anxiolytics to be taken in homeopathic doses. So what I am suggesting you to exorcize this transit is to find out some specific situation in which you may behave so blindly without being too harmful to yourself and to the others.

There you could take those unique, final, extreme decisions – just like if it were the last thing you would do. For example, you may declare your resolution of quitting smoking; you may lie in bed with sedating infusions to detoxify from morphine; or you may resolve seriously to embark on a slimming cure – under the spur of this transit, all these things would lead you to exceptional results.

The same if you are a victim of alcoholism or drug. At another level, you may resolve to run ten miles a day; to join a gym; to do a minimum daily quantity of push-ups. In a word, this is the season of the statements of compromise, in which you are also able to fulfil them. All of your proposals of the kind "from today onwards..." taken during this transit are bound to lead to firm and constructive actions.

During these days no one can stop you: so you had better take advantage of this and jump over any sort of gap – geographical, social, or political ones. If your heart quivers with indignation for anything, for example, you may resolve to join a political party or a mass movement. Take part in environmental campaigns, for example you may join a group of volunteers cleaning up the parks and the hills of your town; or you may even take part in some 'extreme' actions performed y environmentalists, green activists and so on.

For example you may have yourself enchained to the gates of the embassy of a country in which experimental nuclear explosions are carried out. If you have an important surgical intervention to do, or even a mere extraction of the wisdom tooth, well this is the right time to be brave and undergo any sort of torture. And if you feel so brave to take the consequences of this transit to the extremes, you may try to walk barefoot on burning coals, like certain fakirs do. And last, this is a good period for studying astrology, esotericism, parapsychology, Eastern cultures, yoga and so on.

Mars in a dissonant aspect with Pluto

When the worst and deepest energies inside you tend to emerge to the surface, you should try to channel them and keep them under strict control. I can imagine that even psychology would agree with astrology in suggesting you to go to the cinema and watch some film like *Death Wish*. I'm sure that it has happened to you too, to find yourself in a metro coach in the presence of a *gang*, a group of hooligans, drifters behaving in a clearly criminal way.

You know, those dropouts that start singing in chorus obscene songs; but they go further and beat the passengers, spit on them, perhaps they even rob them. In moments like this, the civilized part of you (the Dr. Jekyll) feels uncomfortable, but at most it switches on the mobile phone and calls the police. But during a dissonant transit of Mars with Pluto – including conjunction – the other half of you, the Mr. Hyde emerges and you'd like to shoot with a *Magnum* or any other gun, just like the cops in the American films. This is why I suggest you to go to the cinema and watch that film with Charles Bronson shooting at the head of hooligans. This is certainly not a masterpiece of culture, but by watching this sort of films you could sublimate all of your destructive strength. It would be him, the killing vigilante who does the real thing – not you.

So you'd be happy that the crime rate is dropping and that somebody is doing something about crime, but you won't pay the consequences of your imaginary self-made justice. Somebody, of those who love demagogy, would claim that violence is violence in any case, and that violence produces violence. But I don't believe in allopathy, I prefer homeopathy – *similia similibus curantur*: like cures like. On the other hand I am suggesting this to adult people who are supposed to be perfectly able to discriminate between reality and invention while watching films like *Pulp Fiction*. During this transit also your sexual impulse might improve not only in quantity but also in quality; and you may be led to do something 'weird', strange, morbid.

And if you partner agreed, you'd be able to have unusual experiences in this field. Since this transit also implies a wave of wrath, you may channel it to spoil the friendship between you and somebody that you don't like anymore; or to give a sharp answer to your boss; perhaps to resign after a quarrel. There are days for constructions and days for destruction: these are the days for demolition.

Transit Mars in the First House

This transit takes place approximately every two years. It usually last a couple of months. Keep in mind though, that if the planet becomes retrograde and then it reverts to direct motion again, this transit might last five or six months. This transit gives you an extraordinary stamina; you can behave like if you had taken dozens of cups of coffee; you feel like moving without gravity, like if you were walking on the Moon.

Of course such a surplus of energy must be channelled carefully; otherwise it can provoke real disasters. Those who generally lack of a strong willpower may feel the thrill of being able to take brave decisions on the spur of the moment. On the contrary, those whose basic nature is strong and volitional should make use of particular tactics. My first suggestion is to go to the dentist. I am confident that Mars would appreciate those nightmare-like drilling, scalpelling, root lapping, and bleeding that the dentist's care might imply.

Given that everybody has to visit the dentist on a regular basis, you had better go there when Mars is transiting in your 1st, 6th, or 12th House. In those periods you should also concentrate, if possible, any other lesser or major surgical intervention: such as incisions, haemorrhoids, removal of cysts, birthmarks, tonsils, etc. If you really have nothing to offer from this point of view, then you had better devote yourself to a massive sporting activity.

The more you go in for sport in this period the better you discharge this transit, and the safer you can feel. If you don't feel like going in for sport, or if you aren't accustomed to carry out physical efforts, then proceed gradually, starting with jogging in the woods or on the shore early in the morning. You may also devote some time to the gym. If you are really lazy you may avoid joining a gym club and do it at home. You may buy a rowing machine or a stationary bicycle, or you may simply do push-ups on the carpet. As Woody Allen would say, you may also 'sweat in the sheets': i.e. an increased sexual activity would discharge this transit very, very well.

And if you have got to move pieces of furniture; to empty shelves and rearrange your book collection; to carry out any sort of huge, heavy tasks – well this is the perfect time to do so. Don't you have any heavy task to carry out? Then create them, or help you friends and relatives who are just moving; or help them rearrange the garage or the attic or any other thing like this.

Of course you should avoid the most dangerous tasks such as cutting or sawing wood, otherwise you may run the risk of wounding yourself.

Transit Mars in the Second House

During this transit you stand the chance of having a little but intense haemorrhage of money. In this case it may not be enough to suggest you to be generically careful, to keep alert. You had better try and rule over the symbol, i.e. 'exorcise' it at your best, channelling it in a way that may be even advantageous to you.

To do so you should do your utmost to increase the income of your own personal finance or of the family budget. If possible, accept a second job. This may be a temporary activity and it may last only until this transit lasts. Depending on your field of expertise, you should try to make extra money from giving consultancies, private classes, working as a freelance translator, and so on. So buy the local papers of classified ads and something useful will surely occur to you. For example, you might also earn from selling an old piece of furniture. If there's a chance to work overtime in your company, do so as much as you can during this transit. Perhaps you have never considered getting into high finance and you simply spare your money by leaving it sleeping in a current account? Well, during this transit you might study for days, for weeks, trying a solution for earning more by investing your money in something more productive yet safe; for example you may buy a state bond or transfer your money to another account granting a higher rate of interest.

Or on the contrary, if you have to make expenses and you cannot avoid it, then spend your money exactly during this transit. Buy anything – tools, garment, whatever – provided that meets somehow the symbols implied in this transit. Remember that if you don't do so, you run the risk of losing that money anyway – for example you might be robbed. At another level you had better enhance your physical aspect: so go to the hairstylist, to the barber, to cosmetologists, beauticians, tailors, and whomever can help you improve your looking. Another valid way of exorcising this symbol may be having a little incision made on your body: e.g. to remove a birthmark or a cyst or any other blemish on your skin. You may also invest more time than usual in visiting shops in search for better pieces of garment. This can also apply to any tools connected with the notion of 'image'. Thus you may learn to use a complex software of CAD; study photography; buy a larger monitor, and so on.

Transit Mars in the Third House

During this transit it is a wise thing to become a commuter, or if you already are, increase your daily commuting. This may be connected with an actual need or a changed situation, such as taking your kids to a farther school or your assignment to another branch of your company - but you might also be able to create such a situation of commuting deliberately. In the latter case you may grasp many different occasions. for example you may resolve to assist a course on Shiatsu at the other end of the town; join a gym club far from home; meet a group of friends after work; and so on.

The bottom line is: let it be a larger commuting, a longer way to pass every day. The same if you make it by foot or by car or tramway or train. Each symbol should be 'weighed' in comparison with the individual who wish to constellate it: therefore the distances involved may depend on the natal chart of he, or she, to whom the transit refers. For example, for a native Cancer who spends a lot of time at home, it may be enough a distance of a few blocks; while for an extremely mobile Gemini the distance should involve dozens, if not thousands of miles.

During this period it would be useful to spend also resources, energy, and money to take care of your car from the technical, mechanical and esthetical point of view: So go and visit more often your carwash, your tyre repairer; your auto-body repairer; your mechanic… And if you are so smart to be able to put your own hands in your car, even better! Roll up your sleeves and spend several hours of Saturdays and Sundays with a wrench. At another lever, the transit may be efficiently discharged by diving yourself into a deep study, for leisure or necessity. In the latter case you may get ready for a contest or an exam at university. In both cases the transit gives you the required energy. You may also try and invest your passion in learning a new software programme; studying o reading a book of your favourite author; you may also take benefit in assisting courses, lessons, seminars, lectures. Moreover, you had better intensify your communication – especially the written ones – via Internet or telephone, although you may run the risk of getting quite high bills if you don't pay a flat fee. If you are engaged at a cultural level, grasp the chance and write some important chapter for your next book; or the text of an article, a lecture, an essay… If you had to swallow a bitter pill because of your brothers, sisters, brothers-in-law or sisters-in-law during this transit you have the chance of getting it out off your chest and giving them a piece of your mind. Last, you may take a strong compromise and quit smoking, if you are a smoker.

Transit Mars in the Fourth House

During this transit you have certainly to carry out some work at home. You may do it yourself or have it done by an expert. You may rearrange the whole house or simply have your bathroom repainted. In any case you should spend efforts, compromise and suffering.

The discomforts caused by coming home and finding dust and sand everywhere, up into your sheets; or finding a lime of scuttle left on your best armchair, they should be enough to discharge this symbol properly. If you are smart enough in doing-it-yourself you may spend all of the week-ends of this transit in painting walls and mounting shelves. The bottom line is that you should channel as much stamina and money as you can in this sort of things. These weeks or months are a favourable span of time for you to have a new heating system mounted; or new tiles in your bathroom; or any other lesser or major fixing or renovating or refurbishing job that your place may need from time to time.

The same may also refer to you office, your workshop, your atelier, your shop, your laboratory, your working space whatever it is. The notion of making efforts aimed at your home or house may also refer to a different layout of the furniture, which may be achieved by physical tasks; or simply mounting news curtains, which is a much lighter job. Gardening may also attain to the symbology we are talking about. You may constellate it also by applying for a mortgage loan and start paying instalments for the purchase of a flat.

More precisely speaking, this implies all those direct and indirect expenses relevant to your house or flat, including insurance or the payment of inheritance tax which you may deliberately try to postpone or anticipate so that it takes places exactly during this transit. Furthermore it would be a good thing to deal more with your parents, to take more care for them: go and visit them more often; take them with you on holiday; assist them in a therapy; take them to hospital if they need it, and so on. I can say that this transit can be discharged quite fairly by upgrading the hard-disk of your personal computer.

This seems to be an easy task, but it may be difficult even for an expert technician and it often implies days of reinstalling your favourite software, applications, drivers etc. one by one. But if you do so you may avoid the bad surprise of having your computer infected by a virus, which in certain cases can be solved only by reformatting all of your drives.

Transit Mars in the Fifth House
The ideal would be to sport – to sport very much. If you are already a sportsman or a sportswoman you may simply intensify your activity. If you are not, you had better move somehow: play tennis, dive, swim, and run, make gymnastic at home or in a gym club.

Sports are surely the right activity to discharge this transit in the best way. Yet the Fifth House also refers to anything that may be defined playful and recreational – so dance may be suitable as wall, since it is a sort of 'sport' that one can perform at any age, it is only good for blood circulation, provided that you don't exaggerate – and by the way, exaggerating hurts whatever you do.

The 5th House of the natal chart also refers to love. So in order to tame the transiting Mart claiming for its rights, you can also have a more intense sexual activity, or simply meet you partner more frequently. And remember: if you don't discharge this transit you run the risk of falling into temptation and start frequenting quire dangerous places such as casinos, where the harmful suggestions of the rules of Aries and Scorpio might lead you to spend and losse quite consistent amounts of money. While if you guide this Mars at your best, it may lead you to learn a new sporting activity, such as bridge or chess – you can sweat and loose weight also by playing bridge or chess. These months favour also the practice of teaching.

So if you are a teacher or if you are asked to do a seminar, you should try and concentrate it during this transit. You should also make more efforts in connection with your beloved ones, your partner, you kids: for example, for their medicines, for their spirit. Try and demonstrate in a tangible way how much you care for them. This is also a good time for going to holiday in one of those resorts where the animators don't leave you in peace but make you work even harder than you normally do at work.

Transit Mars in the Sixth House
With this transit, it's a matter of warding off a stronger blow. Whether it expresses itself in your job (i.e. in your relationship within your working environment) or in your health, this is a rather treacherous transit.

In the first case, you had better give it vent by giving a piece of your mind to, say, a colleague whom you can't stand any longer. If you have to quarrel, this is the aptest moment. Certain interpersonal rapports in your working environment can last up to certain point – not forever. At most, during these days you can try and accept harder physical tasks: for example, reallocate the files from one case to another; move huge bulks of heavy folders; do-it-yourself and move pieces of furniture even if those tasks do not fall within your competence.

As far as health is concerned, the dentist is always the best solution: as much 'drilling' as possible and you'll avoid more serious troubles. So visit the dentist as often as possible and ask him to undergo a deep cleaning of your teeth, implying the cutting of your gum and a profound removal of the tartar (this technique is called root lapping). If you are a woman, you may find benefit in an extra visit to the gynaecologist, who might find out some little wound to be cicatrized with an electrosurgical knife. Everybody would find benefit also in chiropractic: hands up those who haven't got any little pain in the bones... Nonetheless, with a transit like this – which in certain cases may last up to several months – one cannot underestimate the problem.

So it would be a wise thing to put into effect all those things that I have gathered under the term of 'a prosthetic technique' in another section of this volume. In other words, during this transit it would not be enough to simply act according to the homeopathic principle *similia similibus curantur* – before anything else you should prevent, and only then combat using certain opposites.

I give a few examples. Those who suffer from chronic gastric diseases know it very well: at any change of season their acid secretion grows; and as a consequence, also their disturbances also grow, making it possible the risk of gastric ulcer. So, as this transit approaches – I mean, already when Mars gets closer to the cusp of the 6th House – you should ask your doctor to prescribe you ranitidine or other similar compounds; stop drinking coffee; stop taking any other substance that may hurt your stomach, such as orange or lemon juice, spirits, and so on.

Similarly, those who suffer from cervical arthrosis would start going out wearing a wooden scarf and a hat; sleeping with an electric heating-pad in their pillow; adopting all those precautions that any patient like them knows very well. In other words, you have to defend rather than attack, for this is a really bad transit and if it happens together with other bad transits, it may imply a very critical period for you. So if you don't want to become its victim, avoid the underestimation of this transit and take all the required steps against it. Above all, remember that during these weeks you'll get all the relapses of the troubles from which you suffer periodically. Of course, if you have to undergo surgery, this is the time to do so, always keeping in due consideration the general astrological rules that refer to any operation; namely, that you shall not undergo an operation when the Moon is in the sign connected with the organ to be operated. Furthermore you should not forget that when Mars passes through your 1st, 6th, or 12th House as well as in any other particularly negative situation, if possible it is a good thing to observe a total, therapeutic fast. If you cannot, a partial fast also may suit.

Eat as little as possible – a small cup of hot clear soup; a few chestnut to fill your stomach; very little bread and cheese, or fresh fruit. Through total fast or a frugal diet it is possible to overcome safely a good part of the aggressions of Mars. This is also valid in general, so you can follow this behavioural direction also in presence of other 'malefic' celestials.

Transit Mars in the Seventh House

Unlike the previous situation, here you have absolutely to attack: the harder you attack the less you'll be attacked. So you should do your best to develop many little battles – or one single war, but be an important one. This may or may not imply legal stuff, i.e. your war may also take place before a court, but it may also have absolutely nothing to do with lawyers, attorneys, or judges. For example you might pick up the phone and call your neighbour to complain against his doggy making poo-poo just before your own door. You may also join a residents' meeting and start fighting for your rights before each of them.

If somebody owes you money, you may also ask for legal assistance to have your money back. And if you really think that you've got nothing to quarrel with anybody (in which case I dare say that you... live on Mars), you can always create or invent occasions of battling: for example you may take part – at least during these weeks – to actions of environmental activists, animal welfare, and so on.

Also having yourself enchained to the gates of the embassy of a country in which experimental nuclear explosions are carried out may be quite useful to discharge this transit. You may also invent or hype a dispute with a newspaper or a magazine, by writing tons of letters to them showing your indignation for one or another subject. So join meetings, protest rallies, public debates, any sort of popular happening. If you are so shy to be unable to speak in public, you may always ask a legal representative to act for you. The golden rule is: the more you produce war, the less damage you suffer from this transit. Ironically, sports may help you. So join a club and make karate or boxing. By giving kicks and punches to an opponent – either for hunger or for sport – you'll be able to discharge this symbol partly or completely. In my experience I have noticed that I have explained these things several times to those who asked for my counselling, yet very few of them took me at my word.

An honest and respected professional, a very good man, did not start any sort of battle or struggle or quarrel against anybody during this transit. One day two young men waited for him before his consulting room; when they saw him they simply asked for a confirmation of his identity; then they assaulted him with kicks and punches. The professional never understood who ordered them to do so. Remember that during this transit you may have your driving licence confiscated; you may undergo the control of a custom officer; you may be interrogated by a judge; you may suffer from little or serious legal troubles. So the only way, let me stress it once again, is to invent wars, and attack, attack, and attack once again. The more you attack the less you'll be victim of attacks. In this case, this rule proves true and works very well.

Transit Mars in the Eighth House

Before anything else, you have to administrate a series of controlled expenses. Since you cannot avoid expenses during this transit, the idea of not spending anything is not really advisable. It is much better starting with anticipation, say when Mars is still in the 7th House: then you should start scheduling your future expenses so that you spend the money exactly when Mars is in the 8th House.

In other terms, it is really advisable to postpone, if possible, your expenses when Mars is in the 6th and 7th House, and then, when it enters the 8th House, you can buy all the things you had programmed. This way you produce that outgoing flow of money that this transit requires. Willing or not, you'll have to spend during this transit, so the clever action consists in spending well. What you have to avoid and ban at any cost is any sort of speculations and games. If you usually play, you had better spend more money for your house or for a holiday rather than wasting money in lotteries or bingos.

In other words, if you really wish to ward off the sinister blows that the celestials may bring to you during this transit, you should learn to programme – and to programme with due anticipation. If during the year you have to have something fixed at home; if you have to buy some electrical household appliance or a new car – you simply have to postpone the event until Mars reaches your natal 8th House. In other words, concentrate your expenses in those weeks or months. The same applies if you have to pay certain bills, such as the dentist's bill, or the psychologist's bill, or the bill for the lessons of piano for your son. In a word: spend, spend and spend once again.

But – only spend for useful things, for things that you cannot avoid. Furthermore, it is possible that during these months you may have to face legal controversies in connection with disputed inheritance or taxes, with the assistance of a lawyer or your bookkeeper. If this didn't happen in a natural way, but you judge that it may happen, you had better provoke such a situation. At another level, you may increase your sexual activity; considering the symbols involved in this transit, this should happen quite naturally.

Transit Mars in the Ninth House

The time has arrived for you to make that journey that you have postponed so far, because you do not see it as a holiday. It may be a displacement for job, for study or to undergo a therapy – so be strong and resolve to leave at least. The longer and more tiring is the travel, the better you discharge this Mars in the 9th House. According to the notion of *exorcism of symbols*, the deal would be to go very far away to undergo surgery, incision, perhaps an aesthetical operation.

I know people that don't trust Italian dentists and they travel periodically to Switzerland to be cured there; they also claim to spend less then here in Italy. And this is exactly what you should do in order to oppose safely this transit. On the other hand, this transit usually takes place every second year and it would be a little bit to wait for this transit to happen until your next visit to a foreign dentist. So what you could do instead is covering a distance of two-three hundred miles to run a particularly annoying errand: for example, visiting some bureaucratic machine in the capital. Or you may travel in order to visit and/or take care of a relative who lives far away.

Or you may resolve to take a plane and struggle with the chief officer of your company in order to attain better working conditions. The bottom line is that you should move against your own will, or in order to perform actions that you dislike. Mars in the 9th House might also be discharged by going in for sports – yet in this case you had better beware of possible accidents, so only go in for the least dangerous sports such as swimming or gymnastic. At a mental level, the ideal would be to learn a new language, or improving your skill in a language that you already know. This may also refer to programming languages.

Hence you may also spend these weeks or months in learning how to use and make profit from a new software package. It would also be a wise thing to channel this particular sort of libido into the so-called 'superior' studies, meaning in this case all the disciplines that go far beyond your daily life: history of religions, Eastern cultures, Zen, yoga, astrology, parapsychology, esotericism, philosophy, analytic psychology and so on. And last, also dealing much (or more than usual) with animals (possibly your own pets) would also be useful to discharge this transit.

Transit Mars in the Tenth House

Under this transit it's a matter of upgrading, i.e. enhancing your social and/or professional position, or more generally speaking – achieving a better emancipation. If you are a young woman you may insist and have your boyfriend engage and eventually make arrangements for your marriage; if you are a clerk you may relentlessly apply for better positions; if you are a teenager you may ask your parents the permission of going out with friends and coming back home later at night. You may also engage a sort of competition with yourself as well.

So you may study harder; learn something new; get more expert and proficient in your job; computerize your activity; produce more; or enlarge the area in which your product is sold. In any case you'd have to work harder for your prestige, particularly at a social and professional level. For example you may pick up the phone and call twenty different persons asking for their vote in a local election in which you are a candidate. Only be careful not to mix up job or prestige with money: they are two completely different worlds.

Cutting your umbilical cord may be another way of expressing the spirit of the efforts required to you by this transit. You may get rid of your chains also by quitting smoking; stopping and resolving a long-lasting therapy of deep analysis; making efforts and channel energies to stop taking a pill that you might consider unavoidable, while it only causes you harm with its collateral effects. A good way to exorcise Mars in your

10th House may also consist in working until late. Do not forget that the natal 10th House also refer to your mother; so if you wish to avoid quarrels and troubles with her, you had better do your utmost for her during this transit.

For example go and visit her more often; take her to the doctor; take her to the blood test; simply devote more time to her. In other words, show her in practice how much you care; she who has spent a whole life in making sacrifices for you deserves that you make sacrifices for her form time to time.

Transit Mars in the Eleventh House

It is very easy to discharge this transit if you are a musician: simply play and play. If you usually play much, well – play more then. If you don't play any instrument you may start learning, although it is clear that not everyone can afford such an ambitious project, also considering that this transit takes place every second year.

So you must do something else. The most logical thing to do during this transit is to deal more with your friends; devote more time to them; spend energy for them; give them your help and support; show them that friendship is not merely a nice word for you. Since transits never arrive by chance, you can be sure that during these months one of your friends will surely need your help: so just give him (or her) a hand if you only can. Otherwise, at the very least you should expect that this transit will cause hostilities from your friends.

Mars transiting in the 11th House may also imply many efforts in making projects, and this doesn't mean wasting time in staring at the infinite, lost in fancies. No, making projects means, for example, taking steps to change your job; write and send resumes; preparing a list of recipients to whom you'll send the catalogue of your products or services... At the same time you may also trying to obtain the assistance or support or sponsor of important individuals who might give you a hand. While Mars is in you 11th House you should knock at as many doors as possible. You have to understand that those doors won't open as easy as when Jupiter passes through your 11th House; so you know that you'll have to knock stronger and louder, if you wish to achieve your goals. Last but not least, you may also live this transit by making practical efforts to make friends with new people; for example you may volunteer in cleaning up the parks of your town, or join the Red Cross, or Caritas.

Transit Mars in the Twelfth House

This transit implies a scenario similar to that of the passage through the 1st and the 6th House. So you should behave keeping in mind that you have to give as much as possible to the planet of war, wounds, and troubles in general. The more you give of your own free will, the less you run the risk of Mars choosing the brick falling onto your head.

Be clear that you may have this transit forty times during your entire life, and not always happens anything serious. But if this transit takes places together with other negative transits of the slower planets such as Saturn, Uranus, Neptune, and Pluto – and if the whole scenario involves an overall negative situation – then you really can run serious risks. So, in the majority of cases you'll simply have to do with less importance events; nonetheless they might keep you concerned for weeks, and you might be able to overcome or avoid them if you only succeeded in discharging this transit well enough.

As I always do in these cases, once again I suggest you to be visited by a dentist or a surgeon: more than anybody else, it's them who might exorcise this transit at best. On the other hand, you may not really need surgical help during these few months. So if you really wish to act accordingly to the symbol implied in this House, you should be hostile with your 'pseudo-hidden' enemies. I say 'pseudo' hidden ones, because if they were really hidden you wouldn't even know about them. No, I mean those people who bury their head in the sand after having done something evil against you, so that you can easily understand who did it. Unlike their way of behaving, you had better act directly, bravely and openly against them. In this period, facing directly those who hate you may help discharge this transit.

So speak aloud if you need, and let them know that it is not your intention to suffer passively any longer. At another level you may enhance your concentration of strength and energy and channel them in esoteric researches, or in search of anything that is – somehow and in the broadest meaning of this term – hidden. For example, if you suspect that your beloved one betrays you, this is the best moment to investigate: you may do it yourself or charge a private eye who will be able to do it more professionally by placing electronic bugs or shadowing your partner.

If you belong to that group of people who love helping the mankind, you might also join associations of volunteers who give assistance to those in the need.

15.
Transits of Saturn

In its classical representation, Saturn is an old, ugly, and battered man, in poor health and covered by bandages. His skin is greyish; he's got long, unkempt beard and hair. A crutch helps him walk and he holds a pruning hook in his left hand – the latter being the symbol of death, subtractions, and suffering. You may try to twist the notion, but the final result is always the same: suffering, pain, and misery. You cannot ignore this bottom line. Putting your finger into the whipped cream and retracting it covered by red, sweet sour-cherry syrup is certainly one of the pleasures of life. Thinking of tasting it and renouncing may provoke a sort of growth inside you, but it surely implies a kind of suffering.

So when you think of Saturn and wonder what you can give to it during its transit, you cannot mistake: you'll have to renounce virtually everything, from the crunchy skin of the roast chicken up to the sports car; from the high-resolution giant monitor for your computer to the handsome neighbour who apparently is courting you. You would give up the brand-new elegant garment, your travel to China, buying or wearing jewels, accepting the news job, and so on. Saturn surely works on a privative basis. I believe that no one could doubt it any longer, not even those who indulge in demagogy.

This characteristic of Saturn seems so obvious to me that I would rather stress on another important aspect of the technique of exorcism of the transits of Saturn. In fact this planet, the ruler of Capricorn and Aquarius, not only implies suffering 'because of need', but also 'because of excess' of something. Let me explain. Let's consider the transit of Saturn over the Medium Coeli of any man.

Often this transit means the loss of job, or a serious hindrance that prevents you from carrying on your work. So, depending on the actual case: if you are a worker in a company in crisis you might be fired; if you are Gianni Agnelli you might suffer from bone fracture or heart attack so that you are prevented from dealing directly with your company for a while; if you are a singer you may suffer from pharyngitis so that you can not sing for the time being; if you are the owner of a company, one of the most productive and reliable employees may retire, and so on... On the other hand, Saturn may also herald certain episodes of success. For example, a teacher in a comprehensive school applies for a post of headmistress and gets the job.

What?, you may argue, *then Saturn also gives presents and not only penalties?* The answer is: Yes, but at a high price. For example, public employees who try to improve their working position by tender, during this transit: they surely have to spend a lot of sleepless nights in study and many other sort of sacrifice. Eventually the common denominator of all those situations, the good and the bad ones altogether, is *suffering*. Saturn promises that you'd suffer in connection with job, and that's exactly what those situations describe.

Nothing else than suffering. So more precisely, we can say that the transits of this planet make you suffer either for what they give to you or for what they take away from you. As you can easily understand, this implies some more chance while exorcising the symbol of its transits, and I'm going to tell you how to take advantage of it. Read carefully what follows in connection with the transits of Saturn.

Saturn in a dissonant aspect with the Sun

It implies any sort of mortification in connection with your career, your personal or professional success, your Ego. So in this period you had better hide yourself, avoid being a protagonist, depress your own visibility, in the broader meaning of the terms.

The less you appear the better. If they announce or promise an advance, renounce or postpone it. If they want to give you an important charge, decline; you should accept only if this implies sleepless nights, a good amount of extra efforts, and much *pathos* in general. If you love to be at the centre of attention, this is a good period to become modest, to avoid speaking in public, to deny your presence when invited.

Mortifying your Ego may also mean showing off your humility: renounce prestige, notoriety, success in every aspect. You had better stop being brilliant. Start wearing with sobriety, i.e. more classic, less luxury, less coloured garments. During this transit you should take care of your *being* rather than your *possessing*. Censure yourself and appear less in public. Act so that the others think that you have disappeared for the time being.

Also sacrifice something in connection with your sons and daughters, or your parents, or your husband or wife, or a brother or sister. Without any doubt you should give up anything that is not essential. Give up any sensuality in a broad sense; be lonelier, more essential, and more modest. Accepting harder physical tasks would also help 'paying' your debt to Saturn. For example during this transit you should avoid lifts and climb the stairs instead; or avoid driving the car and take a bus instead.

You should also visit a dentist more often, as well as the orthopaedist, the gym club, and the expert in chiropractics, in massages to the backbone. Start slimming or detoxifying diets. Read serious, demanding books rather than watching TV.

Sacrifices can be small but constant: do not drink spirits, do not eat sweets, do not eat meat, and so on. Engage yourself in a long-term project involving huge fatigue. Perhaps for the first time in your life you may start wearing a hat in winter, a heavy scarf, knitwear… If you need it you may also resolve to wear prosthesis, for example dentures.

Saturn in a dissonant aspect with the Moon

Under this transit you aren't generally in the mood of talking, and you may suffer for any sort of human contact – even if you really wish to have human contact. What you should do then is to give up your desire of human warmth and remain lonely for the time being.

This is the classical transit that you can exorcise mainly by means of loneliness and isolation. As Dethlefsen used to say, I may also suggest (but it's his original idea, not mine) to dress in black and visit graveyards often. For if you feel the death in your heart and see the world in black and white, you won't see it in colours even if you buy a dozen colour-TV sets. And if it's raining cats and dog and you feel depressed, singing "rain rain go away, come again another way" won't make you feel better. So isolate in loneliness, stay on your own, writing a personal log, reading serious and demanding books.

Avoid telephone calls; postpone meeting your dear ones. Stay with serious, solemn, earnest people, such as the old, the moralists, the priests, the teachers, the masters in general. Embrace suffering and pain, do not try to avoid them. It is probable that you'll have to detach yourself from a dear one of the fair sex during this transit. Perhaps a relative, a girlfriend, a daughter or a sister might wish to leave, to go away – and you had better let her go. Accept any sort of compulsory isolation, enter any sort of hermitage.

Your character, your personality will become a little older – do not try to avoid it. Begin to behave more seriously, accordingly to your age. You may grasp the occasion and learn how to dominate over your gestures, over your own facial mimics. You'll be also able to judge yourself with increased severity, and with less indulgence.

Saturn in a dissonant aspect with Mercury

Above anything else, give up driving your car; also, renounce some journey. If you spend all of your time behind the steering wheel, this is the right time for keeping it parked in the garage. Take the bus or the train instead, especially if they are crowded and always late. If you are a daily commuter, change your way of commuting.

You may resolve to choose a longer, heavier, more expensive route to reach there. For example you may resolve to join a farther gym club, located at the other end of your town: this way you'll give something to Saturn every single day. Also walking much, or jogging or footing a lot, may help. As the last chance, if nothing else can suite you, you may buy a new car (but if you do so, it might not a very good idea). Instead, it may be the best moment for studying and applying for a driving licence or a boating licence.

Also give up telephone and browsing the Internet, if you usually spend much time in those activities. Instead of sending E-mails, you may resolve to pick up a fountain pen and write a traditional letter. This transit may help you start a demanding, serious, and proficient letter exchange with a master or an individual whom you esteem much. You may also compromise to assist a son or a brother or a young friend or relatives. This may happen in any way: you may lend him money, give him private lessons, or visit him at hospital, or give him moral support, and so on.

Saturn in a dissonant aspect with Venus

In this case you have to do something serious, such as parting. If you are accustomed to run with the hare and hunt with the hound, you had better take your decision now – which side are you own? You cannot have it both ways. You must give up something. Usually, if not always, this transit demands you to give up love. And if you love one person only, you should take in serious consideration the hypothesis of separation. If you don't feel like leaving your dear one for ever more, you may consider a sort of 'parting for the time being'.

I have suggested this solution to many people, who proved that it really works, and it works well. 'For the time being' means reaching an agreement with your partner and do not meet until this transit lasts. At the same time you resolve not to get involved with anybody else. If you both do so, there is a fair chance that after the end of this transit, you have given enough to Saturn and you can re-establish a happy, serene relationship with your beloved one. While this solution is more easily feasible if you do not cohabitate, if you are married or if you live together, it may be harder to carry it out in practice. If so, what I suggest is to avoid at least sexual intercourses; for example start sleeping in separate rooms.

If you live in different places and you normally meet, say, once a week, during this period you may discharge the transit by meeting, say, once a month. You may also try to exorcise this transit through a drastic fall of sexual activity. Or you may resolve to face this transit by accepting to make sacrifices for your beloved partner: for example spending money on him or her; or carrying out physical tasks to relieve her/his fatigue. This may also refer to a daughter or a sister or any other female individual whom you care for.

Saturn in a dissonant aspect with Mars

This is the classical transit in which you cannot but visit your dentist. Ask him, or her, to perform any sort of operation on your teeth: dentures, fillings, bridges and perhaps implants. The more often you go to a dentist the better. The same applies to the orthopaedist.

The ideal way of discharging this transit would be wearing a corset that blocks you for a few months. You may also bind your back, your shoulder, your knee... If you have planned to undergo surgery, especially orthopaedic surgery, this is the best moment to do so, for this is a really disharmonic transit and you need to discharge it somehow.

So orthopaedic surgery suits the best (meniscus, herniated disc...) otherwise any other sort of operation, such as cosmetic surgery, the removal of a cyst or of a myoma, or any other sort of gynaecological or anal intervention. If you are in a good health and you have no surgery to offer to Saturn, you may practice remedial gymnastics, especially if it involves pain and suffering. So get prepared to spend long hours at the gym, at the physiotherapist, at the expert in chiropractics and in massages to the backbone. Any sort of physical task would help exorcise this transit, not to mention that after all, it is also good for your circulation.

During these months or weeks, Saturn might also ask you to become nastier, more cynical, and more heartless with your fellows. So within certain limits you should comply with it and, at least, you should try to be less lenient or indulgent with people. If you have to carry out works of carpentry such as cutting or sawing wood, or mounting pieces of furniture, this is the best moment to do so.

Saturn in a dissonant aspect with Jupiter

This transit asks you to look at the world in an ascetic way; so be more essential, more frugal, and more severe. This transit also implies a period of unluckiness, which you should discharge almost provoking a real stroke of bad luck. In practice, this may mean, for example, that you should accept or even provoke a business which is unfavourable for you. You may resolve to sell an object through the classified advertisements, and at a lower price, at an absolutely inconvenient price for you.

This way you would surely give a concrete form to a portion of the bad luck which this transit announces. In other words: in order to avoid more serious damages in this period, you should act in order to suffer a lesser financial or business damage. Say that you have got a video recorder and that you might sell it for 200 Euros.

Well, give it away for 100 Euros. By selling it below its real value you'll suffer a small financial damage, but this is exactly what you should do under this transit. You may also lend a little money to a friend of yours, knowing that he's not going to give it back soon – or that he's not going to give it back at all. This way you make a very bad deal, but at the same time you spare a worse damage. Although this transit is not as bad as the transits of Saturn in bad angles with the Sun and the Moon, you should pay attention if you want to avoid serious consequences.

Saturn in a dissonant aspect with Saturn

If only possible, isolate yourself. If you already live in loneliness, try to be even lonelier. Avoid all simple and easy things, those which could give moments of recreations or joy to you. Engage in solving long, complex, and tiring problems instead. In this period, destiny requires sustained and continuous effort. You really have to live days of sacrifice: especially at a physical, working level, and also in connection with food.

So don't go out at evenings, or go out much less than usual. Devote all your time to work; read a lot; avoid watching TV. Refrain from eating; engage in severe slimming or detoxifying diets. During these weeks or months you should feel the need of being lonelier; of living in isolation; of seldom meeting people; of embarking in prolonged efforts; of performing activities that do *not* imply any sort of gratification.

Abolishing any sort of gratification may also imply avoiding pampering yourself with all those objects that our Western psychology considers as 'joyful' or 'positive'. So do not buy garments or tools that might enhance or make your job easier. Do not take a holiday, do not travel, do not go out for rides and so on. The best way would be to undergo efforts: work and work, over and over again. There is a time for fatigue and there is a time for recreation. This is undoubtedly the time for fatigue.

Saturn in a dissonant aspect with Uranus

This is surely a particularly destructive period of your life. Remember that our bottom line is that you have to give something to the celestials. So be prepared to offer a sacrifice in harmony with this transit. Which kind of sacrifice does this transit requires? Surely – destruction.

For example, if you are not satisfied in connection with a friend, this may be the right time to end your relationship with him, or her. For this transit surely implies some sort of destruction and what you should do during these weeks or months is exactly destroying, alienating, getting rid of things. You should behave in a radical, absolutely negative, and intransigent way.

To do so you may sacrifice a human relationship that was already weak and unsure, and that survived only thanks to your Christian spirit of charity that prevented you from leaving him or her. Sometimes a little bit of cynism is not so bad. So face the reality and get rid of useless junk, false friends, dead weights, people whose friendliness depends on how you do. Be they relatives or friends or former lovers, simply get rid of them and wipe the slate clean.

The world would judge you cynical and bad – but this is exactly what you have to be during a square, or opposition, or conjunction between transit Saturn and your natal Uranus.

Saturn in a dissonant aspect with Neptune

During this transit you may particularly feel the damaging effects of a long-lasting therapy with psychotropic drugs or the consequences of any sort of intoxication. So you should undergo a sort of 'gastric lavage' in the broadest meaning of this term.

For example you could start a detoxifying diet, even if this might cost you real crises of 'abstinence'. For example, stop taking a pill against anxiety or depression even if this may cause you a state of physical discomfort. Or you may be willing to start taking an antidepressant pill, even if you know already that this would make you feel sleepy, confused, uncertain, out of phase. Since this transit may announce suffering because of a 'drug', it would be a good thing if it were you who chooses what drug you suffer from.

So you may ask your doctor to prescribe you a psychotropic drug that might help you overcome a hard period of your life. This transit may also be discharged by making huge efforts, for example, quitting smoking or quitting taking drugs. Since Neptune also involves the symbol of water, you should try to make efforts in connection with water: for example you may fix or refurbish your boat. Or you may transport quantities of liquids, such as bottles of wine or spirit barrels from one place to another.

Saturn in a dissonant aspect with Pluto

Spend money, or more money than usual, on your beloved one. Allocate money, or better, hand out money to your partner without security. This is also a very bad period for sexuality: you had better refrain from sexual intercourses for the time being.

If you have debts, you had better extinguish them during this transit - even better if doing so means spending virtually all your reserves, or almost emptying your current account. You may also spend money in connection with your family chapel at the cemetery; or in any connection with death. For example you may lend money to a relative stricken by mourn. This is a period of destruction; this is how you should live it. This may imply also getting rid of a person with whom you cannot have a satisfactory relationship any more; for example you may have had an affair with a lover and this is the time to truncate this relationship.

Do not worry if during these months you feel anguish, phobia, little neuroses or fears. Let all this flow and discharge the aggressiveness that you feel on your skin by quarrelling of fighting with somebody. You might try to re-establish good relationship with them later on, after this transit has gone over.

Transit Saturn in the First House

On an average, this transit may last two or three years. It usually implies a good growth at a mental level. During this transit you live a process of maturation – you get older both in a positive and in a negative way. Complying with this transit means making efforts to be more sober, more detached from the material world; to focus more on work; to be more productive and efficient; to keep away from superfluous, unessential things, from everything that may give you recreation and joy.

Accordingly to this, you should seriously consider starting a slimming, or detoxifying diet. The moment has arrived to enforce order, to make a 'clean-up' in your nutrition. Avoid anything superfluous; keep chocolate out of the door together with sweets, candies, sugar and similar food. Empty your cupboard, keep your drawers empty. Always get up from table when you are still a little hungry, with a sense of frustration. Obviously during this transit you should avoid the dessert after lunch and dinner, as well as the ice cream that you usually have on Sundays.

If you drink coffee without sugar, you'll provoke (a first of all mental, secondarily physical) condition of frustration, which during this transit may prevent you from suffering from more severe troubles. You may also try to transpose all this at a physical level, i.e. try to loose weight: it might be determinant in order to exorcise this transit. For example, in a nice summer evening, after dinner you might consider the pleasure of sitting down on your favourite armchair watching TV while sipping a refreshing drink or eating one by one the juicy grapes from your favourite vineyard.

Well, exactly by depriving yourself of such pleasant 'finales' you will see your weight decreasing day by day on the balance. It's starting from mental frustration that you end up with having physical frustration as well. Your 'strained face' represents exactly what you need to discharge this transit properly. You needn't imitate those medieval monks or hermits who used to wear the cilice or prayed kneeling on stones! You may simply make small, but constant sacrifices.

For example you may refrain from drinking spirits or you may fast one day every month; or you may quit smoking, eating cakes and so on. You should also wear darker garments, which would testify before everybody else your current mood. You should also embark on prolonged efforts, working on long-term ambitious plans.

During this transit you should stick to the notion that you are a sort of alpine climber who proceeds step by step towards the top of the mountain – not a hundred-metre sprinter. Sweat, panting breath, devastating exhaustion should be the constants of this transit, which may last a couple of years. This is also the right moment to deal with your own teeth. This is actually the best period to visit your dentist, thus giving to Saturn what Saturn requires in terms of calcium (the symbol of Chronos, the old age). Spending a long time under the drill will surely help exorcising the transit that we are talking about. This may also refer to the rehabilitating actions of chiropractics, such as backbone massage.

Dental care, chiropractics, backbone massage is exactly what you need to discharge this transit. Another good idea could be to keep low your heating at home. A couple of degrees should be enough. Above anything else, remember to constellate this transit with a more disciplined behaviour in a broad sense: be more moderate in every detail, and isolate yourself more than you usually do. Staying on your own in meditation would do only good. Also, adopt a way of looking more suitable to the growth implied by this transit. Perhaps you may renounce dying your hair; by keeping them grizzled you'll testify to the world that the time has arrived for you to get older.

Transit Saturn in the Second House

It marks the time of lean cows. You have only two choices then. You 'turn off the taps' of your outgoing money, or you spend all your money and become penniless. Let me try and explain this transit with a metaphor. Once a friend of mine, exactly during this transit resolved to retire for a period and live in a country house.

He then told me that he had eventually learnt the high value of a single grain of corn, on which the entire life of a plant may depend. In other words, he learnt not to waste anything at all. This is what you should do during this transit: become more careful when spending and making expenses; more controlled; and why not? even meaner. You should learn to use the verb 'to spare' in every aspect of your life.

Spare on electricity, spare on heating, spare on your telephone bill, make fewer phone calls and buy fewer garments unless you need it very badly. Keep away from any logic of consumerism, behave like Scrooge

McDuck and keep counting your capital, happy to see your pile of coins grow day by day. Saturn in the 2nd House is certainly a transit of avarice, so you have to exorcise your avarice. Even if many astrologers think so otherwise, it always corresponds to a loss of money.

On the contrary quite often it announces the arrival of inheritance, an important amount of money in connection with selling real estate, liquidation... So rather that enjoying all this incoming money, during this transit you should start managing your new financial situation with increased care and attention. In the early '70s we got to know a widow who received an incredible (for those times) amount of money. Instead of spending more, she did exactly the opposite. While she used to go to the restaurant once a month, she renounced it. She said she didn't want to 'nibble at that money'.

The bottom line of these years is 'spending less': this is the way you can constellate this transit in the less painful way. If not, you may re-channel your expenses in a particularly aimed, constructive way. For example you may take out a long-lasting, painful house-loan. This way you would concentrate all your flow of outgoing money on it, renouncing a sequel of other possible expenses that you may or may not consider superfluous, such as garments, computers, travels, going out for dinner, and so on. If you spend less or if you spend only in one direction you provoke a deterioration of your quality of life.

This is exactly what this transit requires, and this is what you have to do if you don't want that this transit reveals itself through robberies, swindles, frauds, unforeseen expenses and so on. Another way of discharging this transit may be 'sweating more for money'. For example you may work overtime for a little extra salary.

This way you may feel frustration for the striking incoherence between you being underpaid and, say, the authorities and State itself wasting a lot of money. This 'frustration for money' or anyway in connection with money is what properly constellates this transit.

You may also spend money for acquiring a nicer physical aspect. For example you may spend expensive weeks in slimming centres such as those founded by French herbalist Maurice Mességué.

Transit Saturn in the Third House

During the two or three year of the transit of Saturn in your natal 3rd House you had better avoid using your car. By doing so you would offer the utmost sacrifice that a human being born at the dawn of the third millennium could give to the altar of the offerings of this celestial position. In our society of 'steeroholics' in which you use your car even when you go buy cigarettes, refraining from driving would certainly imply the utmost sacrifice that man could conceive in connection with Saturn in the 3rd House. So go by foot, rediscover the human dimension of walking in your town; or use public transportation if you wish, especially if in your town this service is inadequate.

Re-educate yourself to civil behaviour, and stay patiently in queue at the bus stop, even if it's raining or if it's cold. Rediscover the pleasure of long winter Sundays in which you stroll in the town or you ride your bicycle in a car-free zone. If you offered a similar environmentalist-like behaviour to the altar of Saturn, Saturn would appreciate it very much, thus almost certainly avoiding beating you with its painful lash.

You should renounce also your motorbike as well as your car. If this seems an excessive sacrifice, keep in mind that after all this is a thing that you *can* do, and that if you don't perhaps you wouldn't be able to avoid more serious problems, such as your car being stolen or suffering from nose-to-tail crashes, which might cause you serious expenses, if not serious wounds.

But if you really cannot refrain from driving (but why couldn't you, after all?) you may change your car even if it's a brand-new model, with an older vehicle – perhaps such an old car that you had better keep it in your garage. Another way of exorcising this transit may consist in creating a daily or weekly, tiresome commuting.

For example you may impose yourself on travelling many miles every day to go visit a sick relative, a dear one who's in hospital, a parent who needs you. You may also create *ad hoc* this sort of commuting, for example you may resolve to join a gym club at the other end of the town, avoiding the closer ones for the time during which this transit lasts.

Talking about painful or tiresome displacements, there's another possibility, although it's the one that I suggest the least: you may get up to your neck in debts, with a long-lasting loan, and buy a brand-new, expensive car. At another level, you may also refrain from using the telephone.

Use it only if you really need it very badly, especially if you normally have your ear glued to the phone for many hours a day. Learn to spare on the telephone bill, and leave your mobile at home when you go out on

Sundays. Another excellent way of offering a sacrifice to Saturn's transit in your 3rd House is starting a demanding study, for example getting prepared for hard exams or difficult contests, competitions. Going back to school at the age of forty or fifty may be a really painful thing, but it is exactly what Saturn demands from us in this period. Lastly, you may also consider the possibility of quitting smoking.

Transit Saturn in the Fourth House

During these years it would be a wise and convenient thing if you could have refurbishing or rebuilding works made in your habitat. Remember that the habitat to which the 4th House refers may be you house, i.e. the place where you sleep and where you eat; but it may also your office, your shop, your laboratory, i.e. the place where your work.. The extent of the work to do depends mainly on your current financial situation. They could be huge works or simple tasks, such as creating two smaller rooms from a bigger one; a new floor; a more modern heating system; air conditioning; a false ceiling; painting the walls; a new kitchen; a new bathroom... It would also be a wise thing to do your best to have those works last as long as possible: having little tasks performed in a day, and imposing long pauses in between one task and another. In other words, do not concentrate everything in a short period, but spread it over the longest period that you can arrange.

Remember: the longer you are forced to keep your windows open in winter, or to cohabitate with a lime of scuttle left on your best armchair, the more you avoid more serious problems. Even better if it's you who carry out those tasks personally instead of having them made by masters and workers: your physical fatigue would help you very much discharge this transit. Nonetheless the best way of exorcising and constellating this transit remains the haemorrhage of money.

Let a bank or a real estate agent drain your money and buy a house or a flat. It may be the place where you want to live but it may also be a second house at the seaside, or a portion of a time-share flat, or a shop, or a box for your car.

Take into consideration that this transit may last 2-3 years to 4-5 years, and arrange the terms of the loan over all this span of time. Otherwise you may discharge this transit with periods of planned hospitalizations: for example to heal existing problems or simply to have a check-up performed on you. It would also be useful to undergo a 'jailing' for this purpose: for example you may spend this transit cohabitating with your mother, if you are not in good terms with your wife or husband. In fact this transit often marks the periods in which one of the two (the husband or the wife) leaves the house and go to live with his/her parents, a brother or sister, a friend.

Another way of living this period following the rules of Active Astrology is to take more care of your dear parents or grandparents. For example you may take them frequently to a day hospital, or you may visit them daily, do the shopping for them, or simply showing them how much you care. You may also keep order in your database, in your files and folders. For example, you may put order in the contacts of your mailing software.

Transit Saturn in the Fifth House

During this transit of Saturn in your natal 5th House you might let your son(s) go and study abroad. Thus you'd give to Saturn the deprivation that it demands. You'd also face expenses for your kid. For example, say that you let him/her study overseas: this would certainly discharge the negative symbols implied in this transit. In fact any sacrifice that you made in connection with your sons or daughters would lead to positive results, especially if you do them in this special period of your life. Otherwise you should invent something else in accordance with this basic notion or 'sacrifices for the kids'.

For example you may hire private tutors for them; enrol them in a private school or college; let them join a gym club and pay their bill; pay for a training course on computers for them, or any other course in which they could learn something useful. If you did so, if you faced sacrifices and spent money for your children, Saturn would certainly appreciate it. In its classical depiction, Saturn holds a pruning hook in his left hand: it represents the notion of separation, of isolation.

So if you cannot let your children go abroad, you may at least allow them go away from home for a while. For example they may live at your parents, or they may go and study in another town, where a relative or a good friend may host them. If your son is of the age of being soldier, let him serve in the army now; even if he would have the right to do so it wouldn't be a good idea to postpone it.

If your kids (or one of them) need dental braces, this is the best period for having it done: so don't wait! This is also the right period to take your kids to the dentist and/or to the orthopaedist. If they suffer from scoliosis or similar, they may be fitted with a form of corset in order to immobilize and protect the torso.

You may also try and deal more with your kids' problems: talk to them more often, listen to them more carefully, let them reveal their secrets and treat them with higher responsibility. You may also compromise in making their habitat better, more comfortable: for example rearranging the whole layout of your home so that they have more space while you face some sacrifice. For this is exactly what Saturn wants – step aside and leave space to your kids! Take cognizance of their existence, of their needs having more requirements than you had thought until now. In a way or another, during these years you are supposed to spend more money on your kids.

You may also reduce dramatically the quantity of joy and play in your life, for example by going out less often at night; renouncing going to the cinema, the theatre, recitals, and restaurants. Spend less week-ends in the country, travel less, have less sex, especially occasional, extra-marital sex. If possible, renounce having love affairs – this would be the highest sacrifice that you could offer to Saturn in this period. This is the best period if you have to end up with an extra-marital relationship, even if this would cost you pain. It is also a good occasion for quitting smoking, playing cards, gambling, occasional sex, and so on.

Transit Saturn in the Sixth House

During these years you should take particular care of your health, and of your self in general – much more than what you usually do. First of all, this transit requires a special care for your teeth and for your bones. So go often to the dentist, to the orthopaedist, and submit yourself to therapies based on chiropractics, backbone massages, and energy healing (pranotherapy). The more you heal your teeth and bones, the fewer problems you have from this transit.

So engage in long-lasting therapies or cures made by a sequel of tiring and annoying, if not painful, sessions. This is the best way to discharge this transit. Of course any therapy involving time and suffering will suit, even if they are not of a dental type. Nevertheless dental care is the best in this case, because it matches all the symbols of Saturn, i.e. Chronos = time = calcium = bones and teeth.

Even better if your dentist gives you a mobile prosthesis or similar instruments of torture to wear often: they will surely have the effect of discharging this transit if not in full, at least in part. In any case any sort of rehabilitating therapy will suit, even those that imply gymnastics, joining a gym club, mud therapies, or inhalation therapies, e.g. aerosol. This may also refer to slimming and/or detoxifying diets. In certain cases you have to lose weight in order to unburden your bones: you see? this also refers to Saturn. At another level you may intensify a task, i.e. accepting extra work, taking part of your work at home, and embarking on an ambitious enterprise involving physical fatigue. If you constelled symbols relevant to the work together with symbols relevant to physical tasks, you might be sure that you're acting in the right way.

If your occupation is prevailingly of an intellectual kind, try to carry out also some physical work: the harder the better. For example you may help your wife or your mother in seasonal tasks such as spring cleaning; swapping your wardrobe; dismounting, cleaning and remounting your curtains; displace pieces of furniture and so on. Another winning way of living this transit may be, for example, doing it all by yourself without any domestic help. Very often during this transit a collaborator (secretary, driver, maid, daily help…) leaves or resigns and you cannot rely on his/her help any longer.

If this happens, avoid looking intensively for another person in his/her place, because if you do so you may run the risk of hiring and firing in sequence three or four collaborators, one after another. No, you had better take this event philosophically and, for the time being, do it yourself. Say that you are a medical doctor and your nurse or secretary gets pregnant and leaves temporarily: you should carry out also her job for the time being, until this transits ends and/or she returns to the job.

This way you can be sure to be discharging this transit in a very appropriate way. And if you really cannot refrain from hiring a collaborator, choose an aged person.

Transit Saturn in the Seventh House

There's undeclared war at home during this transit, and this is exactly the path you have to follow. This transit in fact usually opens deep wounds between you and your beloved one, or between you and a commercial partner, or with an ally in politics, in your profession, in the syndicate… So the best thing you can do is to declare one or more 'wars' rather than waiting in a defensive attitude for the others to attack you. So get prepared and light one or more conflicts, for example with your neighbours; your colleagues; your relatives... The ideal would be to produce legal paper against somebody, but if it is not possible for you to sue anybody, at least you should call somebody and argue with them on the phone.

If there is a person with whom you don't want to have anything to do any more, this is the occasion for telling him/her openly. When I say 'legal paper' I mean it in the broadest meaning of this term. So it may be an intellectual quarrel on a local newspaper; flaming letters to its director; or a series of complaints to the Police; or a period of militancy in an environmental movement or party; and so on.

To make a long story short, you have to leave for the war in any way and under any form. If it's you who light conflicts during this transit, you stand fair chances that others would not attack you. Otherwise you'll have to defend from all sorts of attack from the law or from other citizens like you. In this period also your relationship with your steady partner runs the risk of getting worse; so you had better be cautious if you don't want to spoil it definitively.

Try not to get involved in anything, act with a degree of indifference; and don't be excessively concerned if you notice that your marital relationship is getting chiller: the good thing of Saturn is that when its transit is over, the implicated situation usually reverts back to the stage in which it was before the beginning of the transit. So you had better accept that there will be a degree of penalties and misunderstanding between you and your beloved one during this transit. Moreover, you may even create a situation in which you become a sort of slave to him or her: fetch the breakfast to him/her, go and take him/her at work, help him/her doing the cleaning, and so on.

Usually during this transit your wife or husband tends to behave with increased conceit or arrogance. Instead of struggling against this, you had better indulge his or her whims – remember that they will be over as soon as this transit also is over. You should also make efforts to give more to the others. So if you usually avoid picking up the phone, during this transit you should do your best to overcome this attitude of yours and become more open with the others. You may also make some sacrifice for a business partner or a collaborator or a colleague: e.g. accepting to carry out certain tasks in his/her place.

Just like any other transit, you should not simply hope that it passes without any consequences and then give a sigh of relief. No, you should give something to the transit, something that the transit itself (i.e. its symbols) requires. In this case you have to offer a sacrifice in your marital life, or to a collaborator, a colleague etc. This is also a good period to embark on a trial, especially if you expect a long legal suit, and if you know that you cannot really avoid it.

If this transit takes place within the frame of other detrimental astrological situations that may affect your marital life, you should take into serious consideration that possibility of a sort of 'parting for the time being' as already explained in another section of this volume: that is to say, reach an agreement with your dearest one and do not meet until this transit lasts.

Transit Saturn in the Eighth House
Almost certainly, during these years you face haemorrhage of money. So get prepared in advance and do your best in order to channel this event as productively as possible. The best way to discharge this transit is to invest in real estate: buy a house or a flat and pay a long-lasting loan. You will be concerned because of the financial compromise you have taken, but you will eventually own a house of your own. It is hardly possible to avoid or to by-pass this transit. There will surely be a flow of outgoing money; and if you will not face any special or particular expense, then there will be a dramatic fall in your income. At the very beginning of this transit it should become clear which way it will take.

In the latter case you had better 'turn off hermetically' the 'taps' of your outgoing money; reduce the expenses to the minimum; spare on everything; become sober; and avoid anything that may be considered superfluous. If you are not greedy, you had better learn to become greedy. If you normally tend to spend much, at least during this transit you had better do your utmost to keep your money under stricter control. This is important: do not underestimate this point, otherwise you run the risk of finding yourself in trouble. If you don't feel able to avoid the expenses that this transit usually heralds, you may always do your best to comply with this transit, of course within certain limits. So, for example, you may apply for a bank loan to be better prepared to cope with an unexpected expense: then you'll repay it slowly and... painfully.

But be careful not to exaggerate, and ask for a loan that you will *not* be able to repay. During this period it may happen that you have to face unexpected, or planned, expenses. For example paying for your daughter's wedding; buying a new car; investing on new tools for your work; undergoing surgery... In all the above mentioned events you have to spend money, so you had better follow the previously detailed pieces of advice. Saturn's transit in the 8th House may also imply a fall in your sexual activity.

Also in this case, it is possible to facilitate the transit by applying a stricter discipline on your self. If you only can, make also sacrifices in connection with your own grave: for example you may have your family chapel refurbished, or you may wish to make your will before an authority. If you have to have excavations done for any reason in a parcel under your property, for example in search of water or anything else, this is the best period for doing so.

Transit Saturn in the Ninth House

During the transit of the ruler of Capricorn in your natal 9th House, you are asked to refrain from travelling – so it would be very wise of you not to leave home for the time being. In fact this is one of the few transits of Saturn in which you are simply required to renounce to the symbols involved. Don't you agree that renouncing a journey is much worthier than having serious problems of health or with your children, or financial troubles, or sentimental crisis? Even if you are a xenophile Sagittarius, one of those who feel alive only when they can travel abroad; and even if you claim that every suffering is only a subjective state of mind; let me underline that this is one of the rare transits that implies virtually no discomfort.

After all, there's no comparison between renouncing a holiday in the Caribbean Sea or inn California, and suffering from serious mourn or receiving very bad news about your own state of health. So I think that every astrologer, even the ones born in the sign of Sagittarius, if they only could, would place a transit Saturn in their 9th House for the rest of their life. The list of the wrongdoings that this 'little rock in the sky' may provoke when it passes through your natal 9th House is extremely long, but it seldom contains events for which you should be really concerned. At most you should renounce a cruise at the last minute because one of your parents is ill.

Or you travel to Maldives but the first day there you have a sunstroke that forces you to spend the rest of your holiday indoor. Or you travel to USA and your luggage is lost in Japan. Or you miss a connection and you are forced to travel back home, and so on. In a word, this transit implies bad luck abroad and in connection with foreigners. So the first system you have to exorcize in this transit is to abort any project of travelling anywhere, and renounce any holiday far from home.

The more serious and important the renouncement, and the deeper your sufferance, the better you exorcize this transit. For the two or three years of this transit you had better resolve not to travel, not even to visit another town; and if you are forced to do so, you should try to transform this journey in suffering. For example, you may travel abroad in order to take a seriously ill relative of yours to a foreign hospital. Or you may sort of 'serve in the army' for a period, i.e. spending a period of time far from home to follow a training course involving a sequel of lodging problems and homesickness.

It may also work well if you refrain from having contacts with a dear one who has left for another town or region of your country, during this transit. You may travel abroad, provided that you go there to carry out a hard, tiresome, mentally compromising work. The 9th House refers to all that is 'far away' from home; but it may be a non-physical distance as well, in connection with unexplored transcendental horizons. So during this transit you may get deeper into a belief, a credo, a particular philosophy or view of life, such as practicing Buddhism and so on.

Another way of 'discharging' this transit may be travelling with discomfort. Say that you have to travel from Italy to Portugal: rather than taking a flight and arrive there after two hours, you had better take a train and arrive there after two or three days. Last, you may also try to give assistance to people of the so-called *Third World*. You may accept a child sponsorship or even better: you may host in your home a poor African, or a Chechen boy...

Transit Saturn in the Tenth House

In this House, transit Saturn expresses a sort of behavioural dualism: here, more than in any other House. It may herald two apparently opposite situations, which reveal to be substantially quite similar if you watch at them carefully. They both have to do with sufferance and your social, professional, or generally speaking: working position.

I give a few examples. Say that you are a worker in temporary layoff: when this transit starts, you stand higher chances to eventually lose your job definitely. In such a situation, Saturn virtually guarantees that you'll be fired. But say that you are a teacher in a comprehensive public school and that during this transit you apply for a post of headmistress. In this case you stand fair chances of achieving your ambitious goal and getting the job. Are you wondering how it can be that in the latter case also Saturn plays a role? It is quite simple: Saturn implies suffering, much suffering.

So in your opinion, how much suffering is required to take part in a public contest, studying day and night, and eventually pass a difficult selection and get a higher job? You can see that both cases involve work, from one side; and suffering, from the other. In the former case you suffer because you lose your job; in the latter case you suffer because you spend 'a lot of sleepless nights to see your name in light'. So when it comes to exorcising or discharging this transit, you have to follow similar directions to those two described in this section.

If you feel that your current job isn't enough or it isn't satisfactory any longer for you, this transits marks the right period for getting rid of it and applying for a better position. Every thing has got a price, so you may run the risk of getting unemployed for the time being – even so, it might be worth if this helps you recovering serenity. Certain things are priceless. And if you realize that during this period you have a chance of growing professionally even if it may cost you trouble and fatigue, make your motor roar and grasp the occasion.

I'm sure that you have caught the basic notion. You have to make sacrifices in connection with the work: I'm sure that everybody knows how to do so. For example, if you work in a factory or in a hotel and Saturn transits over your Medium Coeli, you simply ask to be assigned to the night shift and you'll see that your general working conditions get immediately better! You may also ask to be assigned to a production line, or to an office or a department, whose chief is well known for his grumpy manners. Also in this way you'd give something to Saturn, and if you consider it carefully, this may also save you from dismissal. A poet would say that you have to suffer in order to survive.

So do not hide yourself in order to avoid trouble or fatigue, but volunteer bravely and you'll be 'saved'. Volunteer and accept to carry out even humble or menial tasks, for example cleaning the roof of a congress room. Do not worry about those who would comment ironically that you are a bootlicker: remember that by doing so, during this transit, it's a matter of saving your own post in the company. Other times will arrive when you can allow yourself to play the hero... Under certain circumstances, this transit may refer to your mother. If so, it may imply that you have to take more care for her – much more than usual.

So this is the time to show her how much you are grateful to her for having brought you to life. During this transit you do your best to relieve her pain, to heal her from a disease, to help her overcome a difficult period of her life. This is the time for showing her how much you care: do it in practice, not only with words.

Transit Saturn in the Eleventh House

During this transit, perhaps you are forced to abort certain projects. If so, do it spontaneously and do not try to struggle against the events. They say that you can't win them all. Be aware of this and act consequently. Many times you develop a project and you eventually realize that it isn't feasible, that it could not really become true, that you had to renounce. Well, this is exact what this transit implies.

There is the time for joy and success, and there is the time for deception and renouncement. This is the time for the renouncement. Throw in the towel and look ahead. Perhaps you are mistaken in your calculations, or you have underestimated the hindrances. So be wise and postpone the enterprise to better times, or abort it. But also in this case, Saturn may show apparently opposite situations. So another way of discharging this transit is to follow the opposite direction. For example, you may work on a very ambitious project that requires huge resources of energy and time.

In a word: a 'saturnine' project. A project that starts today and ends up in twenty years, step by step, exactly according to Chronos' logics. In this case, the renouncement consists in giving up the urge to hurry, and being determined to undergo all the sacrifices that such a long-term project demands. In this case, the preconditions match the symbols of this transit and the enterprise will be a success.

This transit may also imply the renouncement of friendship with one person in particular. For example, you might have to renounce a person whose protection could have been extremely useful. If this happens, this event alone may be worth the sacrifice and it may be sufficient to discharge this transit. But you may also try to start a new friendship, especially with a wise, aged, sober person.

This transit may also require you to refrain from music: you may stop playing in a band, or stop dealing with music as a hobby until this transit lasts.

Transit Saturn in the Twelfth House

It is quite easy to exorcise this transit. Everybody with a little brain and fantasy will be able to pursue the following simple rule: the more you give in every field of your life, the more you achieve.

If possible, you should make sacrifices in everything and accept penalties from anywhere. Sacrifices can be small but constant. Refrain from the tastiest food, no sweeties, no candies, no ice creams, no cigarettes, no *spaghetti*, no pizza and so on. In other words, you should leave a sort of monastic life. You should aspire to expiation rather than to the gratification of the flesh. Avoid going out with friends at night. Stay at home. Read serious books, study and do not watch television. You can write a log if you wish, or poems or a novel.

Ignore the telephone, use Internet only for work. Stay at home like a soldier forced to stay in the barracks, refrain from meeting friends and even your girlfriend or boyfriend. Forget about playing and having fun during this transit. Your goal should be being Spartan, essential, sober, austere… Devote much time to meditation; reflect on your current network of human relationships trying to understand which mistakes you are currently making with them, and how you can avoid further mistakes. Sobriety, isolation and meditation should be your key words that lead you during this transit.

Also at a physical level, you should follow the principle of not chasing beauty, but adhere only to essence. Obviously you should also give much; deal with your human fellows; take care of them; worry for the poor; support those who suffer; assist those in need… And do not even try to avoid suffering and pain with prostheses or ointments. If your wounds burn, you had better learn to stand pain. Do not hurry in search of ointments or any other lenitive solution. Be brave. There is a time for joy and a time for pain. This is the time for pain.

16.
Transits of Uranus

You have to understand that with the transits of Uranus you cannot possibly cheat or bluff. What I mean is that, while you can discharge the other transits even with modest half-counteractions, with Uranus you have to do your utmost, and give everything you can for the sake of renovation. At every transit, Uranus asks you to pay very high tolls, and you cannot but fulfil. You cannot behave like Tancredi, the protagonist of Giuseppe Tomasi di Lampedusa's novel *The Leopard*, who claimed: "If we want things to stay as they are, things will have to change". In other words, you cannot act as if you were changing the entire world while your real goal is to leave everything unchanged.

No, Uranus wants you to change effectively, and under its transits you cannot but change – and change dramatically. On the other hand, nobody claims that the changes provoked by this planet are always negative. Often in fact, the renovation caused by Uranus is an evolutionary and positive step in your life. I've seen, for example, aged persons starting studying medicine under its transits. They sacrificed many sleepless nights and in five years they graduated and eventually they changed their life in an absolutely positive and radical way.

I've also seen people re-channelling drastically their libido, quitting their steady but castrating relationship, and flourish to a new life. I might list a long series of examples, but I simply wish to stress that the wind of renovation of Uranus, be it good or evil, simply razes the existing situation in order to leave place for new – absolutely new – directions. Being naturally prone to changing, people born in the sign of Aquarius would accept this better than others.

Particularly Taurus and cancer would suffer more, for they usually tend to struggle against changes. The transits of Uranus require a massive recourse to Active Astrology: above anything else, I mean a series of good Aimed Solar Returns; and secondarily, also by exorcising the symbols in the manner that we describe in the following pages.

Uranus in a dissonant aspect with the Sun

Perhaps this is the strongest transit of Uranus. People who live more than eighty years can be affected by this transit up to four times, taking in consideration only the main angles: conjunction, square, opposition, square, and – if you live longer – conjunction once again.

On an average you can experience a dissonant transit (without considering semisquares and sesquisquares, although they also are extremely important angles) every 20 to 22 years. Usually they correspond to the most intense moments of your life. And considering a possible retrograde motion of Uranus, this transit may last two years. Remember that the Sun, in astrology, is symbolized by a circle with a dot in its centre. This, in the Eastern world, corresponds to a *mandala* – the symbol depicting *the whole*. In fact, when Uranus passes over your natal Sun or when it creates an angle with it, you experience transformations concerning everything – or almost everything.

Provided that you are in the right age, often you can suffer from mourn during the two years of this transit. Mourn itself can be considered as the powerful echo of the hurricane that Uranus provokes in you during this transit. At other levels, this transit always – virtually always – heralds changes in every aspect of your life. So you have to forestall events, with no hesitation and keeping in mind that the stakes are high. You have to offer something important to Uranus even when you see it approaching near your Sun or forming an aspect with your Sun. The ideal would be a complete refurbishing of your own self. Work should obviously be at the first position.

You should try to change your occupation at any cost – or at least you should change the way you carry out your job. If you are a professional (a medical doctor, an attorney, a lawyer, an architect and so on) of course you should not consider becoming an usher! But you might computerize your job completely, for example. If you are in trade, you may extend the area covered by your business. For example, if you are a business agent you may accept to cover another area beyond your current one. If you are a civil lawyer, you may start and deal also with penal cases. If you are an engineer working in a public administration, you may start selling your projects as a freelancer, additionally changing your main job from full time to part time. If you are a teacher you may consider an early retirement, and so on. The list could be infinite, but I am confident that you have already caught the point. Your business card, the way you introduce yourself to the world, depicts what you are. You should change it as well. Have your hair cut or have your beard grow.

Start a slimming diet, join a gym club. Change the contents of your wardrobe as well, e.g. from classical to casual. Undergo chiropractics in order to achieve a better posture. You should also change your character. If you are an introvert you may enrol as an actor in a company of amateurs: this way you'd get accustomed to speak up in the centre of a scene. Or if you are a talkative one, you should compromise to spend hours in silence and meditation, e.g. reading. But above all, you should change your habits – for they are not written down in the 'Tablets of Stone of the Bible'! So you may insert ten minutes of gymnastic in your daily life, for example.

Do not forget to feed your spirit as well: e.g. learn to play a musical instrument, or listen to classical music. Remember that this transit forces you to change, and change...

Uranus in a dissonant aspect with the Moon

One may guess that this transit only has an effect on your sentimental life, but I can assure that I've often noticed its effects also on other aspects of people's life: for example, some people changed their job during this transit. How can this be explained? In my opinion, this can be explained considering that, after all, the final effect of this transit is eventually a hurricane in your sentimental life. I remember a particular event also. A forty-year-old man used to work in tourism.

He was at the height of his career when he resolved to leave his job. He went to live far away, in a remote island, where he started managing a small hotel. Take in consideration that he was an extremely judicious person, I may say he was careful and meticulous; so such a change must have had the effect of a nuclear bomb on his psyche, on his sense of safety, and as a consequence also on his sentimental life. For this reason, most of the things described in connection with the transit of Uranus with the Sun also refer to its transit with the Moon.

On the other hand, to exorcize this transit you should favour or provoke radical changes in your steady relationship or in your loved one. In other words, you should try to have him or her change his/her own habits, the way he or she carries out his/her job, his or her hobbies, his/her favourite food and so on. This is the only way to discharge effectively this transit. Say that you are a jealous husband and that you don't allow your wife to accept a job because you want to know that she is constantly at home. Well, during this transit you should change your point of view completely and allow her – even more: invite her, or help her – to take a job and spend part of the day far from home.

Such a choice should be real, concrete, and visible – so don't limit it to a hypothetical speech. So help your beloved one to apply for a job; fill the forms together with her; if she has to study for an admission test, study with her night and day; if necessary, spend money on her. This may apply not only to your wife, but to any other female of your family: your mother, your sister, your daughter... As I told you, Uranus doesn't content itself with apparent results: he demands authentic revolutions in your life.

So if you are an extremely jealous one and you resolve to calm down, you must do it as if you wrote the headlines of the daily paper of your life, in huge letters. For example, you should accept that your husband or wife spends nights at the restaurant with colleagues at work; give him/her a dedicated room at home where he/she can work and make phone calls without interference; leave him/her in peace without relentlessly questioning him/her about his/her spare time, and so on. All this may imply a titanic effort if you normally suffer from jealousy: on the other hand, the transits of Uranus *are* titanic and they require titanic steps from your side.

Uranus in a dissonant aspect with Mercury

This transit involves events in connection with your displacements, that is to say: your daily or weekly commuting, your moving on the road – or at another level: your intellectual life. This is the ideal period for a mental competition, for mental challenges: such as graduating, taking a degree, taking part in a contest, learning to use a computer, making effort in any intellectual enterprise.

If you have left your studies years ago, during this transit you may resolve to enrol in a course on languages, for example. And if you have developed a special skill in a specific field of expertise, for example if you have learnt to cook following the rules of macrobiotics, you may resolve to write a book or to hold a series of lessons or radio transmissions on this subject. Certainly, the renovation caused by this transit may lead you to write poems or a personal log: in fact this is not necessarily something that leads you to earn more money, but it is simply something that leads you to fulfil your inner needs.

On the other hand, Mercury also represents trade. So during this transit you may create a business of your own, for instance selling garments at home, just to make an example. Without necessarily leaving or reducing or changing your current job, during this transit you may sell many different objects in your spare time: books, jewellery, your used computer, or software programmes. This transit may also refer to displacement, so it would be a wise thing if you invented a commuting execise during this transit. For example choose to join a gym club far from home; or move your shop to another place; or ask your company to transfer you to another branch; or commute to another town to meet your love there; travel often to visit an ill relative, and so on.

If you own a car, you should seriously consider about changing it or refraining from driving definitely. A growing number of persons actually give up their car and achieve a better quality of life. If you don't want to get rid of your car, during these weeks or months you may resolve to buy a new one. This is also a very good period for studying and applying for a driving licence or a boating licence.

You should also drastically change your relationship with the tools of communication and telecommunication: for example you may purchase a satellite dish, a mobile phone, a CB radio set. Mercury and the 3rd House have much to do with smoking: so it would be very wise of you if you quitted smoking during this transit (provided that you smoke, of course). Last but not least, try to deal more with a young person of your entourage: it may be your little brother, a young friend, a cousin, a brother-in-law...

Uranus in a dissonant aspect with Venus

Here comes the bad news. For sentimental life is probably the most critical sector of everybody's life. I don't wish to elaborate this notion at a philosophical level: it would be out of the scope of this volume.

So let me only point at a few things on this subject. In my career of astrological counselling dating back for over twenty-eight years, I have understood that happiness within the frame of sentimental relationship is really one of the principal spurs of libido, perhaps the most important one – at least it is so for the overwhelming majority of human beings. I was about to say: for the majority of women, but this is true only up to a certain point. Actually, there are many-many males who long for a steady relationship and do suffer very much if they don't achieve it. Perhaps you could renounce luxury, holidays, car, money, health – but you couldn't possibly renounce the 'security blanket' of love. We all feel terribly alone here on Earth and – rightly or wrongly – we all are convinced that as a couple you get by much better.

Many people are unfaithful simply because they are convinced that two companions protect them better than one. This is due to a sort of immaturity within the human being, and those who think that way cannot be cured not even through a long-lasting therapy of deep analysis. This is why most of us feel as if the ground is subsiding under our feet, and some of us even panic, when the transit of Uranus arrives in dissonance (and sometimes also in harmony) with Venus.

Yet it is a good thing to realise that against this transit you cannot possibly do anything effectively but *giving* – even if this will cost you very much. As I told you, Uranus doesn't content itself with apparent results: you have to accept that it demands you to produce real, radical, and total changes. You had better not even try to do like Ulysses when he had himself tied to the mainmast of his ship to resist the mermaids – for there aren't ropes or chains strong enough to resist the attraction of Uranus. Is there no means of escape then? Well, the answer is that, according to my practical experience over thousands of people, there are actually two ways you can behave.

The first one is a *timed parting*. If your loved one agrees, you should resolve to part for a quite long span of time (say 8 to 16 months) with the promise of not getting involved in any other sentimental liaison. By doing so, at the end of that period you can stand fair chances to be able to rebuild your sentimental life with your steady partner, while Uranus would be satisfied. Another way of exorcizing this transit is that of performing a little craziness, such as living two weeks of wild love with a much younger partner, for example, and before the eyes of everybody, i.e. without hiding, but on the contrary: feeding the gossips.

In other words, you need an intense yet brief scandal as well as beams of light over that scandal. Of course you can do it if you can rely on a steady partner who is capable of accepting you back in his/her arms after this transit-scandal is over. Do you remember *The Blue Angel*?

With the aim of punishing his students, an old bachelor goes to the local cabaret and ends up falling crazily in love with dancer Lola (Marlene Dietrich). Well, that Professor was surely having the transit Uranus-Venus. Based upon my experience, I believe that there is no other way to exorcise this specific transit.

Somebody may claim that it should be sufficient to change your attitude towards your beloved one, but this doesn't match my experience: and if you leave Uranus leading your life in this period, it may even provoke your definite parting. Coming back to the timed parting, if you live in a different town than your beloved one, you can also carry it out by simply meeting less frequently.

Uranus in a dissonant aspect with Mars

This is a treacherous transit, containing a strongly explosive charge. Since each of them is a real fire-raiser, the flammability mix produced by these two celestials can really provoke violent fires. There is no use in struggling against this transit with mere prostheses, for there's nothing to do: it only has to deflagrate. So you have only two ways of discharging it. One, you can have it deflagrate 'physically' or two, you should start behaving in an absolutely radical way.

The former solution may consist in undergoing surgery (and I think you actually *should*), especially if doctors agree that it cannot be postponed any longer. In many occasions I have met men and women who had to be operated, I mean doctors told them to undergo surgery, but they were frightened at the idea and postponed. I suggested them to be operated during the transit we are talking about, also keeping in mind the rules described in my volume *Astrologia applicata*, ed. Armenia. Things turned out very well for them. In fact that way, Uranus had obtained a very important sacrifice ad those people had got rid of the sword of Damocles over their head.

I do believe that the best thing to do is undergoing surgery during this transit; this is especially true if in your natal sky you have potentially dangerous positions for accidents. In certain cases, when the native has strong elements in the sign of the Lion and/or in the 6th natal House, it is possible to have an intervention of cosmetic surgery: just like any other operation, this would be able to discharge this transit quite well.

Otherwise, a deflagration should happen in your behaviour in connection with others. If so, you should show your claws and fight as wildly as possible. You had better avoid any loving attitude, any prudence; behave decisively and without any compromise. If during these years you have to give a piece of your mind to, say, a colleague, a chief, or an employee whom you can't stand any longer, you had better do it fiercely and bravely exactly during this transit. You run the risk of leaving 'wounded victims on the field'; you run the risk of harming yourself as well. But this is necessary: one can not simply avoid the consequences of the transits of Uranus.

While if you facilitate them you cannot but unsheathe your sword, and this is exactly what I am suggesting to do: unless you have tonsils to sacrifice. And back to surgical operation, many people ask me if going to the dentist may be sufficient to discharge this kind of transit. The answer is No; it is not enough unless your dentist makes an implant into your bone, which can be considered as real surgery.

Uranus in a dissonant aspect with Jupiter
The worst consequences of this transit should be in connection with the last discoveries of technology, electronics, and informatics. So if you wish to exorcise it you should provoke the relevant symbols by embarking in some uncertain enterprise such as, for example, installing a new operation system in your computer machine.

In fact, such an upgrade might have the effect of making your computer freeze; eventually you might even run the risk of losing all of your applications and software and resolve to restore your previous system after a couple of weeks of real drama. If you use the computer quite often you know perfectly what this means: it is something that can be more devastating than software viruses.

So you may ask, "Is it really worth? What's the use in it? Isn't it a little like shooting yourself in the foot?" No, it isn't: because after having repaired and restored your system, you eventually end up by having your whole machine up-graded. If you have caught what I mean it should be easy for you to deploy this notion in other fields of your life, in connection with, say, hi-fi stereo players; the latest model of digital camera; anti-stress equipments based on bio-feedback; and so on. At another level, you may try and discharge this transit by drastically breaking a relationship with a foreigner, or somebody who lives in, or who comes from another town or region of your country (not necessarily abroad). Obviously I refer to situations that you had already resolved to terminate:

you can do it preferably during this transit. Furthermore, following the symbols of Uranus and of Jupiter, you may resolve to cancel suddenly a travel abroad; or on the contrary, to start suddenly for a travel. Jupiter also refers to justice: therefore you can unexpectedly promote a suit and embark yourself on a long trial amidst lawyers, attorneys, and courts. You may also try to carry out a prosthetic action such as a detoxifying diet, or anything that can help you get rid of any kind of toxins.

Uranus in a dissonant aspect with Uranus

This transit may provoke many troubles deriving from the 'old', in the widest meaning of this adjective. Obsolete equipment, outdated electrical household appliances, such as unstable microwave ovens, could damage you during this transit; so what you have to do to neutralize this transit is, before anything else: trying to get rid of them! Get rid of any old, outmoded object in your house and in your work place. You have to be drastic in that: discard generously all the old objects and working tools that you may keep with you only because they are connected with nice memories of your past.

During this transit, on the contrary, you have to throw them away and carry out a complete renovation of your tools and instruments at home, at the office, in your laboratory, in your garage… Also damages may arrive from aging structures such as a roof that does not isolate properly, or a wall with infiltrations of water. This would probably imply sacrifice, an important expense; but you should do it in order to discharge this transit. It is in your own interest. This may also refer to your car or any other vehicle. If it is old-fashioned you may buy a newer model, even if your dear-old one seems to be still fully reliable. *Updating and rejuvenation* should be your motto during this transit. Also take particular care about the date of expiry of packed or canned food, drugs, and any other perishable item around you.

The same may refer even to human beings – so be particularly careful with old people during this transit. Of course I don't mean that old people may be dangerous in general: I simply want to stress that this transit may announce unforeseen, unexpected damages coming from aging people. Foreseeing also means preventing: so try to guess and avoid any possible damages that may derive to you from old persons and/or old objects around you. If you do this way perhaps you'll be able to determine exactly when and where this transit would possible strike. This transit may also involve trouble deriving from bone therapies based on radiations; so I suggest you to consult with a specialist during this transit.

Uranus in a dissonant aspect with Uranus

Similar to the transits of Uranus in connection with the Sun, the transit we are describing here also provokes a strong impulse towards change and renovation at every level, including your sentimental and professional life. You simply feel the need of changing as much as possible, although you may not be willing to turn your life upside down.

This transit will not allow you to do like the ostrich and bury your head in the sand. So if you usually do so, forget about it because Uranus won't forget you. In fact this celestial seems to take account of every single human being on Earth, be it the President of the USA or any John Smith. And this is particularly wonderful, because it also works in a positive way, during its harmonic transits. People born in the sign of Aquarius are the most favoured by this transit, given that their own nature inclines them to changing, sometimes radically. Cancer, Taurus and one by one all the other signs usually aren't happy to face this transit, with its revolutionary consequences. Most of them, in fact, tend to mediate, to reach agreements, to postpone… But doing so will only increase the damage.

What you should do in order to discharge this transit is behaving like a martyr woman who is about to be raped. If this comparison seems too much, well at least behave like people of good will before the unavoidable events of life. It is very rare to find a person who accepts to have everything change: job, home, alimentation, leisure… But this is exactly what this transit provokes! So you had better invent a new life for yourself, otherwise you have no chance: you change spontaneously or you have Uranus change you.

In this sort of struggle or competition against the celestials, you have to understand that in this case you have to submit to Uranus, so it is better that you volunteer and get rid of all your old habits. This is a period in which you feel the need for a general renovation, and you should accomplish with this by having your life turn suddenly and – why not? – dramatically. Like Giuseppe Tomasi di Lampedusa wrote in his novel *The Leopard*, "If we want things to stay as they are, things will have to change". So be brave and do your best in order to be, like the Romans used to say, *the artisan of your own fortune*. In this case: the artisan of your own change... For example you should organize your working activity in a different way – not necessarily *change* your job, but simply *reorganize* it. The same may refer to your hobbies, to the way you spend your spare time.

By doing so you can stand fair chances that your sentimental life and your professional life would not be affected by this transit. Yet, if you feel that your sentimental life also needs restyling, you had better do it during this transit. Sometimes it is possible to have all the changes required by Uranus concentrated in one main revolutionary step. For example some people become a Buddhist during this transit. I cannot really fancy any change greater than this: it certainly is enough to give Uranus what Uranus demands in this period.

Uranus in a dissonant aspect with Neptune

We ended the previous paragraph with the example of the conversion to Buddhism: that example of exorcism of the symbol may refer perfectly also to the transit of Uranus in connection with Neptune. For the previous dissonant transit Uranus-Uranus announces revolutionary changes that make your life turn upside down and inside out. The range of possible changes includes also conversion, among many others.

On the contrary, in this specific case conversion is the most probable change announced by this transit. It must be stressed though, that conversion may not refer to religion only. During this transit people may radically change their political views; they may start volunteering in environmental movements; they may start dealing passionately with esoteric astrology, with parapsychology, and so on. What all these things have in common is an altered state of consciousness. It may be 'altered' by a religious credo – of *any* religion – by political faith, by active participation in syndicates, trade unions, military groups, and so on.

One can also become fond of a new style of life implying – for example – vegetarianism. During this transit a wave of passion should lead you to join mass movements, and it's absolutely the same whether you join the Red Cross, Caritas or CSICOP, the international council of sceptical organizations.

Remember that the altered state of consciousness can be also connected with toxins that you may assume in relevant quantity during this transit, such as caffeine, tobacco, a psychotropic drug, and so on. In another section of this volume I have written about the 'little Chinese acupuncture' whose basic principle claims that 'one pain drives out another'. So if you channel your libido into a huge passion of any gender, you would almost certainly avoid becoming a victim of the chemical slavery that this transit might provoke if you don't do anything to discharge it. Of course a degree of sincerity is required.

You cannot become a supporter of a football team if up to this date you have never cared for football! You had better discover in yourself a secret, sleeping passion that you could apply in your current life, and have it deployed during this transit. You might even consider the possibility of having your blood 'poisoned' voluntarily. For example you may start taking a new medicine to kill a persistent pain that has been affecting you until now.

While you should carefully avoid any dangerous activity connected with the symbols involved in this transit: e.g. water sports, scuba diving... If you are an anaesthetist, you should be even more cautious during this transit, and have a good insurance cover you against possible professional risks.

Uranus in a dissonant aspect with Pluto

During this transit the deepest animal instincts tend to rise to the surface. I'm talking about the least noble spurs, the worst impulses that can be found virtually in every human being. In order to struggle against them you have to understand exactly what 'exorcism of a symbol' means. Perhaps certain psychologists would not agree, but I claim – I am actually convinced – that in order to overcome this transit you have to give free yet controlled way to the most brutal portion of your self.

And in order to do so, you should appoint an external 'killer' to act for you. I try to tell it another way. When you take the metro you often see a gang, a group of hooligans, drifters behaving in a bullying way. You know, I mean those who shout, sing Nazi songs, spit on the ground, annoy passengers, and sometimes even steal from them. Tell me the truth: in those occasions you really like to embrace a gun and shoot at them, don't you? So instead of acting as Charles Bronson in *Death Wish*, go and meet your 'vigilante': go to the cinema or hire a videotape of the series *Death Wish*, watch Charles Bronson blow the hooligans' head with this automatic gun machine.

This way you'll have given free way to your adrenaline without harming anybody. I know that many people don't approve of violence in films, and perhaps you are one of them. But I believe that this behaviour may be cathartic, i.e. liberating, relieving – and exorcising as well. This transit may also provoke an increased desire of 'unusual' sex.

So if your partner agrees, you may try and put in practice all the positions of the Kama Sutra. Remember that in the field of sexual intercourse there is nothing like 'orthodoxy', so get rid of any Catholic influence in your education and experiment unusual or 'unorthodox' positions. At another level, you may tray to discharge this transit by dealing with anything that may be in connection with your future burying. You may wish to make your will, for example. After all, this is something that every human being should do sooner or later.

Transit Uranus in the First House

Please refer to the section about Uranus in dissonance with the Sun, especially if Uranus is very close to the Ascendant, they may apply also to this transit. During these months or weeks you may get ill. In order to discharge this transit, it is very important to try to change either your physic or your character. One of the best ways to exorcise it is to change your body mass, provided that you need a change towards a more balanced condition.

What I mean is that if you are overweight or underweight, this is the time to try to correct your diet and to reach your ideal weight. In modern society there's a risk of obesity pending over virtually all of us, so in the majority of the cases, this transit suggests to start on a diet. If you are in this situation too, take it seriously and change radically the way you eat. Many people resolve to start the diet 'next Monday' every week. Doing so of course is completely useless: roll up your sleeves and be serious this time.

During this transit you have to forget your own weakness and you have to struggle against hunger, if needed. Stop being self-indulgent; behave with rigour, inflexibility, without any pity towards yourself. In order to give Uranus the change that it demands you have to be relentless, intransigent, and even heartless and lose weight sensibly. According to your current overweight, you might need to give up five or ten kilos, perhaps more.

The aim is to be reborn, to become a new person. The same, of course, refers to those who are underweight because of their bad habits in connection with food. Do not follow these pieces of advice though, without consulting your doctor. In any case this transit requires you to give a dramatic turn to your habits in connection with food, and to take care of your body mass. In certain cases, you may consider correcting a slight physical blemish, perhaps undergoing cosmetic surgery.

For example you may consider getting your eyes operated to get rid of myopia, or to remove some bad-looking birthmarks spoiling the beauty of your face. Or you may consider having a tattoo made on your arm, or having an already existing tattoo removed from your skin. Going to the dentist during this transit may be helpful but only up to certain degree. It would be useful if you underwent some more serious operation such as implants in your jaw – which would imply effective surgery. Women may get pregnant during this transit; some women resolve to undergo sterilization during this transit. Male readers may resolve to take advantage of this transit and undergo vasectomy.

Of course whatever sort of surgical operation you may have to undergo, you had better have it performed during this transit. At another level, this transit may demand from you a dramatic change of character, especially if it requires you to show that you possess strong iron will. For example, if you are basically shy and introvert, you should make efforts to become open and extrovert.

Or if you are extremely talkative you should try to talk much less, and when you do you should ponder your words one by one, often stopping to reflect upon what you are about to say.

Transit Uranus in the Second House

This transit opens quite a critical scenario. But there's no way to cheat Uranus, so you have to resign yourself to the fact that the years marked by this transit will herald important events in your financial situation. If you are not careful, you run the risk of losing a good amount of money, although – of course - money may also arrive into your pockets. The whole of your transits and your Solar Returns of these years will help you understand in which direction your money would flow.

Whatever it may be, your attitude shall be resolute and without hesitations. If you have to spend, there's no use in resisting because Uranus will make you spend in any case. What you could do during this transit is to apply for a loan or an advance of your severance pay, or ask a relative or a good friend of yours to lend you money.

Be careful yet, because it's exactly when there's a shortage of money that you can become a victim of loan sharks who act as false friends and eventually strangle you if you don't pay their money back with the highest interests.

So avoid accepting money from people whom you don't know very well, especially if they offer money to you with suspicious easiness. Unless you can rely on noticeable financial reserves, you could hardly avoid applying for a loan – but if you do so, you had better ask a bank and not private institutions or individuals. This transit may last six to seven years on an average: during this span of time you'll be able to pay back your loan or a good amount of it.

On the other hand instead of spending, it could be that money arrives to you coming from the sale of real estate, or inheritance, or severance pay, or gambling win: if so be careful and do no dissipate that amount. If it's not money, then this transit usually refers to an important change in your appearance. For example you may lose ten kilos or you may gain weight. You may grow a beard or shave it. You may resolve to shave your head, and so on. The bottom line is that something will happen to change the image you project.

Also this transit may refer to your increasing interest towards images such as photography, cinema, theatre, television, drawing, design, and computer-aided design: for example you may resolve to enrol in training courses on these subjects.

Transit Uranus in the Third House

During these years you'll certainly face serious news, perhaps even dramatic ones, from your brothers, sisters, brothers-in-love, and/or sisters-in-love. So you had better provoke them somehow: for example you may take the initiative and if you are in bad terms with one of the above mentioned relatives, you should take the first step to re-establish a civil relationship between yourselves.

Show all of your good will and take the first step. Remember that after your parents, your brothers and sisters are the closest relatives, those whom you should care for the most. Sometimes it isn't hard to break the ice: and during this transit, Uranus will help you make the first act of good will. You may even try to change completely your attitude towards them.

For example, if so far you have been quite 'absent' from their lives, now you might show them all your sincere affection, and let them know that you really care and that you really wish to help. Or perhaps it's you who is in dire straits and who feels alone: if so, you may ask them for help setting your pride aside. Often relationship with brothers-in-law and sisters-in-law are a little bit difficult.

But thanks to this Uranus, everything is possible and you should not give up without having at least made a serious attempt. It is possible, or better said: it is probable that your attitude towards the car and vehicles in general will change during this transit. It may be the best time for studying and applying for a driving licence. Or perhaps you might even resolve to refrain from driving and to sell your car. Often during this transit people buy a car or they sell their old car to purchase a new one. The same may refer to motorbikes, vans, trucks, caravans… During this transit it is very probable that your attitude towards movement will change. For example if you are a stay-at-home who never goes anywhere, during this transit you may start commuting every day to go to work, or for any other reason.

Or if you usually drive hundreds of miles per day, with this transit you will probably stop doing so. The bottom line is that you should do your best to play an active role in all this: you should not wait for the mentioned changes to take place – you should project them, if not provoke them. You may also provoke changes in the field of studies, for example by enrolling in training courses connected with your current job, or in absolutely news fields for you such as, say, a foreign language, a course on informatics, and so on.

You may also enrol at a university during this transit. You can take advantage of this transit and start writing something important. During these years you can also quit smoking, even if you are a heavy smoker.

Transit Uranus in the Fourth House

Probably you focused on your car during the previous seven years – now it's time to focus your interest on the place you live. If you cannot rely on your own resources to reach this goal, you should apply for a mortgage loan.

In any case it is almost certain that during these years you would carry out an important transaction in the field of real estate.

You stand actually have three choices: one, you sell or buy a house/flat; two, you refurbish it; or, three, you move. This may also refer to the place where you work, not only to the place where you live. Hence the above mentioned events may happen in connection with your office, with your shop, with your laboratory, and so on. It is virtually impossible that nothing happens in this field during this transit.

So you had better consider whether it isn't worth to take the first step, at least making the preliminary plans and let it happen during this transit. The transit may also herald inheritance or a donation; perhaps one of your parents or another close relative lets you live in a house of their ownership. In the worst event, you may face a situation in which you need to leave your home, perhaps because you separate from your husband, wife, or steady partner.

For example, perhaps you cohabitate with your boyfriend or girlfriend; during this transit you may argue very badly and have to go and live on your own. The worst event of all may imply hospitalization. In order to undergo a therapy, you may be forced to leave home for a while. During this transit one cannot exclude the possibility of even being imprisoned. After all, being jailed implies moving out from home.

Of course, the latter event is possible only if during this transit other detrimental transits take place in connection with your 8th or 12th natal House. With Uranus in your 4th House you may also have to leave your country or your native area, in order to take a job abroad or in another area of your country. This also implies looking for another place to live. Also, this transit may announce important changes in the relationship between you and your parents.

If you wish to exorcise this symbol you have to take the initiative and change actively something in this connection. For example, if until now you have been servile and condescending with them, during this transit you may start behaving like an adult, still behaving with responsibility and keeping in mind that aged people have their own character that you should always respect.

Transit Uranus in the Fifth House

This transit requires you to change something fundamental in your loving relationship. If for example your steady relationship is getting unstable or unsatisfactory, rather than trying to save it at any cost you had better let your partner down.

You should consider separation seriously, as well as starting on a brand new affair. After all, nothing lasts forever and if it does, it must not be considered as a taboo, i.e. untouchable – you can always consider renovation. Only steel is stainless, everything changes, everything can change – and it must change indeed – everything gets older. So you are completely wrong if you insist in believing that there can be anything in your life to which these rules do not apply. Everything can be amended or modified, even if it may hurt very much.

On the other hand, modifying does not necessarily mean changing partner: it may simply imply some sort of renovation in your relationship with her/him. Who said that your steady partner shall serve you breakfast in your bedroom? Once in a lifetime you can do that for him/her for a period! Am I not right? Sometimes you say to yourself, "This will *never* change!" Then Uranus arrives and everything is altered.

Renovation, from this point of view, means basically changing the strategic balance within your steady relationship; bringing into dispute your leadership within your pair, taking in consideration that the roles we play in a pair are usually unwritten and can be renegotiated at any time. So you have to put *yourself* into dispute first of all; and be open to renovation in that specific field of your life. The same may refer to your relationship with your children, where things may even demand an abrupt U-turn. Last but not least you should also reconsider the way you spend your free time, the way you have fun.

Who said that the mechanisms of your playing and sporting activities can not change even radically? Perhaps you have sold your soul to the devil, who in exchange has asked you to go to the stadium every Sunday until the end of your days? So you see – many things can change, and they have to change in fact. Even more: it is the right moment for them to change.

Transit Uranus in the Sixth House

You have to roll up your sleeves and take care of your person – undergo radical therapies, if needed. Perhaps so far you have underestimated certain slight symptoms and you have constantly been postponing serious remedies for your health.

Well now the time has come for you to beaver away. You have to understand that it's time to go to the doctor if you don't want that your health condition gets worse. Of course the practical effects of this transit are different if the subject is a 15-year-old boy or if it is an adult, say: over 40, over 50, or even older. Usually when Uranus enters your natal 6th House it always shows important effects – you had better not underestimate it. You had better discharge this transit by offering something important to Uranus, some sacrifice. For example, if you have been postponing surgery, the time has arrived for you to undergo it.

You cannot face this transit by simply bluffing, you can not try to spare on anything. The more you possess, the more you have to offer, without hesitation. I personally fear from this transit very much, I would like it to never happen to me.

During these years you should take in serious consideration the Aimed Solar Returns every year and you have to relocate it with particular care, but you should also do your best to deploy anything that might exorcise this transit as well as other detrimental transits that may take place in this period. If you are over 60, this period might mark an extremely dangerous time of your life.

So you have to deploy some radical strategy against it. In my life I have met several people who – at a certain point of their life – resolved to go abroad to undergo radical dental care, for example surgical implantation in their jaws. Certain countries are ahead in this field as compared with Italy, but undergoing this surgery can be much cheaper there than in the most important dental studios of one of our larger towns. So during this period you should undergo something radical like this, something total, global, perhaps under general anaesthesia. Furthermore, in order to discharge such a powerful transit you have to change radically the way you eat.

For example it could be a good idea to observe total, therapeutic fast. If you cannot, partial fast also may suit. During these years you should get accustomed to eating less. In fact you should eat the least indispensable: hot clear soups, a few chestnuts to fill your stomach, a little bread and cheese, fresh fruit, or cereals. Under such transit, a healthy diet can make the difference and save your life.

Transit Uranus in the Seventh House

Your steady relationship, your pairing is where this transit demands you to change.

This time serving breakfast in the bedroom to your beloved one may not be enough to discharge this transit – it may be necessary, but it may not be sufficient. In fact this transit requires you to change the philosophy of daily life, the little things on which your marital life relies. If you believe that you have acquired permanent rights on your steady partner, you are badly mistaken.

And you'll have to change much during this transit, the same if it arrives during your honey moon or on your 20th wedding anniversary.

There's no such thing as 'proven' or 'well-tested' for Uranus. During this transit you have to remember an important thing, which is real in general but it is even more important now: namely, that you have to conquer and deserve your love on the field, *every new day*! In a way, the beginning of the end of love arrives exactly when you feel that you are safe and that everything in your relationship is granted.

Conquering and maintaining love is perhaps the most difficult art of this life – only a fool or a conceited person would disagree. Every day you risk losing your loved one a hundred times; if you don't see that you are *really* running this risk! And if you risk a hundred times normally, during this transit you risk a thousand times! Never forget it and deploy a consequent strategy. I have no magical or infallible remedy for it – I can only suggest you a series of little but persistent efforts of unselfishness; much sympathy; and much appreciation towards your beloved one. This is the only way in which you'll be able to conquer and re-conquer love over and over again.

Otherwise your relationship will be definitively spoiled by this transit. So if you care, show it in reality, day after day, moment after moment, and not only with words. Remember: during these years reality is not appearance. When least expected this transit may ruin your love. So you had better show that you really are in love; show that you are aware that your beloved one is a precious present from Heaven and that you don't want to lose him/her. If you act so you stand fair chances to maintain your steady relationship for the seven years of this transit, and probably for ever more.

Of course things are different if your natal chart has Uranus in the 7th House, and if during its transit in this House, Uranus also creates a detrimental angle with your natal Venus. There's no harm in trying though. *Active Astrology* may teach you removing mountains, if needed. So beaver, beaver away, over and over again.

You can change false and unstable balances; you can do it. 'Giving' is the verb of this period: if you aren't willing to give, and to give much, you had better renounce any effort because you stand no chance of discharging this transit. For example, if you are a jealous guy who has never let your wife taking a job and leaving home every day, during this transit you should reconsider this habit. If you are one of those who believe that if you wife is locked at home she will never be unfaithful, I can tell you of that jealous man's wife who had an affair with the plumber for twenty years! And this is not a funny joke – it is a real event. This may show you the stupidity of certain human beings.

Transit Uranus in the Eighth House

This transit brings you expenses, a real haemorrhage of money. But you had better not be greedy. Instead you should be prepared to spend a good amount of money on positive and unavoidable events such as your daughter's marriage; buying your first house; applying for a mortgage and have your home refurbished; and so on. Normally there's no use in defending against this transit. In fact acting passively would be the worst solution, for if you don't spend your money on regular, classic ways, during this transit your money might escape from your hands in a dramatic way – e.g. because of theft, burglary, swindle, fraud, robbery, wrong investments. Spending is the *leit motiv* of this period.

So even if you are avaricious or greedy, there's nothing that you can do but spend, spend, and spend over and over again. Be open to the changes in this specific field of your life and also open your pocket, your wallet and your chequebook in order to face any foreseen or unforeseen expense. In 90% of the cases, during this transit people spend directly or indirectly on their home. Direct expenses may mean purchasing, refurbishing, or moving. Indirect expenses may involve paying inheritance tax on inherited estate, which usually means a huge amount. As I told you before, the last thing to do is to play in defence, trying to avoid or to postpone expenses.

These would be efforts that would not lead you anywhere. There would be no use in that. The only thing to do if you haven't got money enough to afford expenses during this transit, is to ask for a loan, a mortgage, a financial help from a friend – of course, being extremely careful about whom you ask money from, since there are plenty of loan sharks around.

Perhaps, in order to cope with the expenses of a piece of real estate, you may need to sacrifice another piece of land or building, or all the money left in the bank. In a word, be prepared for a huge change of your financial situation during these years. I repeat that playing in defence is absolutely useless, which also refers to all the transits of Uranus. Some times this transit announces death; which also may involve expenses. Perhaps one of your close relatives would be stricken by unexpected mourn and you would be expected to help him/her financially.

Perhaps you may resolve to prepare your own passing away, for example by producing clear administrative documents in connection with your last will, in order to avoid litigations among your heirs after your death. You may also spend on your family's chapel or on your own grave. This transit may also imply a change in your sexual habits.

You have to be prepared and open also in this connection. Some people stop having sex during this transit; some others start having sex during this transit.

Transit Uranus in the Ninth House

If there's a time for play, a time for love, a time for health, and a time for money, this is the time for going away, for migrating with your soul and body. During this transit a marvellous season of travels my start for you and for your beloved one.

You may take a plane for the first time in your life, or you may discover or re-discover the pleasure of travelling. You may resolve to start on learning a news foreign language, or improving your skill on a language that you already can speak and write, but not so professionally as you wished. You may join a tour operator and travel the world and the seven seas, thus fulfilling a desire of all your life. After all, travelling has becoming cheaper every day in the last decades. Even travelling overseas is not a dream any longer. During this transit you learn travelling and you start travelling more than before.

You make become accustomed to spending a fixed portion of your yearly budget on travels: so why not start with the aimed birthday? If you have never taken a flight, this is the perfect occasion for doing it. Perhaps, if you really fear from flying, in order to break the ice you may ask an expert traveller, a veteran of international travels, to come with you. I am sure that during the third millennium not only the costs will fall dramatically, but also the times of flight.

But you can also travel with the spirit. This means that during these years you may start on a course on yoga; you may get closer to Buddhism; deepen your Christian faith; perhaps taking a degree; deepening your knowledge of astrology, parapsychology, esotericism… During these years you may also have the chance of moving to another town, another region of your country, or abroad. Even better: you may promote this sort of change. You should take in serious consideration all these things; make them real not only in your mind, but also in reality.

You may also start frequenting a relative of yours, who lives far away, or a spiritual guide or a cultural reference, who lives abroad.

Transit Uranus in the Tenth House

It appears very much probable that during this transit you have to review completely the way you work – during this transit you are asked to change virtually everything in this field. Of course I am not suggesting you to study architecture if you are a dentist: you should simply reorganize your activity. For if you don't change the way you organize your work, the way you perform or execute your profession, it will change anyway under the spur of Uranus, and in a way that you may not like at all. It's up to you finding the best way to do it.

Be creative. For example, if you are a dealer you may try to advertise you business by fax or on the Internet. If you are a successful dentist, you may consider computerizing your study. For example, you may have a laser scan the alveolus left by a molar that you have pulled out and a software application can reconstruct it perfectly on the desired material. Do you think it is science fiction? It may appear like science fiction, but it's reality.

Discover new materials, new technologies, and new techniques of sales. There are vast horizons before your eyes that let you change, I don't say you work, but at least the way you work. During this transit it may also become necessary to move to another working place; to start on a daily or weekly commuting, perhaps by train or by plane; to take part in virtual conferences via Internet; and so on. During these years your approach towards your mother will also change for sure. This is another aspect of your life which Uranus demands you to change. Please it: you won't repent.

Your emancipation would be marked – and it should be marked – by many a different, and potentially interesting step.

Transit Uranus in the Eleventh House

During this transit you are demanded to face a U-turn in friendship. Get rid of old, unstable, unpleasant relationships. Build up new friendship with new people, and/or renew your friendship with the old people as well. You may write a new chapter with them, refounding your friendship on new bases. Certainly those who knew you well since ages, they will be surprised and astonished to see that you become friendly with, say, original, eccentric, or even suspicious persons.

In fact this transit may provoke a real change in your very approach towards certain categories of persons. If for example, until now you have been detesting bonzes or hippies, during this transit you may start considering them with the same respect as any other human being. And if some of your old friends aren't able to accept this, well he is not obliged to be with you when you are with them. If you are an architect, during these years you may work on odd, ambitious projects. For example you may consider building a house without inner walls, or a house without inner doors, a house in which people may share virtually anything.

But above all, remember that during these years what has to change is your friendship with people. Your sense of possession, your notion of property, your jealousy: that's what has to change. If they don't change radically during this transit, you run the risk of losing virtually everything: from love to friendship; and virtually all of your most dear ones.

Each of us is accustomed to conjugate our own relationship with the others by declining the verb *to have* or the verb *to be*. Whatever verb you have preferred so far, during this transit you have to invert their usage. Hopefully you chose to be unselfish; to help your neighbour; especially if you fear from losing the most important ones from around you.

Another way of discharging, or exorcising this transit consists in starting on studying a musical instrument, or music in general. You may also wish to start singing, for example in a choir.

Transit Uranus in the Twelfth House

This is surely one of the most dangerous transits; yet it is not the most dangerous of all: consider for example a transit over the conjunction of Sun and Mars in a natal 6th House! At any rate, you had better not underestimate this transit. In order to overcome the hard times that this transit heralds, that may last up to ten-twelve years, you have to rely on all your mental resources and on all the pieces of advice that you can find in this volume.

Some people may be appalled while reading these lines. But if I say that during this transit John Smith may be jailed for 15 years in, say, Saint Quentin – which is not really a sort of Paradise – could you claim that this is not a tragedy? So I ask to those who criticize me for writing such 'terrorizing' things, give to me in public examples of transit Uranus in the 12th House having wonderful consequences – possibly excluding paralyses, strokes, serious surgery, mourn, bad health condition of the native or of some parent of the native, loss of money, and so on... Well, some people argue that the damage caused by this transit may simply be limited to, for example, a broken TV set that makes you miss the last 10 chapters of *The Bold and the Beautiful*... Some claim, "Nothing bad has happened to me during this transit" – I would like to inquire from them on certain details. Of course certain people claim so in bad faith, but I don't wish to deal with them.

This transit implies similar events as those described in the sections of transit Mars and Saturn in the 12th House. You may tray to discharge it by means of a voluntarily hospitalization and/or by undergoing a surgical operation that you have postponed so far.

Also declare open war on your enemies, especially the ones who pretend to remain hidden, but whom everybody knows. Undergo drastic, painful, and long-lasting diets and therapies.

17.
Transits of Neptune

They are really important transits – extremely important indeed – so do not underestimate them. If you are an artist, a musician, a composer they can determine exceptional states in which your consciousness opens to the influence of suggestions, poetry, and fantasy.

Otherwise you have to beware of them, because if you aren't lucky they might only bring confusion and anxiety into your life; but if you are not, they might even be responsible for serious states of depression and anguish. If you wish to antagonize (i.e. discharge, constellate, exorcize) them you have to dive deliberately into some sort of credo. For example you may become an ardent football supporter, a kind of hooligan; or you may follow a highly humanitarian ideal deploying a potential spirit of nursing assistance, thus vibrating in harmony with the positive vibration that astrology can give to you.

You can also deploy the technique of prosthesis: in this case it mainly means taking psychotropic drugs, antidepressant pills. They may be chemical ones, such as *Prozac* or natural ones, such as melatonin.

Neptune in a dissonant aspect with the Sun

This is possibly the most treacherous transit of Neptune in connection with the Sun. When this transit arrives, you usually feel depressed and this usually corresponds to 'real' depression: although it may be due to inner (i.e. subjective), rather than to outer (i.e. objective) reasons.

Often this sensation may be caused by the sense of loss for a deceased relative or by the separation from your beloved one, or by unemployment. Whatever the cause be, you usually feel down, blue, knocked-out, hopeless... So the first thing to do is ask your doctor for some synthetic or natural antidepressant. Perhaps you'll have to try before you find the aptest remedy. Some people prefer *Ignatia*, the homeopathic remedy derived from St. Ignatius beans which is said to heal the pains of love; some others would require *Prozac* and so on. In any case you would probably need taking some pills, for it would be hard to rely on your own strength alone.

For certain people a cup of coffee every day may be sufficient to cope with this transit. In any case you have to struggle against this transit by finding your 'prosthesis': do not even try to antagonize it face to face. The symbol deployed by this transit is usually clear – it may be treachery, unfaithfulness, the loss of your beloved one, or any other loss associated with somebody or something that will never come back again. The only thing that can work as a prosthesis during this transit is that you 'unleash' some sort of passion or credo such as becoming a supporter or cheerleader for a team; a political, environmentalist, or religious activist; joining whatever may elevate your heart in a more or less fanatic way, thus leading your sleeping libido towards a great operational commitment. There's nothing else you can do.

For example, if you have ever considered volunteering in any field, this is the right time to do it actively: the results will be important.

Neptune in a dissonant aspect with the Moon

Also this transit implies anguish; but this time they can be provoked by situations of tension or uneasiness in relationship with your female acquaintances. You mother or sister or daughter or wife may be ill or may face some discomfort during this transit, which feeds your state of anxiety, depression, anguish, fear. If so it could be useful for you to embrace a credo; to 'draw your sword' and start on a 'crusade'; to show your commitment to civil rights; to join animalist or environmentalist movements – although in the majority of the cases it might be sufficient to start taking some antidepressant.

Ask your doctor for this, but remember that it's not necessary to go to the neurologist or to the neuropsychiatrist: even your homeopathic doctor may be able to help you with some natural remedy. This transit makes you believe that you are in a death trap seizing you by the throat; you also feel like this moment will last forever.

Of course this is not true: but it is true that this sort of transits may last up to four or five years. So it would be good for you to dive into religion, but beware of false magicians and false prophets, otherwise you run the risk of being swindled by some 'faith-healer' who might convince you to purchase some extremely expensive amulet... On the contrary, during this transit you have to face reality and understand that nothing, nobody could really save you from this long-lasting transit. The only realistic solution may consist in psychotropic drugs, but you have to ask the doctor for this.

Neptune in a dissonant aspect with Mercury
It is usually a period of some weeks or months in which you may feel anxiety or depression because of one of your sons, or a boy, or a brother, a cousin, a brother-in-law, or any other young relative or acquaintance. In order to discharge the transit it should be sufficient for you to 'artificially' deploy this anxiety, being aware that it is not seriously based on real events, perhaps because it is simply a gossip.

To be clearer, assume, for example, that people start spreading rumours about your son allegedly taking drugs. Say that you are perfectly aware that you can trust your son and that people are not right. If you are certain that it's only gossip and hearsay, rather than claiming publicly that your son is a saint and that your neighbour Mr. Smith is simply a backbiter, you should fake anxiety instead.

What I mean is that you may pretend that you believe in those rumours and let those people spreading rumours believe that they are right, doing your best in the meanwhile to eventually demonstrate that they are only people in bad faith. Justice will eventually triumph and everybody will see that your boy has never done anything wrong, and during this entire quarrel you would have taken your time and exorcized this transit. Similarly, but at another level, you may also act as if you were supporting some strange, unclear, shady affair of your brother-in-law or sister-in-law, while in reality you are simply collecting evidence that people spread gossip also against them.

I hope that with these examples you may have deduced that the exorcism of symbols does not imply a crystal-clear truth guiding you: it can also consist in a strategy made of dummies and feints as if you were playing a football match.

Neptune in a dissonant aspect with Venus
This is one of the worst transits of all. It may announce that you are in love with someone who does not return; or that you suffer for jealousy and you are convinced that your partner is being unfaithful; or that your

beloved one is having a very bad ill or disease. It doesn't matter if your fears are justified by real suspicion or if it's only your imagination: the result is the same – a very deep anguish that you cannot avoid. Some claim that the pains of love are the most intense ones – it is probably true. Some homeopathic doctors in these cases, suggest you to take *Ignatia* because it seems to be the ideal treatment against the pangs of love – although there's no remedy against certain pains.

So it is a very bad transit indeed. In my opinion there's only one way to face it: and you have to strike the ball on the early rebound, otherwise there's no use in trying to free yourself from the tentacles of this terrible Neptune.

So what you have to do is: when you foresee the approach of this transit, i.e. when Neptune is approaching the orb of the disharmonic angle with your natal Venus, you have to create a story of fantasy, a sort of storyboard of a movie film or of a graphic novel. For example, you may pretend to have an affair with a colleague at work, who knows absolutely nothing about this story.

So when your wife or husband sees you in the company of this colleague of yours, she/he will be sure to grasp certain allusion in your colleague's words, certain surreptitious glance in your colleague's eyes, while in reality there is nothing – absolutely nothing – between you two. If you think that you can go farther, you may even ask your colleague to be your partner in this play of jealousy. For example you may have dates with him/her in public areas where everybody can see you together, and spread rumours.

The more scandal there will be, the better you can discharge this transit. And do not fear from consequences, because since you are not *really* being unfaithful, there simply *cannot* be consequences. Similarly, you might provoke a similar atmosphere of suspicion and distrust at home. Of course, you have to be careful and deploy all of your skill; otherwise you run the risk of harming your family and yourself.

Neptune in a dissonant aspect with Jupiter

In the majority of cases it heralds problems with money; little scandals; or perhaps intoxications of your blood. In all the aforementioned events, the cause is usually the same: excess. Jupiter leads you to go too far, to exceed the mark, to overstep all limits.

I have met many people who ruined themselves by simply being given a loan during a transit of Jupiter. In fact it was a loan that they could not really afford, and that could hardly repay.

The keywords in connection with Jupiter are inflation, exaggeration, and hypertrophy. All these mean that you lose the control over your self-moderation – and this is exactly what a bad transit of Neptune in connection with your natal Jupiter may bring to you. So during this transit you had better take care not to get into troubles. You run the risk of biting off more than your can chew; so the right strategy may consist in 'talking big', perhaps telling stories or telling lies. For example you may ask for some entrepreneur's financial support by proposing him/her real boondoggles: i.e. incredible, unfeasible projects.

The worst that can happen to you in this case is that the entrepreneur takes you as a fanatic and everything ends up without any consequences. The real problem is if you have such qualities like those hucksters in the TV, who may be able to sell refrigerators in Alaska. If you are so, during this transit you run the risk of convincing people to really give you a lot of money for virtually nothing – and you won't probably be able to ever repay that money. That is why I suggested you to 'talk big': the bigger you talk, the less risk you run.

Neptune in a dissonant aspect with Saturn

This transit provokes anguish or confusion in connection with the old: I mean the obsolete things or aged people. But also, whatever is getting older in your own organism. So the best thing to do during this transit – and during other transits described in this volume – is going to the dentist, even better if you dilute the visits into homeopathic doses: I mean, going there every week for a longer period, in which the dentist would do little work at each session. Another way may be in having the old tubes fixed at home, in your heating or hydraulic system.

Even in this case, you had better deploy this as a strategy made of a long sequel of little steps. Day by day, little by little you'll be able to discharge this transit, thanks to the anxiety associated, for example, with the costs of repair. In connection with aged people, you had better focus your attention on your aged relatives. Show them that you care; take care of them; remember that Neptune is the ruler of the sign of Pisces and that it conveys symbols of self-sacrifice, self-abnegation, Christian charity in the widest meaning of this word, and spirit of nursing assistance. Be as careful and loving with them as you wish your sons and nephews to be careful and loving with you when you become as old as your parents or grandparents are now. Mortify your body through prayer, and refrain from unessential material goods. Perhaps you can fast or have an experience of spiritual retreat or collective prayer. There's a time for material good and there's a time for spiritual goods – this is the latter.

Neptune in a dissonant aspect with Uranus

In this period you mainly tend to be the victim of sudden 'verdicts' of magicians, false astrologers, priests, healers, and so on, who might provoke serious damage upon you. For this reason I suggest that during these weeks or months you keep away from the aforementioned categories of professionals who might really be detrimental for you. During this transit you should also avoid anaesthesia, so if only possible – postpone any surgical operation until after this transit.

This is the right moment for getting rid of obsolete gas boilers or electric heaters which are not even legal any longer... At the same time, you had better avoid taking new drugs because this transit exposes you to side effects more than ever. Do not be friendly with astrologers, magicians, and drug addicts during this transit. An 'active' way of exorcising this transit may consist in resolving to eventually computerize your interest in astrology: you may buy a better computer machine, or you may install a more professional software package for casting astral maps, transits, and Solar and Lunar Returns.

This would probably provoke anxiety and some weeks of sleepless nights: but it will eventually prove to be extremely useful for you. Probably during this transit you'll feel an inner tension provoked by the fear of flying. Perhaps you have to take an international flight and you would like to avoid it. But don't fear: statistics assure that in the overwhelming majority of cases, this transit provokes fear and anxiety which is absolutely groundless.

Neptune in a dissonant aspect with Neptune

It marks a hard period for you at a subjective level. On the other hand, Carl Gustav Jung claimed that the subjective reality may be as hard as the objective reality, especially if your psychological attitude is wrong. So whatever are the ghosts and the monsters that you feel creeping inside you, you'll probably judge them to be 'real'. For example you may feel that your dad is about to die and it would be the same whether he is *really* going to die or this is a mere obsession of your mind. So during these weeks or months you had better avoid frequenting magicians or bad astrologers or bad priests, who might provoke such fears that you won't be able to overcome for the following months.

Also be cautious about the pills and the toxic substances that you may take in this span of time. Perhaps in this period you had better ask for the professional help of a psychologist, a good astrologer, a neurologist; a good homeopathic doctor; someone who knows officinal herbs well, and so on. Keep also away from gas, from water, and from the travels on the sea or on rivers. Also avoid any sort of psychological stress such as distressing readings. If you have quarrels with your wife or husband, ask her/him to postpone them for the time being. The truth is that to overcome this transit you need all the affection and the understanding that your beloved ones can give to you.

Neptune in a dissonant aspect with Pluto

The notions expressed in the former section may also apply to this transit, although in this case the effects would be amplified. In this period you tend to suffer from neurosis, anguish, phobia, fears of any kind. So you have to keep away from all sources of anxiety and depression. You had better frequent happy people instead, who enjoy life and who live in thoughtlessness. Also avoid crime stories, film noir, and dark stories of séances, zombies, and similar thrilling subjects.

You should do your utmost to avoid being directly or indirectly involved in the death of a member of your family. For example, if a relative of yours is suffering from cancer at its terminal stage. Despite all of your Christian charity, during this transit you may be unable to give him/her assistance because in fact it is *you* who need help very badly in this period. If so, you had better ask for the help of a homeopathic doctor or a neurologist, who will suggest the best pills that you can take to overcome this bad period of your life.

During this transit it is highly advisable to aim all of your birthdays (i.e. to relocate all of your Solar Returns (and deploy all the strategies of Active Astrology.

Transit Neptune in the First House

Neptune can pass through each natal House only once in a lifetime. Its passage through the 1st Natal House is virtually equal to the transit over your natal Sun: so please refer to what has been described in the relevant section. If this specific transit has a peculiarity, it is an excessive recourse to alcoholic drinks or to drugs – and for 'drug' I usually mean *Valium, Prozac*, but it could also be coffee or tobacco.

Furthermore you may suffer from excessive indolence, laziness, self-abandonment, and a general fattening of your body. In other words, you have to be wary of all the kinds of manifestations of Neptune: from the most banal ones to the most treacherous ones – the latter being strong anguish, heavy depression, phobia and so on.

The best way to exorcise such transit is to dive into a 'religion' in the widest meaning of the term: into astrology, into analytical psychology, parapsychology, esotericism, Eastern cultures, or any other discipline to which we often refer as 'New Age'. The harsher you struggle for your credo, the less Neptune in the 1st House harms you. Beware though: yours shall be a 'healthy fanaticism'. What I mean is that you can try to spread your own 'gospel' on any subject of public interest, but you shall not try to have your personal ideas prevail over the others'.

Transit Neptune in the Second House

Some people start earning money by selling drugs or in similar way. But let us ignore them and let us deal with the overwhelming majority of people instead, who during this transit start feeling anxiety or phobias because of their deep concern of being unable to cope with a financial situation – for example they are afraid not to be able to repay a loan. The best way to exorcise this transit is: doing your best not to fall into debts, avoid applying for a mortgage loan.

If you are in dire straits, you had better apply for a lesser loan from a reliable company; or ask for money from a close relative of yours (parent, brother, brother-in-law...). Absolutely avoid people whom you do not know very well. The newspapers are full of articles about false friends who eventually reveal to be sharks who strangle you if you don't pay their money back in due time and with the highest interests.

And if you cannot avoid taking out a loan, do it for a positive goal, such as refurbishing your bathroom; renovating the water pipes; repairing the heating system in your country house; purchase a boat, and so on. You may also consider starting on depth analysis. This latter is perhaps the very best way to act in accordance with the symbols carried by transit Neptune in your 2nd House.

Transit Neptune in the Third House
If you have similar symbols expressed in your natal chart, you have to pay particular attention during this transit because you stand fair chances to become a victim of road accidents. So be extremely cautious on the road; if possible, refrain from riding motorcars and mopeds.

Be also careful while driving. Especially during winter and if you live in a cold place where fog, ice, snow is frequent. Also be extremely cautious if you happen to move on the surface of water (such as sailing on sea, lake, or river) or if you do scuba diving.

During this transit you should take more care of one of your brothers or sisters or brothers-in-law or sisters-in-law. They (or one of them) may need your help because they (or one of them) run the risk of becoming a victim of drugs or psychotropic pills. Perhaps during this transit your relationship with brothers, sisters, brothers-in-law or sisters-in-law, cousins etc. may become confused. Beware, you might even be involved in a love affair during this transit, which would provoke a sequel of serious troubles. Also avoid studying or dealing with astrology, magic, esotericism etc. during this transit.

Transit Neptune in the Fourth House
During these years your home may be spoiled by flooding or gas escape - provided that also in your natal chart there are elements that confirm so. Perhaps you resolve to move and go to live by the seaside, or close to a lake or a river. Also it may happen that one of your parents or grandparents starts showing psychological problems such as depression, anguish, phobia, fixed ideas, and so on. As you can see, this transit may imply either positive or negative events.

Only the overall reading of your natal chart, your transits of this period, and of each Solar Return of these years could tell you what you have to really except from this transit. In order to 'curb' these energies, I believe that the best way is to try and purchase a home at the seaside, or anyway to move and live in a place close to the water (a lake or a river). By doing so you will be able to 'discharge' many of the energies unchained by Neptune in the 4th House, and at the same time you will be able to avoid the spreading of worse symbols. Furthermore, you can also take better care of your parents, without showing excessive concern from your side.

Transit Neptune in the Fifth House

If you are a musician, a film director, or a writer this transit may bring years of flourishing artistic production to you.

On the other hand, this transit may also mark hard years for your kids. They may face real troubles or you may simply be concerned because of them, without any real cause. For example, your son may start frequenting bad company such as drug addicts. Or he may become a drug addict himself. Or he may simply face a period of depression, anguish, fears, negative moods connected with taking psychotropic medicines, or smoking too much, or drinking too much coffee, or drinking and so on. If you are a teacher 'your kids' may not refer to your son & daughters: it may refer to your pupils as well. During these years 'your kids' may face some trouble in connection with water – so avoid organizing holidays at the seaside during these years, if you know that the natal charts confirms this potentiality in some of them.

This transit may also herald problems in connection with an unhealthy passion for gambling. It may announce loss of money, if you find other elements confirming so in the 2nd or 8th House. Last but not least, you may also face troubles in connection with love. Perhaps your steady partner betrays you, or he/she wants to leave you – or hopefully it's only your imagination: but you are convinced that something is going on and this makes you suffer, during this transit. Perhaps the right step to take in this case may be inventing a fictional affair with a real individual, even better if she (or he) has evident features of a Neptunian kind. If you feel able to spend a couple of years by playing cat and mouse with him/her, by nudging, winking, hinting and so on... you will thus create a Neptune-like atmosphere without really harming your social or marital life.

Transit Neptune in the Sixth House

The ghosts living in your heart often move to your mind or to the most unforeseeable organs of your body: thus you may become convinced of having cancer or liver diseases or any other pathologies, while in fact your health is as fit as a fiddle and all this is merely a creation of the transit of Neptune in your 6th House.

If your natal chart shows that you are slightly valetudinarian, this transit surely stresses your concern and you will be dealing with your own physical and psychical health. Since it is a long-lasting transit, you may spend years in anguish. During these years you will show the desire of meeting many doctors (and you'll probably do), especially the specialists in any branch of medicine. You will fill your drawers with pills and you'll undergo a long sequel of medical test.

By applying the saying 'one worry drives out another', you may even hope to have some lesser pathology detected in your body, so that you could concentrate on that for the rest of the transit. At least, thus you would focus on a single, real problem and you'll avoid being concerned because of many other, unreal pathologies. Nonetheless, as it usually happens in connection with the transits of Neptune, you might consider taking psychotropic drugs or homeopathic remedies that might help you to overcome these years more easily. If needed, you may even ask for neurological help.

Your concern of these years may also have something to do with an employee or collaborator. For example, one of your workers may sue you or you may simply fear that this may happen. I know that some employers ask their workers to undersign an agreement in which they renounce any unpaid arrears of salary or similar; but in case of legal trial, of course, all those papers are useless.

Transit Neptune in the Seventh House

It is probable that during these years your steady partner suffers from phobia, persecution complex, neurotic behaviour and so on. So you have to take particular care for him/her because (at least in theory) he/she would do the same for you. So show that you support him/her and take him/her to the doctor (better if homeopathic doctor) often. You can pay for his/her psychotherapy if you wish. In the last years I have realized that this is preferable to the classical depth analysis: you can have a session every fortnight and, what's more important, the analyst talks, gives suggestions, practical advice, support to the patient.

Probably the doctor will suggest you to take medicines or other lighter pills, perhaps melatonin. In any case you should be prepared to be a good nurse to your beloved one.

At another level, what may also happen is that your own neurosis or fixed ideas lead you to believe that your wife or husband is manoeuvring because he/she wants to let you down eventually, perhaps in order to live together with his/her lover! If so, and provided that you have no reason to believe so, in this case it is you who may need psychotherapy.

This transit may also announce real or imaginary troubles with law and justice. This may be neutralized by appointing a good lawyer and by a good Aimed Solar Return. Otherwise, according to the principle that 'one worry drives out another', you may create a little war of your own – for if you attack somebody during this transit, you avoid others to attack you with even worse consequences.

Transit Neptune in the Eighth House

You may become upset because of the death of a relative, or simply because you *are convinced* that this will happen, even if you have absolutely no reason to think so.

Or perhaps this anguish may have a real trigger, such as for example your beloved one having a heart attack. But in the majority of cases this transit actually refers to something completely different. It refers to fears for your financial situation: you may face menace because you have taken out a loan and you fear being unable to repay it. Or perhaps you foresee an important expense (for example you may have to purchase a car, or a flat) and you fear being unable to afford it. The best piece of good advice that I feel like giving to you in this case is to start manoeuvring in anticipation.

A few months (or why not a few years?) before this transit arrives, you apply for a loan at your bank, so that you can repay it slowly, without being in a hurry, and without panic, during the following years. You may fear from your own death – if so, your anxiety is particularly strong and you had better ask for a specialist's help: a psychologist or a neurologist.

Transit Neptune in the Ninth House

One of your relatives abroad may suffer from serious health troubles during this transit. This is the most probable scenario that you may have to face during these years. Perhaps it's not a relative who's ill abroad – it may be a friend, a former boyfriend or girlfriend, or simply someone whom you regard as a guide for you.

Sometimes this transit expresses that you feel anxious because you have to take a relative of yours abroad, frequently, on a regular base, to a doctor or to a hospital, to undergo surgery or any other special therapy. So if you wish to discharge this transit, this is exactly what you have to do. If for example others volunteer to take your relative abroad, or to another region or town for therapies or medical tests – do your utmost to ensure that *you* are the one who goes with him/her. As emphasized by the Latin motto, s*imilia similibus curantur*, you had better follow this golden rule too. In other words, you have to exorcise this fear through a remedy which is identical to the 'pain'. Also, during this transit beware of the dangers deriving from accidents, especially in water. You run serious risks of being shipwrecked.

Transit Neptune in the Tenth House

Often this transit talks about your mother facing a period of deep depression, demoralization, dejection, phobias, fears of all the kinds. So you have to show how much you care for her, and let her know that you'll never forget what she has devoted her entire life to you. Show that you really care and that you want to help her with facts as well as with words.

For example, you may resolve to pay for a psychologist or psychotherapist to assist her, or a neurologist to prescribe her a pill. Be with her in any case to support her. Neptune does not imply real troubles but it announces that you simply fear from something that may not even take place. Remember that it's Uranus that usually heralds real change, while Neptune simply 'menaces' change. During this transit you may show this sort of concern also in connection with your profession. So be realistic and if you have real reasons to fear from practical changes, you may consider asking a doctor for some pill to help you overcome this troubled period of your life.

But if you only can, you should change your work actively, for example you may start dealing with psychology, or liquids, or herbs, essential oils, natural drugs such as coffee.

Transit Neptune in the Eleventh House

In the majority of cases this transit happens in coincidence with mourn. Usually this is in connection with the death of a close relative or a beloved one, and it usually has serious consequences on your soul. In those cases there's nothing we can do: only time will heal your wounds.

Other times, this transit means that you are in anguish but only because you *fear* from loosing some dear one, even if you have actually no reason to feel so. The transit may also announce that a friend – a close friend of yours – starts showing symptoms of serious psychological disease such as neurosis, anguish… If so, you have to take care of him/her just as if it were your mother or your beloved one. Give to your friend all your loving support and help him/her in coming out of the critical period. Perhaps you may pay for psychotherapy or for the medicines prescribed by a neurologist or a homeopathic doctor.

Following the notion of the exorcism of symbols, during this period it may be a good thing to become friendly with artists, neurotic people, or even drug addicts – but beware of not becoming involved in their troubles.

Transit Neptune in the Twelfth House

This is undoubtedly one of the heavier transits. In fact it may be that your fictional phantoms overlap your real troubles, with absolutely real and serious consequences.

You may feel fears virtually in every field of existence, but especially in connection with bad astrologers or magicians or priests. Keep away from all kinds of drugs: alcohol and smoke; coffee also may be detrimental to you if you over-indulge.

Also absolutely refrain from trying to take new pills, especially psychotropic drugs which may hurt you very badly in this period. I am aware that it may be hard to follow the latter piece of advice, since this transit may last many years – but at least you should try.

During this transit it is almost certain that you need the psychologist's help – do not try to avoid it. The main source of your anxieties may be hidden enemies – in which case there's virtually nothing to do.

18.
Transits of Pluto

Similar to the characters of Fëdor Michajloviè Dostoevskij's notorious novel *Crime and Punishment*, those of one of Woody Allen's most known films intertwine in a plot whose background seems to be the same old question of all times, i.e. "Does crime pay?". In fact, it goes much farther beyond the tearing grief of Dostoevskij's peculiar character, the young student and killer Raskolnikov, who questions himself on wide-ranging doubts about human existence, the mysteries of life, the existence of God, the 'voices inside you' and so on…

These words are a short introduction to my review of Woody Allen's *Crimes and Misdemeanors*, but it could also be the introduction to this chapter about planet Pluto. This celestial stands as a symbol of crime, death, inner grief, mental disorder; similar but even more serious than those to which Neptune refers.

Furthermore we can claim that Pluto works at a higher octave, by means of mental mechanisms of obsessions, phobias, anguish and whatever puts people in a state of self-torture. Often blocking or 'freezing' situations derive from Pluto's 'tortures'. Such situations enchain you in a very bad manner, so that you feel projected into a world mainly made of ghosts.

And as Carl Gustav Jung claimed, subjective reality very often corresponds to the objective reality. This means that it doesn't really matter whether you only *see* an unreal abysm, or if there *really* is an abysm before you. The transits of the last known planet of our solar system should be exorcised by trying to extract all of your inner monsters to the surface, perhaps by means of those therapies that make use of the theatrical representation of your own inner dramas within the frame of a psychoanalytical therapy.

Also every sort of intervention with the aim of melting together your psyche and your body would be helpful. I am aware, by claiming so, that you haven't necessarily to be a follower of reiki to understand, for example, the importance of orgasm as a liberating experience for man and woman.

On the other hand, in my opinion there isn't only one way - there must not be one way only to find relief for all those who suffer and are in dire straits. Sometimes the right therapy isn't really a healthy and liberating sexual activity. Sometimes it's the sublimation through an altruistic activity, within the spirit of Christian brotherhood, in the field of nursing assistance to others. In other words, I don't think that always the very same healing method may be good for everyone: those affected by the transits of Neptune and those affected by the transits of Pluto must be 'treated' in different ways.

Surely Shiatsu may be considered to be the elective exorcising activity for the transits of Pluto, because it makes your body express itself, together with sex, dramatization of your inner phantoms, a more classical supporting psychotherapy, psychotropic drugs, homeopathic medicine, and above all the aimed relocation of your Solar Returns.

Pluto in a dissonant aspect with the Sun

We can surely claim that affliction is the common ground of all the transits of Pluto in a dissonant angle with one's Sun. These will be months or years of self- destructive behaviour, or even masochism. Sometimes during this transit people become fixated on a precise, manic point of self-destruction, without being aware that their fears are magnified by this transit in fact. You really have to discharge this transit, even better: you have to 'vent' it out. Physical activity may be good, especially in a gym club; even better if you do some martial arts.

Also an intense sexual activity may contribute to discharge certain type of tension, if you have the rights features in your natal chart to do so. At any rate a supporting psychotherapy or a Gestalt or Gestalt-like analysis, which would help you bring your phantoms to the surface; for example through the theatrical representation of your inner nightmare, as I already said.

Also the right herbs or homeopathic medicines or Bach flowers can help very much. Surely there are right 'drugs' for these cases, but of course only competent persons should handle them. But I remain convinced that during the years of this really treacherous transit, you can do your best to exorcise these dangers and overcome these tough situations, only if you relocate every single Solar Return according to the rules that I've detailed in my volume *Transits and Solar Returns*. In other words, only if you can't leave for your birthday you may face really dangerous situations.

Pluto in a dissonant aspect with the Moon

In order to explain this transit in a proper way, here is a short passage taken from my portrait of Luigi Pirandello, published in 1979 in my volume *L'oroscopo di 25 VIP*: "In Pirandello's biography, she [his mother] appears to be just like all the other female figures who disastrously forged the model of his soul that is to say, in a negative way.

In fact Caterina Ricci Gramitto lived constantly in the background in respect to her husband Stefano; the latter might be well defined as a male chauvinist, nowadays. The cross-section of his sad life may be summarized by the position of the Moon in his son's natal chart – conjunct with Pluto, in the 12th House, and opposite to Saturn in the 6th House. This is a fundamental point of the natal chart we are examining: femininity, feeling, soul – and all of them at their negative, in the extremely sensible Cancer. As I'll show you in brief, his sister suffers from craziness for a period; also crazy was his wife Antonetta.

He had only two important love affairs in his life: A platonic and never really satisfactory one, with actress Marta Abba; and another with her daughter Lietta – and he suffered very much when the latter got married and followed her husband to Argentina. As for femininity as a feeling is concerned, there was a single event in Pirandello's childhood [therefore still during the period of influence of his native Pluto-Moon] which can help throw light on his future, definitive views of woman and love. One day curiosity led little boy Luigi to creep into a mortuary room where there was a corpse on the slab, ready for burying. Already frightened at the macabre scene, the little boy got scared when he realized that he wasn't alone in the room.

As his eyes got accustomed to the darkness of the room, he saw a man and a woman winding themselves; she had the skirt up; they made a rhythmical movement that his young soul could not simply accept. Later on Leonardo Sciascia commented upon this event in the following terms: "In Pirandello, love would always be somehow linked with death. Not the notion of death, but with death itself, with the physical presence of death. Otherwise, love would be troubled by craziness. Or poisoned by lack of understanding and infidelity. In his characters, you never find a moment of self-abandonment to the heart, to the feelings. And there's never a woman – not even among the most beautiful ones – whom the author does not depict, more or less evidently, with a shadow of repulsion." Later on – not much later though – Luigi would face another drama of a similar kind. I refer to an adulterous relationship that his father had when Luigi was fourteen years old, with a widow relative [by that time Pluto was transiting over Luigi's Ascendant].

Blind with repugnance towards his father and with pain because of his adored mother, Luigi did something of an extreme gravity – he spat on the face of his father's lover. This was the beginning of a progressive cooling of relations between him and his father. They would never reconcile."

I find this double evocation of a transit of Pluto in connection with the sphere of feelings that also reminds one about the conjunction between Pluto and the Moon in Luigi Pirandello's natal chart. In everyday practice, when this transit takes place, you should mainly expect a deformation in your view of the sphere of feelings, or a negative stage for the psyche of one of your close female relatives: your mother, your sister, your daughter, your wife... So you have to show them how much you care, and do your utmost to minimize their trouble in connection with this transit. They would surely feel an amplification of their mental troubles, of their anguish, phobias, perhaps a serious neurosis and – in the worst cases – they might even fall into psychosis – but only if the natal charts of their close relatives justify this forecast).

You had better ask for a psychologist's help; also consult a neurologist or a homeopathic doctor, an expert of herbs, or of energy healing. But also in this case, the very best option is the aimed birthday.

Pluto in a dissonant aspect with Mercury

It may mark long months or years in which you feel phobias in connection with displacement such as the fear of travelling on an airplane or the mental fixation of dying in a traffic accident.

If your practical life allows you to do so, you may also be indulgent with this phobia and refrain from taking a plane or driving the car until this transit is over. Sometimes anguish may refer to the telephone: e.g. during this transit you might be persecuted by an anonymous voice who calls you in the middle of the night. Still, also in this case you may resolve to play the game by amplifying the thrilling atmosphere: instead of having your phone number changed or privatized, you may keep listening and/or try to hold some conversation with your insane and nameless caller. At another level this transit may imply a sort of compulsory, painful and perhaps macabre commuting: for example - you'll have to visit a relative in jail or at a hospital.

It may be a good idea to accept bearing this cross. In the worst cases perhaps during this transit your son may show symptoms of serious neurosis, if not of psychotic and/or morbid tendencies towards sex, death, crime, detective stories, magic, and so on. Do not pretend you don't see it; on the contrary, you had better face the problem up.

So talk to him often, take care of him, take him to the psychologist, help him also with money, and lend him your own energy to solve his troubles. The danger could be well exorcised through a sort of 'full immersion' into dark literature of all the times and of all the countries, before the problem arises in reality.

And if you happened to feel morbid desires of perversion towards teenagers of one or of both sex, you had better have your insane passions deflated in other ways: for example, by joining some erotic chat or hotline.

Pluto in a dissonant aspect with Venus

Lovesickness is perhaps unbearable, and a dissonant aspect between Pluto and Venus can bring much trouble in this specific field.

Often it is only trouble of an endopsychic origin, i.e. subjective, only due to your imagination; but sometimes it can be real trouble, i.e. your most inner nightmares becoming true.

Perhaps in this period your steady partner may have an extramarital affair; your beloved one may express his/her intention of letting you down to go and live with another. Unluckily, if this is your case, there's little to do except avoiding doing like many others, who end up in the hands of magicians or similar people who claim to be able to cast your 'negativeness' away. In my opinion this transit needs much more than a talisman or a spell to avoid the crisis that this transit may herald in you sentimental life.

As I always repeat *ad nauseam*, the only and most important talisman is the displacement of your aimed birthday, also known as the active relocation of your Solar Return – but you have to do it before the fire is lit, not after. Sometimes something can be done even after the fire is lit, by relocating the following Solar Return. I must confess that this way I have achieved interesting results.

At least, the betrayed one set his/her mind at rest and realized that nothing could be done to save their broken relationship. Although I do not exclude the possibility that through the exorcism of symbols something even more positive could be done. After all, this transit implies a sort of morbid fixation, which can be easily discharged – provided that your partner agrees – by experimenting certain sexual behaviours that might channel your strongest erotic, transgressive, sadomasochist spurs, which on the contrary might be the right way to constellate – in certain cases – the couple 'sex & violence' or 'sex & depravation' implied by this transit. According to this logic, also having an affair with a 'bad lot' may be useful to discharge this transit.

For example, if you had an affair with a prostitute or with a gangster, you'd be able to attenuate the poison of this transit, which otherwise would probably be detrimental for any 'healthy' relationship of yours. This transit may last very long; and in some cases, also autoeroticism may be able to counterbalance this transit. Many other aspects of this transit should be exposed, for example in connection with money or with your health or with a daughter.

I could only make a quick reference to it. But in my volume on *Transits and Solar Returns* you can find many other aspects in which this transit may express itself. I am confident that you'd be able to find logical solutions to your specific, practical problems by simply following the ideas explained in that volume.

Pluto in a dissonant aspect with Mars

Great is the destructive force that this transit may unchain. If you are a violent one by birth, you can show a real peak of aggression during this transit. Being the two involved planets in connection with the sign of Scorpio, their brutal mix may produce real criminal instincts.

At any cost you should try to work on your own psyche so that this stream of unhealthy feelings may flow into a safe direction avoiding its worst consequences. The cleverest thing to do, however old you are, is to join a gym club and go into martial arts. In fact during this transit you may desire to destroy your enemies, to ''tear them into pieces' – so you had better do so fictionally, inside a gym club. Be aware though that in this case it may not be enough to punch a sandbag.

This transit implies a sadomasochist mood that should not be ignored. So what you have to do is choosing your opponent, and deprive him/her from all his/her energies, still following the rules of Pierre de Coubertin's 'athletic chivalry'. You may also play in football or soccer matches, but keep in mind that by doing so the risk of physical wounds and accidents increases significantly.

Men may also indulge in an increased sexual activity. Although the very best way to exorcise this symbol (as well as other powerful and dangerous symbols treated in this volume) remains surgical intervention.

Pluto in a dissonant aspect with Jupiter

For sure this transit might favour irregular or abnormal growth of cells, thus favouring or contributing to possible tumours. Thank God, this is not the outcome in all cases, so if this transit happens to you or to a loved one, don't panic. Normally this transit simply magnifies all sorts of exaggeration, for example you might simply get fatter.

On the other hand it appears illogical to start on a diet until this transit is not over. In a more realistic scenario, you might simply unchain your desires, especially if you generally put them under strict control. So you may go more often to the restaurant; have more fun; spend more; indulge in games and sports; have much more sex.

You may also spend for unessential things; this is not the time for sparing money. You should resolve to exaggerate in something, willing to do so. For example you may purchase something whose price is a little beyond your affordability; and pay it by monthly, expensive instalments. Thus, if in the worst case you'll be simply unable to repay the purchased good, you might give it back, thus losing the good and the money – but at least you would have done your utmost to try and discharge this transit.

Pluto in a dissonant aspect with Saturn

This transit may herald serious financial troubles, for example an expensive tax to pay, or expenses connected with mourn, separation, divorce... It is not so important 'why' you'll lose money, but 'how' – this is the essential theme of this transit, which may strike you with real wickedness.

While Pluto usually symbolizes something 'big' and 'important' in a negative way, Saturn usually implies something chronic. Thus a good way to exorcize this transit may be to accept an entrenched, long-lasting trouble. For example – I am not joking – you might accept that your mother-in-law come and live with you, at your place for the rest of her life. Or you may volunteer in a long-term activity in the social field.

Or you may undergo an extremely long and tiring medical therapy, say for example that your doctor suggests you to run 10 miles every day on uneven terrains. You may adopt a child in need; say a teen-ager, and take care of him or her for the following decades.

Pluto in a dissonant aspect with Uranus

At any moment you may be stricken by an important trouble which comes out of the blue during this transit. It may have something to do with your sexual sphere: in this case it may point to the beginning of trouble at your prostate, impotence, frigidity, psychological blockage towards sex, a venereal disease… But it also may have something to do with mourn or money – the typical symbols of the 8th House.

But it may be virtually anything else, so what I keep on suggesting for over thirty years with satisfactory results is to exorcise the symbols, and in this specific case I suggest you to perform a sort of sudden and sensational *hara-kiri*.

Say for example that you are the top manager of an important society and that you don't like any more the atmosphere in which the top meetings are held. So you wait for this transit and then you resign, even if this costs you money and power. Or say that for all your life you have been bearing a nasty, ungrateful husband (or wife, or steady partner). Now, during this transit, you can end this story with a neat cut and part – definitely.

Or perhaps you have always dreamt of becoming a free-lancer but have never had the heart of leaving your job as a clerk. Now you can kick it, leave the 'safe and sure job' and suddenly discover that you may have to sweat blood in order to have all your bills paid.

Pluto in a dissonant aspect with Neptune

This may be one of the most devastating transits at a moral level, for it may bring you depression, anguish, phobias, prostration… Perhaps you are one of those who usually suffer from 'pill-o-phobia'? I am sorry, but I'm afraid that at least during this transit you cannot simply avoid taking pills. If needed and your doctor agrees, you might even consider taking psychotropic drugs: after all, they can really help. Psychotropic drugs have saved the life of many-many people, and I am sure that they will save even more lives in the future.

For a good portion of the population, they are simply unavoidable, in certain periods of their life. In the first chapters of this volume I have already mentioned the pseudo-heroic attitude of those who pretend to be superior, to be able to face problems by means of a psychodrama and to overcome them.

Perhaps this is possible, but why make a short story long, if science – this time: a good science – can really help? Perhaps you simply need the help of a psychologist. I would personally suggest undergoing – during the entire duration of this transit – supporting psychotherapy and not depth analysis.

Pluto in a dissonant aspect with Pluto

The consequences of this transit are quite similar to those of the previous one, but in this case the 'phantoms' may become more specific and direct, such as sex, death, crime, the world of after-life, etc. Also in this case, I suggest you the two kinds of defence depicted in the previous paragraph. Although the very best way – I'll never stop saying so – to exorcise any negative transit is the Aimed Solar Return.

Transit Pluto in the First House

This is something similar to the transit of Pluto in an angle with the Sun. You tend to magnify your inner nightmares and to behave in a tormented, anguished way.

This transit implies torments and it may express itself through very powerful, tense and perhaps unhealthy sexual spurs as well as through neurotic behaviour in connection with death, crime, the occult… You had better ask the help of a doctor; undergo pharmaceutical therapies, go to the psychologist. Physical activity in a gym club may help as well, especially if it's martial arts. Also, an increased sexual activity, perhaps by experimenting erotic fantasies that you have been repressing so far.

Transit Pluto in the Second House

In the majority of cases, during this transit your financial situation is shaken deeply – but not always in a negative way! Many times you may also become rich, for reasons about which only the analysis of your natal chart may allow you to throw light. Yet this volume is about dissonant transits, and to struggle against them – so let us ignore the possible positive meanings of this specific transit.

You may fall into debt, and serious ones, perhaps in connection with real estate – if so you should be able to detect similar meanings in other transits: for example transit Saturn or Uranus in your 4th natal House. Some other times, getting into debts is connected with the beginning of a new professional activity in which you wish to engage yourself; or with the purchase of professional tools for your usual job. In this case exorcising means simply swimming with the current: ask for a loan, perhaps a mortgage loan – it will keep you concerned but it eventually result in a good thing for you.

On the contrary, these lines intend to keep you concerned or even 'frightened' so that you don't waste all your money in gambling. Listen to what happened to a lady once. She was accustomed to play lottery. She ran into debts and sold her house for 700 million Liras. She planned to pay her debts with that amount. She did so, and still 500 million Liras were left. Unluckily she resolved to go on playing with the hope of being able to re-buy her house. In one year she lost everything.

Transit Pluto in the Third House

It may correspond to a serious state of depression of a brother or a sister. Perhaps one of your brothers or sisters may be involved in a crime during this transit. So you should do your best to show them how much you care; still keep in mind that during these years perhaps you won't be able to avoid those incurable wounds that arise between you and them – or some of them.

Often people say "No, such things do not happen in our family!" Still, before money many people – virtually any person – may become a Cain; and do not forget the Latin motto: *homo homini lupus*. If your birth chart shows the serious risk of a traffic accident, you should also take in serious consideration refraining from driving during this transit. This is what *I* have done, and believe me, I am not repented.

Transit Pluto in the Fourth House

I meet this transit very often when people suffer very much to purchase a house or a flat; or when they sweat blood because they have inherited real estate but for some reason they can not take possession over it.

Some other times this transit implies refurbishing works at home or in the place where you work – and this is exactly what you can do in order to discharge this transit.

You may plan works at home, and you may have them last for decades, giving any little detail of your place refurbished or renewed or replaced: the door knobs, the electrical system, the baseboard... Deal with every single detail as if you were one of those who spend entire years in model-making of ships, airplanes, cars etc. If you only can, also deal more with your parents during this transit.

Transit Pluto in the Fifth House

Those couples who suffer from partial or total infertility may resolve to do whatever they can in order to have a baby, during this transit. In fact if both compromise, during this transit it is possible to achieve this goal by investing huge resources, a good amount of energy, and above all, having exorcised the symbols involved in this transit. In other cases, this transit may ask you to assist one of your sons or daughters who is in need, even if this will cost you very much.

I've seen people who visited hell, during this transit, in order to help a son recover from the tragedy of drug addiction. They lost whatever they had to do so, but at the same time not only their son: they too were reborn to a new life; they became spiritually involved, they became better from many points of view.

At another level, if you are a gambler be informed that during this transit you run the risk of falling into the vice of gambling with obvious negative consequences. Also, beware of not falling in love with dangerous people: promote or perform a private investigation before starting on a new relationship with anybody.

Transit Pluto in the Sixth House

Beware of whom you accept into your house; also be cautious when hiring somebody during this transit. You run the risk of making an incautious choice and paying the consequences. What you can do to discharge this risk is provoking a huge trouble at work – provided that you are able to cope with it without damage.

For example you may accept more work than you could bear; then you may bend over backwards, perhaps hiring more personnel in order to fulfil. You may also do something extraordinary for your own body.

Deal with your own health in an exaggerated way: gymnastics, massages, saunas, mud therapies and so on. During this period you should do it in a rather compulsory way, and become real hygienists.

Transit Pluto in the Seventh House

Consider getting married seriously, even if you normally believe in remaining single. Yes, during these years even the most convinced single may become a potential member of a fixed, stable, long-lasting relationship. On the other hand, this transit may also imply the risk of divorce; so ponder it well, because when Pluto strikes it's always 'breaking news', not mere menaces.

So if you care for you existing marital life, try to re-conquer your beloved one, keeping in mind that there's nothing granted for a lifetime – you have to re-establish it day by day. During these years it is also possible that you are involved in a long suit in a court.

If not, you may consider getting involved in a suit, i.e. provoking it somehow – better if it's going to last for decades. If you ask, 'How much would it cost me paying a lawyer for years?' I say, 'How much would it cost you to get involved in a penal suit?'

Transit Pluto in the Eighth House

Perhaps an important death – or simply your fear of death – could keep you alright during this transit. I suggest you the classical remedies: psychotropic drugs and/or homeopathic remedies against anguish, and/or the psychotherapist's help.

You had better avoid frequenting terminally ill people during this transit; also refrain from visiting hospitals and any other place which is directly or indirectly connected with death: morgues, churchyards and so on. Relax and take your mind off those things by reading optimistic novels, watching entertaining TV shows and so on. Be together with happy people, and avoid facing serious subjects with them. Since this transit also refers to finance, similar to the transit of Pluto in the 2nd House, in this case also you may face loss of money. So please refer to the relevant section *Transit Pluto in the Second House*. To avoid possible sexual troubles, consult a specialist: an andrologist, a sexologist, a psychologist. You may also face troubles in connection with inheritance with possible legal implications. This may not be a real trouble: you can consider it a sort of toll – and not a very expensive one – that you have to pay to Pluto.

Transit Pluto in the Ninth House

If you have ever dreamt of emigrating alone or with your family, abroad, and in a definite way, you should consider this chance seriously during this transit. But if you have not, well in this case you run the risk of being obliged to go abroad or far away from home, and to stay there for several years, and in an unpleasant way.

A good way of exorcising – within certain limits – this risk may be starting on a long-lasting metaphysical and transcendental journey. What I mean is that you may start studying yoga at a higher level, Buddhism, Eastern cultures, astrology, philosophy etc. By doing so you stand fair chances that the symbols involved in this transit follow the psychic path and not the physical one, thus limiting or avoiding all the afore mentioned risks.

You may deploy another attempt of exorcism by frequenting distant places, for a long period and more or less on a regular basis. This can be done for work, for love, for healing, for any reason. The bottom line is to perform a sort of 'commuting' over a long distance. It would be perfectly aligned with this transit.

Transit Pluto in the Tenth House

In this case the right direction to follow within the frame of that 'aimed behaviour' explained in this volume, is to make any possible attempt to potentiate your working activity, even if this costs huge sacrifices to you. Be ambitious and do your utmost to achieve a better place in the sun. This transit requires you to exaggerate and make relentless efforts in order to reach your goals – on the other hand, it's this 'overdoing' that will consume the symbols involved in this transit.

A very practical example of what I mean may be the clerk who starts studying to graduate at the age of 40.

By coming back home every night and opening your books instead of relaxing or having fun with your kids; devoting virtually no time to play; living once again the old emotions of the school times; these are things that might discharge this transit very well. At another level, you may engage yourself to take care of your mother, whom perhaps you have been neglecting so far.

Transit Pluto in the Eleventh House

As I have already underlined it in several volumes of mine, only a blind person cannot not see the strict connection between the 11th House and death. You can also refer to the section on *Transit Pluto in the Eighth House*, as well as to the previous section on *Transit Pluto in the Tenth House*.

Besides the suggestions given there, you may try to attain something important from a friend, from an acquaintance, form a high-ranking person. Day by day, virtually on a daily basis, you should try to exorcise this Pluto in your 11th House. By the way, this does not seem to be a particularly detrimental transit, except in that it may announce mourn – but of course, you cannot avoid mourn.

Transit Pluto in the Twelfth House

Pluto in this House might strike you with an extremely wide range of events. It is truly a potentially risky transit and I suggest you to relocate as many Solar Returns as you can during this transit.

Keeping in mind that this transit may last 20-30 years, perhaps it is not necessary to relocate all the 20 or 30 Solar Returns – but at least, the most menacing ones.

Since this transit usually has consequences at a psychic level, another suggestion is to have antidepressant, anxyolitic pills help you. If possible, undergo supporting psychotherapy as well.

Appendix

A few astrological portrayals of celebrities
that can help you understand the theory explained in this volume

19.
Astrological portrayal of Giacomo Casanova

Casanova's life, which was extremely singular and extraordinary, can be compared - analogically - to the rhythm of the movie - *The Empire of Senses* (1976), by Oshima Nagisa, which in its turn, corresponds to a sexual intercourse: gradually escalating at the beginning; very strong in the middle stage; condemned to an irreversible catabasis in the end. The movie of the Japanese director, considered here like a metaphor to the expression of libido of the subject, explains that the life of this Arien has been very intensive between twenty and thirty years of age and has changed later to a slowly descendant parable at maturity/old age, where energy transformed itself in aggressiveness and the phallic power was exhausted through the countless daily diatribes expressed towards the servants (the Sun, as we can observe later is in the sixth House in his horoscope.)

This man, characterized by genital and libido hypertrophies, was primarily a "rapist". For him we can say, going by both Freudian and Jungian analyses, that his mental energy was totally of the libidinous and psychosexual kind: when he saw a woman he felt an uncontrollable desire to possess and "rape" her; and immediately after that his greatest interest would be to compensate her in some way and to get rid of her.

His life story is out of the ordinary because he was out of the ordinary and even if he was a liar, a cheater, a libertine, a deceiver, a gambler, an adventurer and many other things, we cannot restrict his character to anyone of these labels; we have to consider them projected upon a universe of heterogeneous features that show him up to be a gentleman, a generous man, a man very learned and with taste, one of the greatest men of letters of his time.

According to some people, like Carl Gassaner who composed the theatrical text *Casanova in the Dux's Castle*, enacted a few years ago by the *La Rocca's Group* in Bologna - Casanova would have invented all of his incredible past, while according to Ugo Foscolo, the man would not even have existed. But, the most famous Venetian of all times, together with Marco Polo, lived and left deep foot prints in his wake. Even if his biographers demonstrated that there are some false facts in the legends about him; that there are unfounded shreds of memories obscured by the severity of senescence that doesn't spare anyone, his life is yet representative of the lifestyle of the century that he lived in; it is the story of the world seen through the eyes of a man definable in many different ways.

Casanova was variously portrayed - as a "big turd" by the film playwright Armando Papa; as a big goat whose mechanical repetitiveness was comparable to that of a piston - able to do only up and down movements - in the Fellini's movie; as a "monster of total physicalness" by Alberto Moravia.

In our opinion however, Casanova epitomizes many things together, as we will see through his horoscope. But over all, as we said before, he represented a sustained, rhythmic and accelerating coitus at the beginning, which became very strong and explosive in the middle, and in dying contraction in the end.

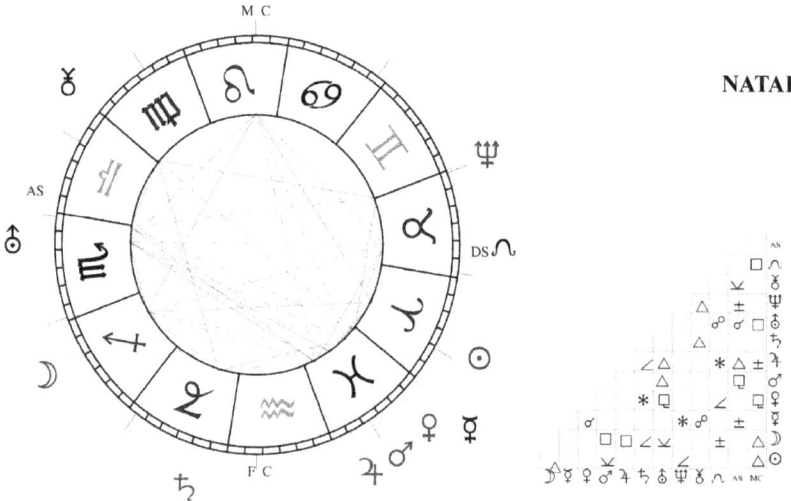

NATAL

Going by his self-declaration, Giacomo Casanova was born in Venice on April 2, 1725. His natal hour it is not known, but from a speculative reconstruction proposed in the book *The American Book of Charts*, by

Louis M. Rodden, we comprehend that he came into the world at 8:00 PM (LMT).

This natal time is very convincing for us, very much indeed. His natal chart, in this way, comes to have a Sun in the VI House, the Ascendant about 1° in Scorpio, an extraordinary stellium in Pisces, in the fifth House, and a dominant Uranus that explains the enormous instability of his destiny, the highs and lows of his life, the dramatic turns, the turning points at square angle, his originality-eccentricity, the enormous need of freedom that always punctuated his choices, the unpredictability of any of his decisions.

We have to note his Sun in the sixth House that pushed him to shave three times a day, to dress as a dandy and to pay a salary a personal hairdresser even when there was a paucity of funds, to always appear well groomed in public. The same Sun in the sixth House represented a very particular relation with servants who abandoned and robbed him or who haunted him with a thousand malice and daily perfidies in his old age.

The first luminary in the House corresponding to the sign of Virgo, expressed itself in the manner of his very great interest for the subject of medicine, that he would have studied when he was young and that he practiced very often in his adulthood and old age; with the diets that he often imposed upon himself and with the exasperating critical sense that made him become, at the sunset of his life, an old grumbling troublemaker.

His Ascendant Scorpio together with the values attributable to his Pisces/fifth House and Aries, provides ample evidence that his energies were particularly inclined in a sexual direction and justifies the numerous gonorrhoea and haemorrhoids that afflicted him. Ascendant Scorpio also vindicates his assertion: "my dominant passion has always been revenge" (edition Dall'Oglio of the *History of My Life*, 1946, page 558/II).

The strong values associated with Pisces and Jupiter-Mars-Venus-Mercury between the fourth and the fifth House, were clear indicators of his indulgence, of his enjoying life: he ate like a king, beginning with dozens of oysters and precious game birds at every meal and washing them down with a copious flow of very excellent wines.

A great part of his life was spent at the dinner table, in the arms of women and at the gambling table. He slept very little and even that is quite Scorpio-like and his amorous escapades were legendary.

He was insatiable, to the extent that when he over-indulged - and it happened quite often - he ejaculated blood; it was something that horrified his women but left him satisfied and very proud.

He loved with an incredible intensity and for very long periods, as he proposed to one of his lovers - that desired to abort - the aroph's cure, a very bizarre coitus to be repeated 5 or 6 times a day, for many days. But, if his virility was as a page from the Book of Guiness World Records, not less was the sexual fire of his women, as was the case of the young Elena: "… in the time that I spent for only one, she passed 14 times from life to death" (cited work, vol. II, page 300).

The balance of his sexual-love life tells us of almost two hundred women seduced and of half dozen children begotten and spread all over Europe. This, despite the fact that, as he himself narrated, he copulated without condoms that were "… a recent English invention".

But if we were to see Casanova to be essentially a sex maniac, obsessed and driven by a solitary purpose, then such a view appears to be too simplistic and unfair.

As some of the great Venetian scholars have stated - scholars such as Maynial, Zottoli, Kesten, Rives Childs, Bàccolo, and more recently Piero Chiara and Roberto Gervaso - this great seducer, was also a refined literary man and intellectual who left us one of the most precious frescos of the eighteenth century. His Memoirs, translated into many languages, were appreciated by big literary talents who praised it for its simplicity of expression, fluent style and surging spontaneous outpourings (the Sun in Aries).

It is true that Casanova had both admirers and denigrators, but in general, he went down in history as a great one. Here is a little anthology of spiteful critics from Gervaso's essay (Rizzoli publisher).

"Men such as Casanova - says Molmenti - brought for a walk through the world, the show of the Italian's shame, affirming that the old Italy derided, sold and prostituted everything, from the ancient heroes to the new saints". And D'Ancona says: "As a man, the Venetian was an indirect and genuine product of the city's own social putridity in the last period of the Serenissima's life". Closer to us, Jonard condemned him as a "wizened false moralist; a reactionary - full of bile; a boaster seducer - who prostituted his own pen, selling it to the inquisitors". Bozzòla defined him: "a nomad with an open and alert mind, whose only liberty was the one to live in accordance to his talent and without worries". And, to the contrary, Piero Chiara who edited a beautiful but not authentic edition of

Memoirs for Mondadori, together with Federico Roncoroni, has this to say: "Everything that Casanova obtained from life was only by the merit of his ambition, intelligence, studies, undaunted courage and sense of honour; to tell you the truth a little subjectively, he taught himself to practice nobility and constituted himself as a role model of the most unprejudiced and intrepid characters of that time, encompassing the attributes of a wide spectrum of individuals from the cardinal of Bernis to general Branicki. His name, as those of Don Giovanni or Doctor Faust or the marquess of Sade, came out from history to enter into modern mythologies".

Reading the over 2600 pages of memoirs, we see him living a constant paroxysmal existence – every inch of his almost seven feet tall frame - to invent his life each day, to speculate, to gamble, even to cheat, to trade, to work - with success – on high financial stakes, to loose himself voluntarily in the idiocy of pseudo magic, to practice a thousand jobs, to travel more than one of his contemporaneous homologue, to be, in one word, what we would call today a "shady businessman".

Every strange enterprise or audacious activity stimulated him - from charlatans to the marquess of Urfé to the acrobatic defloration of a humped woman; from the dialectic duel with Voltaire to the practical representation of the 35 love positions suggested by Aretino.

His Piscean values were the excessive bad habits that plagued him all his life and which brought upon him many great afflictions: he was many times in penury and as many times in prison. He knew and had dwelt in the prisons of half of Europe and his sensational escape from the Piombi prison in Venice established him as a legend in his lifetime.

He had incredible highs and lows with money all his life, as his Sagittarian Moon in the second House in dissonant aspects with Neptune, Mars and Jupiter, predicts. Being in such a position, the lady of Cancer spread a veil of imprudence on his financial dealings: he was a spendthrift and, during the period of his life, spent several million francs. He left shocking tips, invited whole theatre companies for dinner, indemnified generously all his "victims", most of whom he made rich and happy, "settling them" shrewdly.

But did he love them? Evidently no. He loved over all and uniquely his own pleasure (fifth House values). His physical exuberance constricted him to search continuously for himself some sexual "bleedings". But it is evident that his desire, before being physical, was mental. And what can be at the top of the combination among a Sun in Aries (the hyper-male) with a Scorpio Ascendant and with Piscean fifth House values? Pleasure, primarily pleasure, absolute sexual pleasure. It was a nail that he had in his head.

When he saw a female he only thought of undressing her. It was like a sickness.

A few women attempted to resist him; among them was the perfidious Charpillon whom Casanova came to the point to threaten with a knife to obtain her favours; but he had to go through a lot of trouble later to expel her from his life. He vent his frustration on her by buying a parrot and teaching it to say, every morning: "Miss Charpillon is a greater bitch than her mother". Teresa (the supposedly castrated Bellino), Paolina and Enrichetta were his greatest lovers, but probably they were categorised so only because destiny took them away from him before he got tired of them.

He fell in love every day, but he never got married, exactly in accordance with his Virgo values (the Sun in the sixth natal House).

He had a pleasant taste in his mouth and took every kind: fine, beautiful, ugly, old, the one that he had in front of him; even if he always had a predilection for Lolitas whom he collected in a great measure (he began to love mysteriously even twelve or eleven year old girls).

In his relation with the "Crazy Sublime" he lived a long love afternoon with this woman who was the marquess of Urfé; over seventy years old and to whom he let believe, among other things, that he could make her pregnant. According to some persons, he even descended to the immorality of incest and gave a child to his daughter Leonilda.

He was virile until very late in life, even though from the age of forty he faced a long and painful physical decline that manifested itself in many sicknesses, among which were serious sight disorders, during the last part of his life (the Sun in the sixth natal House).

He was convinced that fortune helps only young persons and he was so fixated with this idea that he lived in a paranoia the last years of his existence, in voluntary exile at the Dux's castle, in Boemia. Here, apart from the hatred of the terrible butler Feltkirchner and of his lover (the coachman), Casanova was treated very well by the count Giuseppe Carlo of Waldstein, who put him in charge of a 40.000 volumes library and gave him a good hotel settlement that the Venetian appreciated a lot: "I eat and drink like a horse", he wrote to a friend of his in that period.

His Saturn in the third natal House expressed itself in many ways. For example, he had a very bad relationship of overflowing reciprocal hatred, with his minor brother, who was a priest. Saturn also left its characteristic stain in the matter of his literary works. If we exclude two minor books that he published at ages of 27 and 32 respectively (Zoroastro, a tragedy translated from French, and Camilla Veronese in the Mercure of France), the most important of his works were written during the later part of his life. He wrote 'The Histoire de ma vie' from 1789 until his death on June 4, 1798, at the age of 73. But Saturn conspired to interrupt this activity on the eve of his return in Venice (September 14, 1774), after about nineteen years of exile (after having escaped from Piombi prison on November 1, 1756).

Some researchers believe that he he voluntarily decided supress further details of his life when he was at the threshold of his fiftieth year while others believe that they were written and had some mysterious content which were intentionally made to disappear by vested interests. What ever may be the truth, the fact was that there was an interruption which corroborated Saturn's presence in the third natal House.

This same Saturn continuous to haunt him even after his death and causes his Memoirs to be censured.

Here are the two versions of an identical situation in his life, the first in the most circulated edition today in Italy (Mondadori) and the other in the more comprehensive edition of Dall'Oglio of which only 3195 copies were printed 1946.

1. "The last night that I spent entirely with my angel, was very sad. If love did not come to our rescue once in a while, we would have certainly died of pain. When we appeared in the family ...".

2. "The last night, that I spent entirely with my delightful countess, was very sad; we would have died of pain, without the voluptuousness of love that comforted us. No night was ever spent so wonderfully than that one. The tears of pain and of love alternated themselves without any break, and I renewed nine times the sacrifice at the altar of the god that revived my strengths every time that pleasure consumed them. Blood and tears wet the sanctuary; the sacrificer was exhausted as much as the victim was; but the desires said: " More!". We had to separate ourselves, commanding ourselves with an effort as much painful as had been the sweetness our union of eight hours... When we appeared together in the dining room..." (work mentioned, volume II, page 438).

A lot has been said and very wrongly too, about his presumed association with Astrology. It was merely a mix of esoteric Astrology mingled with magic and fraudulent boasting, with which Casanova cheated the marquess of Urfé and many other persons. But he read a lot and possessed great refinement, taste and discernment which permitted him to identify, on the winding path of his adventurous life, even the minutest particle of gold in a heap of scrap and, not considering the date of his escape from Piombi prison, that he chose by Cabala, it is very interesting to note what he writes about his birthday. "… I observed that it was April 2nd, 1744, the anniversary of my birth, a date that for ten times in my life coincided with a fact worthy of note" (Casanova, Memories Written by Himself - Garzanti Publisher, page 244).

From every point of view, there is much to be understood about his character. Polemics grow and develop around him. One of these is the manner in which Casanova has been characterized in a television show by Comencini where he appears as a shy and short young man and it is proposed that he is a priest turned a libertine through life's circumstances and that his qualities are not attributable to the astrological and genetic imprinting received at his birth.

But his horoscope and his DNA are there to bear testimony to his true personality. And he himself is reported to have remarked: "I only blush because I am not able to blush".

Translated by Ciro Discepolo and Anna Mellone
Edited by Ram Ramakrishnan

Giacomo Casanova

20.
Astrological portrayal of Luigi Pirandello

How could you explain that the son of a rude and uncultured seller of sulphur; one who was born and grown in a poor suburb of South-Western Sicily in 1867, would soon show such a great love for letters that led him to winning the Nobel prize for literature? You can explain it only through his ruling Venus close to the Ascendant in the sign of Gemini.

By those times, people often inherited the father's arts and crafts, or they used to take over the profession of the environment in which they lived. Some people were forced to choose their field of activity taking in consideration the narrow possibilities of the local market – for example, the fishermen of an island. In certain cases, people chose a profession as a reaction against an inner problem, such as Gavino Ledda, the author of the autobiographical work *Padre Padrone*. Ledda became a professor of glottology – the science of verbal communication – to compensate long years spent in a compulsory silence as a herder on the hills of Sardinia. And what about Pirandello? In his case there evidently was a steering reason, much stronger than any other environmental influence that was – seemingly – prevailing. Luigi Pirandello's steering force was his natal Venus: a sort of anode, capable of magnetizing Luigi's 'libidic electrons' towards a very specific direction – towards the arts.

Ruling Venus in Gemini, close to the Ascendant is not the only astrological element marking Luigi's case. You have to take in due consideration also his Mercury, the ruler of his Ascendant, in his natal 3rd House; and his natal Sun, trine to Jupiter, the ruler of his 6th House, occupying the 10th House, on the throne in Pisces. The latter combination clearly states Luigi's huge success in literature.

Luigi Pirandello's astrological analysis is definitely a stimulating task, for the astrologer can detect a couple of decisive factors in his natal chart. First of all, we know his time of birth with a good degree of precision. He produces a huge amount of literary work that are the reflection of his own soul, so that we can compare it with the information proceeding from his natal chart. He has a life full of significant events, which can also be helpful for comparison with his transits and Solar Returns.

I would suggest the reader to refer to Pirandello's biography written by Gaspare Giudice (the Italian edition is by publisher UTET), in which can be found the main events of his life; a criticism of his works; the biography of people who knew him personally and were in close relationship with him; the joys and pains that moved him; the list of pros and cons in the image he projected to the outer world... In the following lines I am going to comment upon Pirandello's astral chart following the chronology of the events, as listed by Mr. Giudice.

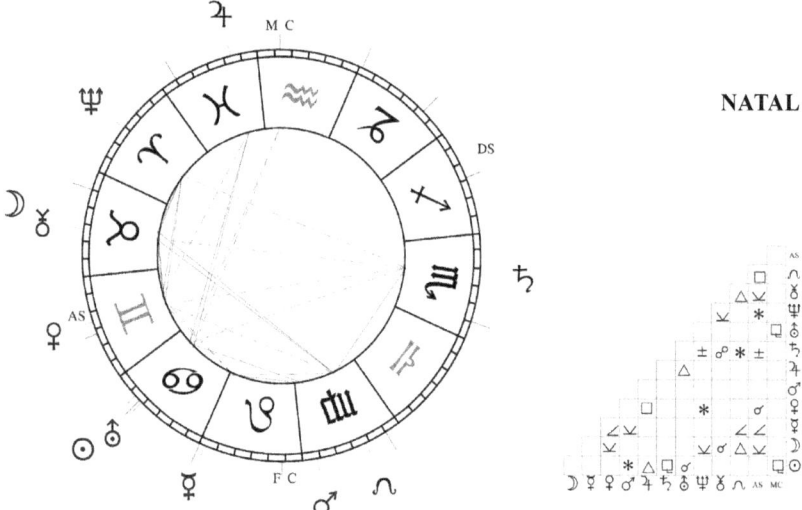

NATAL

In Mr. Giudice's volume you can read that Luigi was born in a village with the curious name of Kaos (Chaos), in the country surrounding Girgenti (today's Agrigento, a town in southern Sicily) on the 28th of June 1867 at 3:15 am. His mother had to deliver in a secluded area out of the main town to avoid any risk of cholera, which used to be a serious plague by those times in Sicily. The second son of Stefano Pirandello, Luigi had to be delivered without the help of a midwife; and he would face another important trouble soon after his birth. I am referring to the fact that his mother got frightened for some reason and lost her capacity of producing milk, which forced Luigi to an early weaning.

In Pirandello's biography, his mother appears to be just like all the other female figures who forged the character of his soul in a negative way. In fact Caterina Ricci Gramitto lived constantly in the background with respect to her husband Stefano; nowadays the latter might be well defined a 'male chauvinist'. The cross-section of her sad life may be summarized by the position of the Moon in his son's natal chart – conjunct with Pluto, in the 12th House, and opposite to Saturn in the 6th House. This is a fundamental point of the natal chart we are examining: femininity, feeling, soul – and all of them at their negative, in the extremely sensible Cancer. As I'll show you in brief, his sister suffered from craziness for a period; his wife Antonietta was crazy too. He had only two important love affairs in his life: a platonic and never really satisfactory one, with the actress Marta Abba; and another one with her daughter Lietta – he suffered very much when the latter got married and followed her husband to Argentina.

Concerning femininity as a feeling, there was a single event in Pirandello's childhood which can help throw light on his future, definitive views on women and love. One day curiosity led little boy Luigi to creep into a mortuary room where there was a corpse on the slab, ready for burying. Already scared at the macabre scenario, the little boy got more frightened when he realized that he wasn't alone in the room. As his eyes got accustomed to the darkness of the room, he saw a man and a woman winding themselves; she had the skirt up; they made a rhythmical movement that his young soul could not simply accept. Later on Leonardo Sciascia commented upon this event in the following terms: "In Pirandello, love would always be somehow linked with death. Not the notion of death, but with death itself, with the physical presence of death. Otherwise, love would be troubled by craziness. Or poisoned by lack of understanding and fidelity. In his characters, you never find a moment of self-abandonment to the heart, to the feelings.

And there's never a woman – not even among the most beautiful ones – whom the author does not depict, more or less evidently, with a shadow of repulsion."

Later on – not much later though – Luigi would face another drama of a similar kind. I refer to an adulterous relationship that his father had when Luigi was fourteen years old, with a widow relative. Blind with repugnance towards his father and with pain because of his adored mother,

Luigi did something of an extreme gravity – he spat on the face of his father's lover. This was the beginning of a progressive cooling of relations between him and his father. They would never reconcile.

From the abode depicted you can understand above all Luigi's attitude towards the image of a woman. You can notice a singular polarity between the coarseness of virtually all his literary plots, and the Puritanism emerging in every manifestation of life. As far as Luigi's Puritanism is concerned, do not forget his hostility towards Gabriele d'Annunzio, whom he considered to be a womanizer – although he also had personal reasons of friction with him connected with their prestige. Pirandello also got disgusted at Benito Mussolini's behaviour – whom he had formerly admired – when the Italian Duce proposed to him to satisfy his platonic love for Marta Abba by simply 'laying the actress on a sofa'.

This contrast reflects the already mentioned astrological elements as well as the position of his natal Mars in the 4th House, opposite to Jupiter. This clearly refers to his father, Stefano: a physically strong man, rude and severe; a former soldier of Giuseppe Garibaldi who also had struggled against the local mafia, refusing to pay 'protection money' in connection with his business of sulphur. Luigi's father was a tough man, one who never accepted to submit. For this reason he suffered from several ambushes and attacks in which he was wounded and in which he often risked his life.

These were Luigi's parents; this was the environment in which our sensitive and delicate writer grew up, collecting the pieces of a jigsaw made of huge pessimism, which he later on would apply to man and life in general. Little boy Pirandello had to face also two more serious troubles: the already mentioned mental illness of his sister, and his father's financial breakdown. Luigi's father-in-law gave over all his goods to Luigi's father, Stefano, who later on had another financial breakdown – even worse than the previous one. This event marked also the beginning of his wife Antonietta's mental illness. Pirandello had to face financial troubles quite often in his life, although not constantly: this is testified by his natal Moon, ruler of his 2nd House, blemished in the 12th House.

On the other hand, the financial troubles that he had to face were not always of a negative kind. In fact he actually took advantage from certain periods of dire straits: he had to abandon poetry in order to write more lucrative genres, and this led him to write his masterpiece, the novel *Il fu Mattia Pascal* (The late Mattia Pascal).

In Luigi's first twenty years we can also see quite a serious disease and his deep love for cousin Lina. His affection for Lina became weaker and weaker in the course of the years, and it ended up in nothing.

In November 1887, Luigi left Sicily and moved to Rome, then to Corno, then to Bonn. This was only the beginning of his endless migrations all over the world, amidst shorter happy periods of staying in Rome at the time of his marriage, crowned by the affection of his kids, his daughter Loretta above all. Hence we can perceive the typical childish side of life of a Cancerian – one who escapes when he doesn't have love. Also his natal Mars in the 4th House stresses Luigi's misadventures in connection with his domicile. Furthermore Mars is the ruler of the 6th House: being in the 4th, refers to Luigi's frequent travelling for professional reasons. He surely moved more often for work than for study.

His first stay in Germany was very much positive for study, but he was forced to come back to Italy quite often due to his bad health conditions. His natal chart speaks up also on this subject: Saturn is blemished in the 6th House. In fact he suffered very much in his life from bad health. On the other hand, during the above mentioned period he had mainly problems of a psychosomatic kind (in his stomach) as a consequence of his traumatic transportation out of the Sicily of the XVIII century to the Northern Europe of XIX century. Of course that area was still conservative, yet it already perceived the novelties of the coming century, and it was surely light-years farther from Luigi's native land.

He then graduated in literature on the 21st of March 1891; then he came back to Italy; expressed his deep love for arts and paintings in particular – how could he ever ignore them, with such a gorgeous ruling Venus in Gemini, close to his Ascendant, and ruler of his 5th House? Then he married Antonietta Portulano – and another terrible event struck his life.

In 1903 Neptune's transit passed over his natal Sun on the cusp of his 2nd House, while Uranus transited his natal 8th House. His father, who used to back him with money, had his financial breakdown and his wife first got paralyzed, then she got crazy.

In the following years Luigi was deeply involved in his literary production, which sponsored him and his family. In this span of time he deals with different activities. He was a teacher at university. He used to write criticisms and essays in various newspapers. He wrote novels and short stories, and of course he wrote plays for theatre. In writing plays, which was his main activity, we can detect once again his very strong, ruling Venus, also ruler of his 5th House - the House of entertainment, show, and performance. Mr. Giudice describes Pirandello's eternal contradiction – full of passions inside, yet cool-headed – which is reflected in his way of dressing: "he mostly dressed in grey", says Giudice. Also during those years his wife showed an absurd jealousy, actually closer to paranoia. Luigi suffered very much because of this continuous torture, which led him to seriously consider suicide in 1903. Deep suffering, heavy burdens marked Luigi's entire existence. He used to be self-sacrificing and always accepted troubles with abnegation, as his natal conjunction Moon-Pluto clearly shows. In his biography, Gaspare Giudice writes, "Really, Pirandello has always suffered in his pride. When he was a child, it was his father who wounded his pride. As an adult, it was his frustrated hope for sublime achievements, far beyond his real capabilities. He accepted troubles from life with dogged, inveterate patience." Undoubtedly his patience was given to him by his natal components of Taurus – he had the Moon in Taurus and the Sun in the 2nd House, which is in connection with the second sign of the Zodiac – i.e. Taurus. At the same time, those components gave him obstinacy in struggling always sustained by a basic wave of optimism (being marked by his strong trine between the Sun and Jupiter) and strong will (the latter underlined by his natal conjunction between the Sun and Uranus). Now certain considerations are required. Many people described Pirandello's 'nihilism'; his eternal view of man being squashed by destiny, man whose lot makes him obligated to be a character – not a person. If it's true that this sense of annihilation has marked his thought – which could not be otherwise, considering the life he lived – it is also true that he showed himself to be incredibly optimistic, having found the strength to rebel against 'fate', starting over and over again after every single setback. I believe that this point can be read quite clearly in his natal chart, yet it has never been put in evidence by any biographer. In fact, despite having a generally pessimistic view of the world (Moon opposite to Saturn) his strong natal trine between the Sun and Jupiter made him optimistic in his actions.

With the beginning of the WWI, his troubles extended to his kids. His first-born child Stefano volunteered in July 1915. In November of the same year, he was wounded in his chest in a heroic action and he became a prisoner. He was then deported to Austria, where he remained imprisoned until the end of the war, amidst deep troubles. His brother Fausto was already serving in the army; he also had troubles and both had tuberculosis. It is quite surprising to notice that the above mentioned ruling Venus also expressed clearly in the depicted events: furthermore Venus, as the ruler of Luigi's 5th House, also expresses the deep love that he felt for his sons. During those years he also lost his mother; his daughter attempted suicide because Luigi's wife – in an excess of jealousy - accused her of having an incestuous affair with her father; Fausto came back from prison; while Antonietta Pirandello was placed in a psychiatric institution where she remained for the rest of her days. On the 16th of July 1921 his daughter Lietta got married. After seven months she migrated to Argentina. That was the 'finishing blow' to Luigi Pirandello, who could not cope any longer with such a sequel of dramatic events. On the other hand, those events forged him as a new creator, and led him to write very original works (at least, original for those times) such as *Six Characters in Search of an Author* (*Sei personaggi in cerca d'autore*), perhaps his most famous and celebrated play.

1923 was the year of his top success, ten years later he was awarded the Nobel Prize for literature on the wave of that success.

Those were the years of Fascism here in Italy. Pirandello adhered to it, but later on he rejected it; in the previous years he also had joined and then rejected other political movements. Probably he was originally drawn toward the radicalism of the early Fascism, for he was a radical himself somehow, in harmony with his native Uranus in conjunction with the Sun. On the other hand, as many other Cancerians, he was obviously unsteady in his political beliefs. Also changeable were his relations with the other celebrities of his time, especially in the world of literature: he constantly had frictions, partings, and manifestations of hostility against them (blemished Saturn in his 6th House).

Pirandello spent the last period of his life in intentional exile, having suffered several manifestations of hostility in his native country (conjunction in the 12th House); he used to live especially in Germany and in France, in a rather nomadic state, demoralized and morally burdened. In 1931 he wrote to his daughter, "..., Your father, Lietta, has to spend the few days still left to him in loneliness, with no fixed abode and without home anywhere. Besides being required by his spirit, which at this point is irreconcilable with any habit of life, this is a necessity because destiny has already excited against him the enemies of his talent and of his value; so strongly that there is no place at home for him any longer. He has to gain life – and not for himself any more – outside, here and there. I hope to die standing on my feet, not in a hospital in France or in America. But I don't care. For the time being I am thinking of working and I'll be working until I can. Death doesn't frighten me, for I am prepared for it since a long time, for it as well as for any other thing of life. This very bitter serenity I have acquired at the cost of having accepted everything. And I don't see any liberation any longer, not even in death..."

He died on the 10th of December 1936. Following his last will, he was prepared naked, only wrapped in a white sheet. Then he was cremated without funeral. He had also asked to have his ashes scattered in the wind. Nonetheless nobody dared following his will up to that point, so his ashes were put in a rock monument which would be erected years later in Agrigento, close to his ancestral house.

The austerity of his death is astrologically expressed by his natal 8th House in Capricorn; its ruler Saturn – opposite with the Moon – informs us about the 'unpopularity' of his death, given that nobody could follow his coffin. Among the Solar Return charts for Pirandello, the most interesting ones are those for the following years: 1915, 1918, and 1922. They refer to the periods of his son's imprisonment, his wife's admittance in a psychiatric hospital, and his own success on an international scale. It's three periods of his life which you can astrologically read quite well not only with transits, but also with Solar Returns. As far as transits are concerned, in 1915 there are three important ones: Pluto approaching the orb of conjunction to his Sun, Neptune within the orb of conjunction with his Mercury, and Uranus in perfect square with his Moon.

In his Solar Return we can see a stellium in the 7th House, the House of war and of declared enemies; and Mars in the 6th House. The Ascendant of that SR falls within his natal 6th House, close to the Descendant. On one hand this gives strength to the reading of the 7th House of SR; and from the other hand, it may refer to Luigi Pirandello's bad health conditions, which became even weaker due to his son being wounded followed by his imprisonment – and in any case, an Ascendant of SR falling in the natal 6th House indicates a detrimental year.

The parting from his wife is ticked by the transit of Saturn on the Imum Coeli, while Uranus was in transit at the Medium Coeli. Also the Solar Return of that time is meaningful, having a stellium in the 10th House, and the Ascendant falling in his 5th natal House; the latter referring to his son coming back from Austria. Furthermore, Mars is in the 1st House.

And lastly, success is marked by Jupiter in the 6th House, trine to the Sun. The Solar Return has the Sun, Mercury and Pluto in the 10th House.

Luigi Pirandello

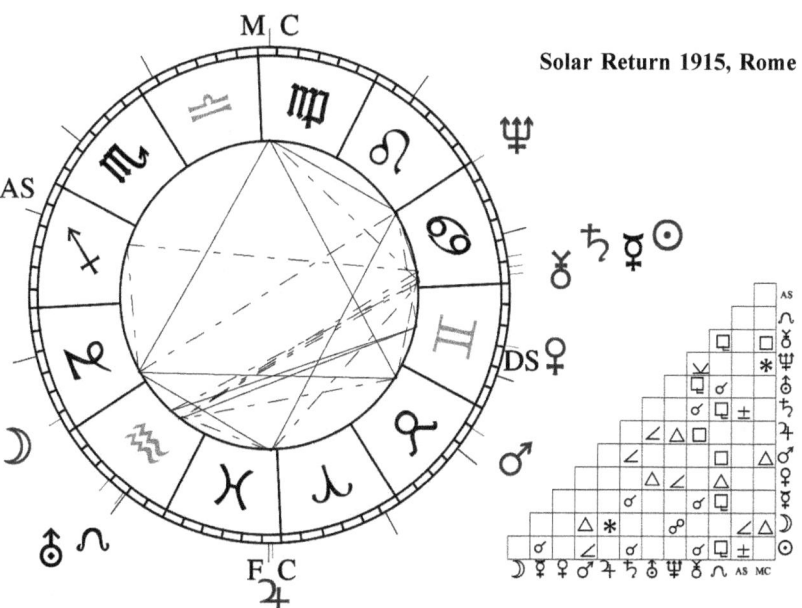

Solar Return 1915, Rome

AIMED SOLAR AND LUNAR RETURNS

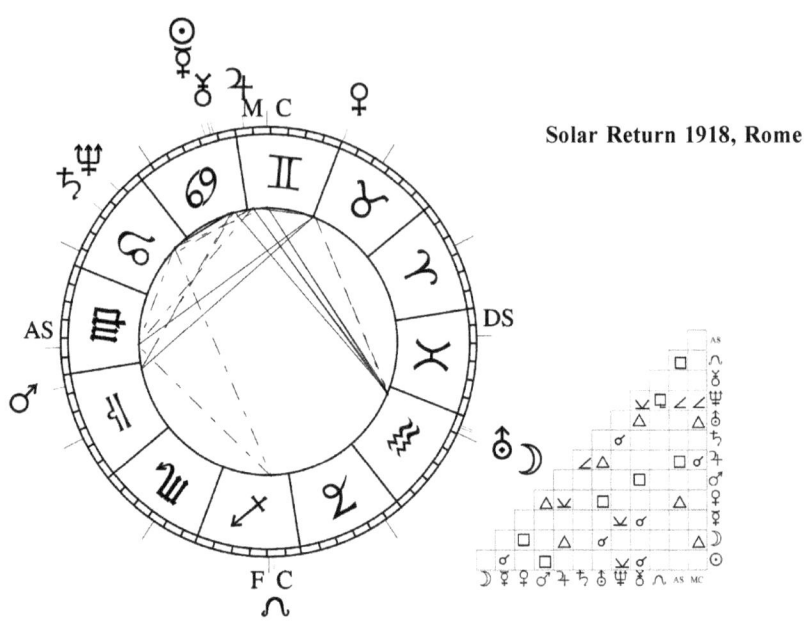

Solar Return 1918, Rome

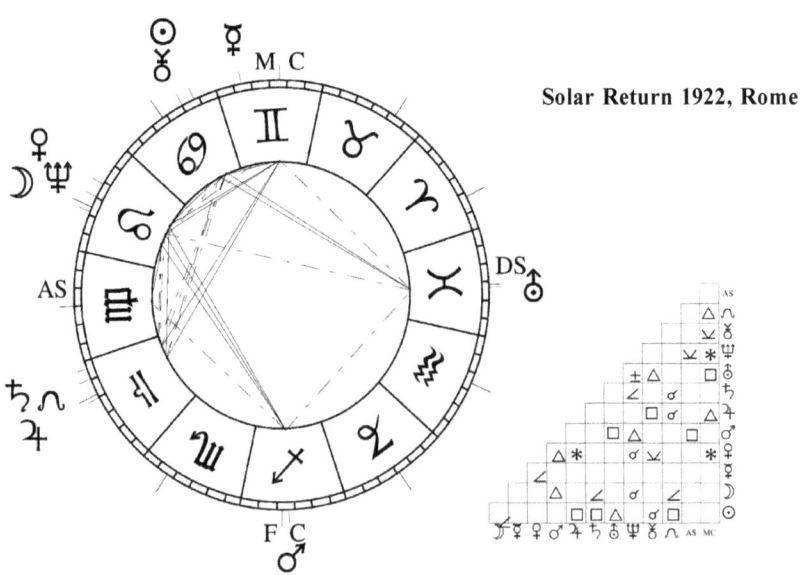

Solar Return 1922, Rome

21.
Astrological portrayal of Ernst Hemingway

"Man is not created for defeat. Man can be killed, but never defeated". These are the words of old Santiago, the protagonist of the 'The Old Man and the Sea'; words, that better then many others, express the world of fights, of competition, of unlucky failures and providential deliverance, of the jungle law within whose ambit he operated - wrote the great Hemingway. And it was for 'The Old Man and the Sea' that the American writer was to earn, in 1954, the Nobel prize for literature.

The novel, though simple and brief is very intense, with high dramatic tones, rich with the principal ingredients of Hemingwayan literature: strength, competition, fight, blood, violence and death. The old fisherman, who goes fishing for the eighty-fourth time, consecutively without catching even one sea vertebrate, meets a very large fish, bigger than his own sail boat that, hooked on his bait, fights for three days before being killed by the man. He never debases the animal's dignity and considers the fish to be a noble creature, saying to himself during the entire fight: "I'd like to feed the fish. He is my brother. But I have to kill him and I need to remain strong to do it". And when, almost exhausted, he doesn't know if he will be able to save his own life in this adventure: "I never saw anything so great and wonderful and calm and noble as you, brother. Come and assassinate me. I don't care which one of us will eliminate the other". At the end, it will be for the old man to win, but destiny, as in most of his stories and novels, will be his enemy: the sharks will attack and kill his fish before devouring its carcass and he will return from this extraordinary adventure bringing with him only a skeleton. Life, for Ernest Hemingway, was a plaza de toros, an arena for gladiators where blood, dust and death blended, presenting a arrogant and gory spectacle and which was for man to behold but not to combat. The image of this bullfight is entirely attributable to the presence of Mars in the first house and squared to Saturn, in the writer's horoscope.

Reading his books we cannot avoid comparing them to Victor Hugo's novels; for example 'The Laughing Man', an immense scenario of human miseries, of the titanic fight of people against a omnipotent destiny. That destiny would bring the author of 'Fiesta' to suicide.

All his life, Hemingway wrote about weapons, wounds and killings.

On July 2, 1961 he became protagonist of one of his stories when he shot a rifle bullet into his head. His was a great Cancerian pessimism, the pessimism of a kind soul that recognizes the law that governs the whole world: "Homo homini lupus (man that is wolf to man)", man devours his own kind, competition is not a sport but battle for survival. The hyena of the story 'The Snows of Kilimanjaro' that lurks around Harry's tent symbolises both creeping death and the pangs of regret at having wasted his artistic gifts.

The Moon of the American novelist was in Capricorn and the combination Cancer-Capricorn is one of the most munificent bestower of unhappiness. The pessimism of Hemingway, however, has something more to it, very often encompassing death or at least violence and blood; and this, as I wrote earlier, is certainly attributable to Mars in the first House. We remember that the same position was prevailed in the natal charts of the Mahatma Gandhi, Indira Gandhi, Rajiv Gandhi, Aldo Moro, Pier Paolo Pasolini, Grace Kelly and many other personages who met violent deaths.

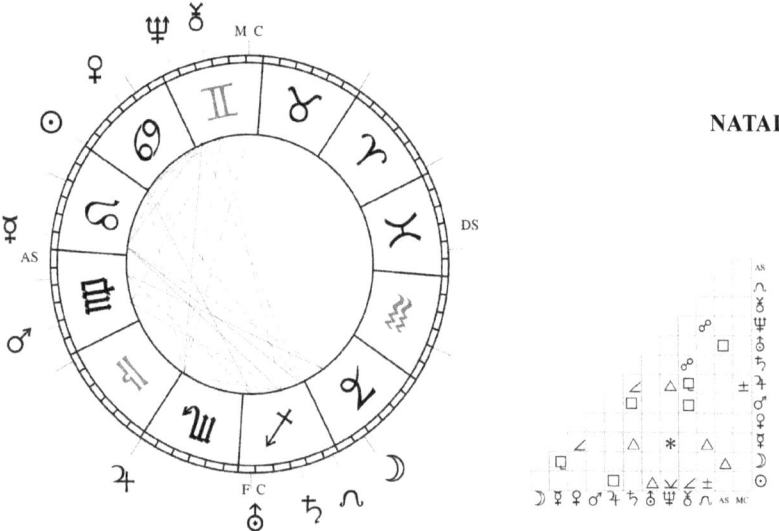

NATAL

The natal chart of the subject was calculated for 1899, on July 21, at 8:00 A.M., in Oak Park (Chicago). Some biographical writings indicate 1898 as the year of birth, but the date considered here was confirmed by many American and Italo-American writers (special thanks go to the USIS at the American Consulate of Naples). Even the Britannica Encyclopaedia reports the year 1899. Also, from the examination of the two different horoscopes from a historically perspective, it appears that the Moon has to be about 10 degrees in Capricorn. This Moon is in the fifth House, opposed to Venus in Cancer and describes to us the falling in love and its frustrating outcome, as the theme of the semi-autobiographical 'A Farewell to Arms'; the love between Henry and Catherine that knew the clandestine emotions of the dark rooms of the American Military Hospital in Milan, to live together afterwards, a quiet life in the beautiful mountains of Switzerland and finally the birth of a still born son and the death of Catherine which leaves Henry devastated.

Hemingway got married four times and in at least three of them, he was unhappy. A Moon in the fifth House, in Capricorn and in opposition to Venus, corresponds to a "saturnized" Moon, penalized by destiny. And what can be sadder for a Cancerian than his sentimental life goes wrong?

The Sun and Venus together in Cancer is the factory label of an extraordinary sensibility, of a restless soul, enormously in need of affection.

The author of 'For Whom the Bell Tolls' would have liked to live in a world of vegetarian pacifists, with a great blind fold on his eyes, so as not to see the horrific world. But instead, in his life, he was many times in Africa in contact with beasts and with men more sanguinary than the beasts; he was at the bull fights in Spain and everywhere where there was war and death, battle and blood, pain and horror. Even his story 'The Short Happy Life Of Francis Macomber' has an African scenario - of the wounded and ferocious lions, of the unjust and fearful hunters, of the adultery indulged in according to the laws of the jungle, of the apparently accidental homicide that is subordinated to a miserable objective. This same world of unjustness and evil, of battles and defeats, that has 'cruel destiny' as a common denominator, is what permeates all his literary works, from 'The First Forty-Nine Stories' to the 'Death in the Afternoon' published in 1932. It is the same theme that was developed in the short story 'The Capital of the World' in which the boy Paco is knifed to death while simulating a bull fight. For Hemingway, life was certainly a bull fight and quite contrary to the notions of Eduardo De Filippo (the Italian dramatist) the subject thought that the 'long dark night' would have never passed and that only the pitiful veil of death would have covered that big square of pain that was life. A psychiatrist today, would have been able to combat the depression of the novelist and with a few grams of Benzedrine or something similar, would have been able to show the world to him in a brighter light, but if this would have deprived us of his masterpieces, let's say: "Viva depression!". This same depression, however, killed Hemmingway and the transits of that event bear testimony it. Pluto was in conjunction with the Ascendant and so was Mars (2° in Virgo); Jupiter gave an opposition to the Sun and Saturn was sesquisquare to the Ascendant and in opposition to the Sun; Uranus, at 23° in Leo, was on natal Mercury, in sesquisquare to the Moon.

Yet again, the aspect of 135° shows up with arrogance: this aspect is erroneously ignored by many colleagues while I believe that it is very important, in the same measure as that of a semisquare. Both the German and American schools of astrology utilize a lot these aspects, while they give very little importance to the sextile and no importance to the semisextile. My personal practice guides me in perfect accord to this vision. Coming back to our author, it is necessary to remember two "significant circumstances" that accompanied the penning and publication of 'A Farewell to Arms'. While Hemingway was writing this book, his father killed himself (Saturn in the fourth House in opposition to Pluto and square to Mars) and on the day the novel was published, there was the great crash at the American stock exchange. Here too, I would like to mention in the context of a comparison, the words of Eduardo De Filippo: "War is not over, nothing has finished". The theme of 'A Farewell to Arms' is particularly suggestive of the Hemingwayan thought: love that is confronted by the absurdities of war, of destruction, of death. The escape of the two protagonists to Switzerland, a country considered to be an island of peace, an oasis of safety is a typical argument indicative of a Cancerian mindset, as in the case of director Ingmar Bergman and his extreme northern island or Piero Chiara's (an Italian novelist) lake in his novel The Bishop's Room (the lake is like an island in reverse, in whose waters the protagonist of the romance hides himself to escape the traps of the world represented by the coasts of the land all around).

But, now, let's speak about Hemingway the writer. Note, first of all, the presence of Jupiter in the third House that although being in Scorpio and square to the Sun has so strongly influenced his ability to write and his literary success. Many people, reading him, have had the impression that his style constitutes rough and uncultured prose, inspired certainly by the Virgo-Capricornian values, values of frugality and essentiality. But Agostino Lombardi (an Italian critic) writes so: "A prose controlled and conscious, cultured and even precious". But people love Ernest Hemingway not for his style of writing but for the substance of his novels, because being a Cancerian, he touches to the bottom of the reader's heart, involves them, makes them emotional participants in the drama of his characters without any abstraction. He was not the greatest writer of all times, but a fantastic protagonist of our world, "a ferocious and violent world, without faith and without love, where man tries to grab and hold onto some fixed point passionately, in his vain search for life's meaning".

Translated by Ciro Discepolo and Anna Mellone
Edited by Ram Ramakrishnan

Ernst Hemingway

22.
An essential astrological bibliography

- Various Authors: *Articles appeared on the quarterly* Ricerca '90 *from 1990 to 2008*, Edizioni Ricerca '90, 128 pp.

- Various Authors: *Dodici monografie sui segni zodiacali* [Twelve monographs on the zodiacal signs] *edited by Serena Foglia*, Armenia, 124 pp.

- Various Authors: *Special university issue (#45-46) of* l'astrologue, Éditions Traditionnelles, Paris

- John M. Addey: *Ritmi armonici in astrologia [Harmonic rhythms in astrology]*, Elefante ed., Catania, 1979, 352 pp.

- André Barbault, H. Latou, B. Rossi, G. Simon: *Kepler*, Éditions Traditionnelles (l'astrologue *issue #52*), Paris

- André Barbault and Various Authors: *Soleil & Lune en Astrologie [Sun & Moon in Astrology]*, Publications du Centre International d'Astrologie, Paris, 1953, 280 pp.

- André Barbault and Various Authors: *La luna nei miti e nello zodiaco [The Moon in the myths and in the Zodiac]*, Nuovi Orizzonti, Milan, 1989, 190 pp.

- André Barbault: *Ariete [Aries]*, La Salamandra, Milan, 1985, 160 pp.

- André Barbault: *Astrologia e orientamento professionale [Astrology and professional orientation]*, Edizioni Ciro Discepolo, Naples, 1984, 93 pp.

- André Barbault: *Astrologia mondiale [World astrology]*, Armenia, Milan, 1980, 272 pp.

- André Barbault: *Dalla psicanalisi all'astrologia [From psychoanalysis to astrology]*, Morin, Siena, 1971, 224 pp.

- André Barbault: *Giove & Saturno [Jupiter & Saturn]*, Edizioni Ciro Discepolo, Naples, 1983, 214 pp.

- André Barbault: *Il pronostico sperimentale in astrologia [The experimental prediction in astrology]*, Mursia, Milan, 1979, 210 pp.

- André Barbault: *La Précession des Équinoxes et l'Astrologie [The precession of the equinoxes and Astrology]*, Centre International d'Astrologie, Paris, 1972, 32 pp.

- André Barbault, *La scienza dell'Astrologia [The science of Astrology]*, Nuovi Orizzonti, Milan, 1989, 186 pp.

- André Barbault: *L'astrologia e la previsione dell'avvenire [Astrology and the forecast of future]*, Armenia, Milan, 1993, 308 pp.

- André Barbault: *L'astrologia e l'avvenire del mondo [Astrology and the future of the world]*, Xenia, Milan, 1996, 212 pp.

- André Barbault: *Toro [Taurus]*, La Salamandra, Milan, 1985, 153 pp.

- André Barbault: *Trattato pratico di astrologia [A practical treatise of astrology]*, Morin, Siena, 1967, 317 pp.

- Armand Barbault: *Technique de l'interprétation [The technique of interpretation]*, Dervy Livres, Croissy-Beaubourg, 1991

- Angelo Brunini, *L'avvenire non è un mistero* [Future is not a mystery], published by the Author, 525 pp.

- Charles E.O. Carter, *An encyclopaedia of psychological astrology*, The Theosophical Publishing House Ltd, 200 pp.

- Charles E.O. Carter: *An Introduction to Political Astrology*, Fowler, London, 1951, 104 pp.

- Charles E.O. Carter: *The Astrological Aspects*, Fowler, London, 1930, 160 pp.

- Charles E.O. Carter: *The Astrology of Accidents*, The Theosophical Publishing House Ltd., London, Unknown date of publishing, 124 pp.

- Charles E.O. Carter: *The Principles of Astrology*, The Theosophical Publishing House Ltd., London, 1925, 190 pp.

- Marco Celada: *Articles appeared on the quarterly* Ricerca '90 *from 1990 to 2009*, Edizione Ricerca '90, 128 pp.

- Yves Christiaen: *La Domification [Domification]*, Dervy Livres, Paris, 1978, 40 pp.

- Thorwald Dethlefsen, *Il destino come scelta* [Destiny as Choice], *Edizioni Mediterranee,* 202 pp.

- Nicholas De Vore,: *Encyclopedia of Astrology*, Littlefield Adams and Co., New Jersey, U.S.A., 1977

- Arato Di Soli: *I fenomeni ed i pronostici [Phenomena and predictions]*, Arktos, Turin, 1984, 120 pp.

- Ciro Discepolo and Luigi Galli: *Supporto tecnico alla pratica delle Rivoluzioni solari mirate [Technical support to the practise of Aimed Solar*

Returns], Blue Diamond Publisher, Milan, 2000, 136 pp.*

- Ciro Discepolo and Andrea Rossetti: *Astro & Geografia [Astro & Geography]*, Blue Diamond Publisher, Milan, 1996, 102 pp.

- Ciro Discepolo and Pino Valente: *Ci siamo con la datazione informatica degli avvenimenti? [How far have we gone with the computerized dating of events?]*, Edizioni Ricerca '90, 2007, 168 pp.*

- Ciro Discepolo and Various Authors: *Osservazioni politematiche sulle ricerche Discepolo/Miele [Polithematic remarks on the researches of Discepolo & Miele]*, Edizioni Ricerca '90, Naples, 1992, 196 pp.

- Ciro Discepolo and Various Authors: *Per una rifondazione dell'astrologia o per il suo rifiuto [For a refoundation of Astrology or for its refusal]*, Edizioni Ricerca '90, Naples, 1993, 200 pp.

- Ciro Discepolo: *365 nap alatt a Föld körül a szolárhoroszkóppal*, DFT-Húngaria, Budapest, May 2006, 190 pp. B5*

- Ciro Discepolo: *Astrologia applicata [Applied astrology]*, Armenia, Milan, 1988, 294 pp.

- Ciro Discepolo: *Astrologia Attiva [Active Astrology]*, Edizioni Mediterranee, Rome, 1998, 144 pp.*

- Ciro Discepolo: *Come scoprire i segreti di un oroscopo [How to unveil the secrets of a horoscope]*, Albero ed., Milan, 1988, 253 pp.

- Ciro Discepolo: Die Transite und das Solarhoroskop, German edition of "Transits and Solar Returns", 2008, 646 pp.

- Ciro Discepolo, *Effemeridi e Tavole delle Case* [Ephemerides and Tables of Houses], various volumes, Armenia

- Ciro Discepolo: *Enquête sur l'hérédité astrale*, issue #67 of *l'astrologue*, Éditions Traditionnelles, Paris, 1984

- Ciro Discepolo: *Esercizi sulle Rivoluzioni solari mirate [Exercises of Aimed Solar Returns]*, Blue Diamond Publisher, Milan, 1996, 96 pp.*

- Ciro Discepolo: *Guida ai transiti* (prima e seconda edizione) *[A guide to transits – 1st and 2nd edition]*, Armenia, Milan, 1984, 510 pp.*

- Ciro Discepolo: *I fondamenti dell'Astrologia Medica [The fundaments of Medical Astrology]*, Armenia, Milan, end of January 2006, 246 pp.*

- Ciro Discepolo: *Il sale dell'astrologia [The salt of astrology]*, Edizioni Capone, Turin, 1991, 144 pp.

- Ciro Discepolo: *La ricerca dell'ora di nascita [The quest for the time of birth]*, Edizioni Ricerca '90, Naples, 1994, 64 pp.*

- Ciro Discepolo: *L'Hérédité astrale sur 50 000 naissances*, and *Astrologie activiste – Réflexions sur l'astrologie*, issue #125 of *l'astrologue*, Éditions Traditionnelles, Paris, 1999

- Ciro Discepolo: *L'interpretazione del tema natale [Reading the natal chart]*, Armenia, Milan, September 2007, 336 pp.*

- Ciro Discepolo: Lunar Returns and Earth Returns, Ricerca '90 Publisher, 2009, pp.304, English edition, modified and expanded, of "Rivoluzioni Lunari e Rivoluzioni Terrestri"

- Ciro Discepolo: *Nouvelle recherche sur l'hérédité astrale*, issue #106 of *l'astrologue*, Éditions Traditionnelles, Paris, 1994

- Ciro Discepolo: *Nuova guida all'astrologia [A new guide to astrology]*, Armenia, Milan, 2000, 818 pp.*

- Ciro Discepolo: *Nuovo dizionario di astrologia [The new Dictionary of Astrology]*, Armenia, Milan, 1996, 394 pp.*

- Ciro Discepolo: *Nuovo trattato delle Rivoluzioni solari [The new treatise of Solar Returns]*, Armenia, Milan, 2003, 216 pp.*

- Ciro Discepolo: *Nuovo Trattato di Astrologia*, Armenia, Milan, February 2004, 784 pp. Never translated in English. The first section covers the rectification of the time of birth. The second section is about the dating of events between a given Solar Return and the following one. The third section is a miscellany of quite technical subjects (for example "The praise to Placidus") Finally, this large-size book –that belongs to the blue series of Armenia's (a series in which there are 8 texts from the same Author)– offers a postface of epistemological nature. REMARK: This text is not a new edition of GUIDA ALL'ASTROLOGIA. In fact, it does not contain a single page from that book. *

- Ciro Discepolo: *Prontuario calcoli [Ready reckoner]*, Edizioni Capone, Turin, 1979, 72 pp.

- Ciro Discepolo: *Piccola guida all'astrologia [A concise guide to astrology]*, Armenia, Milan, 1998, 200 pp.

- Ciro Discepolo: *Quattro cose sui compleanni mirati [A few facts on Aimed Birthdays]*, Blue Diamond Publisher, Milan, 2001, 104 pp.*

- Ciro Discepolo: Russian edition of the 'Nuovo Trattato delle Rivoluzioni solari', May 2009 (http://www.astrolog.ru/)*

- Ciro Discepolo: *Statistique sur 834 nominations ministérielles,* issue #67 of *l'astrologue,* Éditions Traditionnelles, Paris, 1986

- Ciro Discepolo: *Suite of software modules ASTRAL*, developed by the Author and Luigi Miele, Naples, 1979-2003

- Ciro Discepolo: *Temelji medicinske astrologije: osnove za razumevanje* èlovekove patologije s pomoèjo nebesnih teles, Zalozba Astrološkega inštituta, Ljubljana, 2007, pp. 262*

- Ciro Discepolo: *Traité complet d'interprétation des transits et des Révolutions solaires en astrologie*, Éditions Traditionnelles, Paris, 2001, 502 pp.*

- Ciro Discepolo: *Transiti e Rivoluzioni solari [Transits and Solar Returns]*, Armenia, Milan, 1997, 502 pp.*

- Ciro Discepolo: *Tránsitos y Retornos Solares*, Spanish edition of "Transits and Solar Returns", Ediciones Ricerca '90, 2009, 664 pp.

- Ciro Discepolo: *Transits and Solar Returns*, Naples, Ricerca '90 Publisher, September 2007, 560 pp.*

- Ciro Discepolo: *Trattato pratico di Rivoluzioni solari [A practical treatise of Solar Returns]*, Edizioni Ricerca '90, Naples, 1993, 208 pp.*

- Ciro Discepolo: *Various volumes of ephemerides*, Various publishers

- Ciro Discepolo: *Various volumes of Tables of Houses*, Various publishers

- Luciano Drusetta: *Articles appeared on the quarterly* Ricerca '90 *from 1990 to 2009*, Edizione Ricerca '90, 128 pp.

- Reinhold Ebertin: *Cosmobiologia: la nuova astrologia [Cosmobiology: the new Astrology]*, Edizioni C.E.M., Naples, 1982, 208 pp.

- Henri F. Ellenberger, *La scoperta dell'inconscio* [The discovery of the unconscious], Universale scientifica Boringhieri, two volumes

- Michael Erlewine: *Manual of Computer Programming for Astrologers*, American Federation of Astrologers, Tempe (Arizona), 1980, 215 pp.

- Hans J. Eysenck, S. Mayo, O. White: *Un metodo empirico sul rapporto tra fattori astrologici e personalità [An empirical method on the relationship between astrological factors and peersonality]*, issue #42 of *Linguaggio astrale*, Turin, 1981

- Serena Foglia: *Prolusione al convegno di studi astrologici tenutosi a Napoli nel 1979 [Opening speech at the congress of astrological studies held in Naples in 1979]*, issue #37 of *Linguaggio Astrale*, Turin

- H. Freiherr Von Klöckler, *Corso di astrologia [Course on Astrology]*, ed. Mediterranee, Rome, 1979

- Erich Fromm, *Psicanalisi della società contemporanea* [Psychoanalysis of contemporary society], Edizioni di comunità, 348 pp.

- Luigi Galli and Ciro Discepolo: *Atlante geografico per le Rivoluzioni solari [Geographical Atlas for Solar Returns]*, Blue Diamond Publisher, Milan, 2001, 136 pp.*

- Luigi Galli: *Articles appeared on the quarterly* Ricerca '90 *from 1990 to 2008*, Edizioni Ricerca '90, Naples, 128 pp.

- Françoise Gauquelin: *Problèmes de l'heure risolus en astrologie*, Guy Trédaniel

- Michel & Françoise Gauquelin: *Actors & politicians*, Laboratoire d'étude des relations entre rythmes cosmiques et psychophysiologiques, Paris, 1970

- Michel & Françoise Gauquelin: *Méthodes pour étudier la répartition des astres dans le mouvement diurne,* Gauquelin ed., Paris, 1970

- Michel & Françoise Gauquelin: *Painters and musicians*, Laboratoire d'étude des relations entre rythmes cosmiques et psychophysiologiques, Paris, 1970

- Michel Gauquelin: *Il dossier delle influenze cosmiche [The file of cosmic influences]*, Astrolabio, Rome, 1975, 232 pp.

- Michel Gauquelin: *La Cosmopsychologie*, Retz, Paris, 1974, 256 pp.

- Michel Gauquelin: *L'astrologia di fronte alla scienza [Astrology face to science]*, Armenia, Milan, 1981, 312 pp.

- Michel Gauquelin: *Ritmi biologici e ritmi cosmici [Biological rhythms and cosmic rhythms]*, Faenza spa, Faenza, 1976, 226 pp.

- Luigi Gedda and Gianni Brenci: *Cronogenetica [Chronogenetics],* Est-Mondadori, Milan, 1974

- Henri J. Gouchon and Jean Reverchon: *Dictionnaire Astrologique – Supplément Technique*, H. Gouchon Éditeur, Paris, 1947, 40 pp.

- Henri J. Gouchon: *Dizionario di astrologia [Dictionary of astrology]*, Siad ed., Milan, 1980

- Henri J. Gouchon: *Les Directions Primaires Simplifiées*, Éditions Traditionnelles, Paris, 1970, ca. 150 pp.

- Henri J. Gouchon: *L'Horoscope Annuel Simplifié*, Dervy Livres, Paris, 1973, 214 pp.

- Hadès: *Guide pratique de l'interprétation en Astrologie*, Éditions Niclaus, Paris, 1969, 228 pp.

- Robert Hand: *I transiti [The transits]*, Armenia, Milan, 1982, 512 pp.

- R.F.C. Hull and William McGuire, *Jung parla* [Jung speaking], Adelphi, 592 pp.

- Aniela Jaffé, *Ricordi sogni riflessioni di Carl Gustav Jung* [Memories, dreams, reflections of Carl Gustav Jung], Il Saggiatore, 432 pp.

- Eugen Jonas: *Articles appeared on the quarterly* Ricerca '90 *from 1990 to 2008*, Edizioni Ricerca '90, Naples, 128 pp.

- Eugen Jonas: *Il controllo naturale del concepimento [The natural control of conception]*, Blue Diamond Publisher, Milan, 1995, 76 pp.
- Carl Gustav Jung, *La dinamica dell'inconscio* [The dynamics of the unconscious], Boringhieri, 606 pp.
- Carl Gustav Jung, *La sincronicità* [Synchronicity], Biblioteca Boringhieri, 124 pp.
- Carl Gustav Jung, *L'uomo e i suoi simboli* [Man and his symbols], Edizioni Casini, 320 pp.
- Carl Gustav Jung, *Mysterium coniunctionis*, Boringhieri, 288 pp.
- Carl Gustav Jung, *Opere - volume nono* [Works - ninth volume], Boringhieri, 314 pp.
- Carl Gustav Jung, *Psicogenesi delle malattie mentali* [Psychogenesis of the mental illnesses], Boringhieri, 322
- Carl Gustav Jung, *Psicologia della schizofrenia* [Psychology of schizophrenia], Newton Compton Italiana, 218 pp.
- Carl Gustav Jung, *Psicologia e alchimia* [Psychology and alchemy], 548 pp.
- Carl Gustav Jung, *Simboli della trasformazione* [Symbols of the transformations], Boringhieri, 596 pp.
- Carl Gustav Jung, *Tipi psicologici* [Psychological types], Boringhieri, 612 pp.
- Luciana Marinangeli, *Astrologia indiana* [Indian astrology], Edizioni Mediterranee, 200 pp.
- George C. Noonan: *Spherical Astronomy for Astrologers*, American Federation of Astrologers, Washington DC, 1974, 62 pp.
- Pietro Orlandini, *L'acupuncture cutanea* [Cutaneous acupuncture], Rizzoli, 218 pp.
- Tommaso Palamidessi: *Astrologia mondiale [World astrology]*, Archeosofica P., Rome, 1941, 588 pp.
- Johanna Paungger and Thomas Poppe: *La Luna ci insegna a star bene [The Moon teaches us how to be fine]*, Frasnelli - Keitsch, Bolzano/Bozen, 1995, 260 pp.
- Johanna Paungger and Thomas Poppe: *Servirsi della Luna [To use the Moon]*, Frasnelli - Keitsch, Bolzano/Bozen, 1995, 166 pp.
- Claudius Ptolemy: *Descrizione della sfera celeste [Description of the Celestial Sphere]*, Arnaldo Forni, Bologna, 1990, 96 pp.
- Claudius Ptolemy: *Tetrabiblos, Le previsioni astrologiche [Tetrabiblos – the astrological predictions]*, Mondadori, Milan, 1985, 490 pp.
- Claudius Ptolemy: *Tetrabiblos*, Arktos, Carmagnola, 1980
- Claudius Ptolemy: *Tetrabiblos*, Arktos, Turin, 1979, 270 pp.
- Andrea Rossetti: *Breve trattato sui transiti [A concise treatise on transits]*,

Blue Diamond Publisher, Milan, 1994, 125 pp.

- Andrea Rossetti: *Transiti, rivoluzioni solari e dasa indù [Transits, Solar Returns, and Hindu Dhasas]*, Blue Diamond Publisher, Milan, 1997, 188 pp.

- Alexander Ruperti: *I cicli del divenire [The cycles of becoming]*, Astrolabio, Rome, 1990, 301 pp.

- Frances Sakoian and Louis Acker: *Transits of Jupiter*, CSA Printing and Bindery Inc., USA, 1974, 72 pp.

- Frances Sakoian and Louis Acker: *Transits of Saturn*, CSA Printing and Bindery Inc., USA, 1973, 76 pp.

- Frances Sakoian and Louis Acker: *Transits of Uranus*, CSA Printing and Bindery Inc., USA, 1973, 78 pp.

- Vanda Sawtell: *Astrology & Biochemistry*, Rustington, Sussex, England, 86 pp.

- Françoise Secret: *Astrologie et alchimie au XVII siecle*, Studi francesi, new serie, vol. 60, issue #3

- Nicola Sementovsky-Kurilo, *Astrologia* [Astrology], Hoepli, 887 pp

- Nicola Sementovsky-Kurilo: *Trattato completo di astrologia teorico e pratico [A complete theoretical-practical treatise of astrology]*, Hoepli ed., Milan, 1989

- Heber J. Smith: *Transits*, American Federation of Astrology, Tempe (Arizona), Unknown date of publishing, 42 pp.

- Kichinosuke Tatai: *I bioritmi [The biorhythms]*, ed. Mediterranee, Rome

- George S. Thommen: *Bioritmi [Biorhythms]*, Cesco Ciapanna ed.

- Alexander Volguine: *Tecnica delle rivoluzioni solari [Technique of Solar Returs]*, Armenia, Milan, 1980, 226 pp.

- Herbert Von Klöckler, *Astrologia, scienza sperimentale [Astrology – an experimental science]*, Mediterranee, Rome, 1993, 183 pp.

- Ritchie R. Ward: *Gli orologi viventi [The living clocks]*, Bompiani, Milan, 1973

- Lyall Watson: *Supernatura [Supernature]*, Rizzoli ed, Milan, 1974

- David Williams: *Simplified Astronomy for Astrologers*, American Federation of Astrologers, Washington DC 1969, 90 pp.

* These are writings that deal – partly or extensively – with the subject 'Solar Returns' and 'Lunar Returns'.

Index

Preface to the English Edition	pag. 7
Preface	pag. 9
1. Praise of escape	pag. 15
2. The reasons for a vocation	pag. 21
3. To antagonize and to potentiate	pag. 23
4. The problem of expectations	pag. 27
5. Jeoffrey's theorem	pag. 37
6. The added value	pag. 41
7. A complete failure	pag. 43
8. On the precision of the time of birth	pag. 47
9. The 'gap'	pag. 51
10. When the natal Sun is in the 10th or in the 9th House	pag. 55
11. The case of Mrs Smith	pag. 59
12. An easy case and a hard case	pag. 63
13. Stardust	pag. 71
14. Transits of Mars	pag. 83
15. Transits of Saturn	pag. 107
16. Transits of Uranus	pag. 131
17. Transits of Neptune	pag. 157

18. Transits of Pluto ....pag. 171
Appendix
19. Astrological portrayal of Luigi Pirandello ....pag. 187
20. Astrological portrayal of Giacomo Casanova ....pag. 195
21. Astrological portrayal of Ernst Hemingway ....pag. 205
22. An essential astrological bibliography ....pag. 211

www.ingramcontent.com/pod-product-compliance
Lightning Source LLC
Chambersburg PA
CBHW060514100426
42743CB00009B/1316